THE EXCURSION

A STUDY

BY

JUDSON STANLEY LYON

ARCHON BOOKS
1970

[*Yale Studies in English, Vol. 114*]

SBN: 208 00924 8
Library of Congress Catalog Card Number: 77-91184
Printed in the United States of America

To

ROBERT J. MENNER

PREFACE

THE EXCURSION has long been generally neglected by readers, teachers, and students of English literature. There are many possible reasons for this near oblivion, such as the great length and occasional difficulty of the poem, a shift in sensibility which has brought into disrepute anything which can conceivably be classified as a long didactic poem, the fame of the principal critical condemnations of *The Excursion,* and the widespread belief that if one is to read a long poem of Wordsworth's, *The Prelude,* with its occasional great brilliance and its more directly historical and autobiographical interest, is the poem one should read. But perhaps the most important single reason is to be found in the influence of Matthew Arnold.

With his well-known essay on Wordsworth, Arnold fixed the course of Wordsworth criticism for a generation or more. Reversing the previous critical tendency, he emphatically denied the value of Wordsworth's philosophy and directed attention to the short pieces. It is obvious that this critical injunction was injurious particularly to *The Excursion,* both because it is long and philosophical and because Arnold selected it specifically as an example of all that he considered least valuable in Wordsworth.

It is possible that in the long run more generations will hold Arnold's view than any other. However, as a matter of historical fact, Wordsworth criticism for the last twenty-five years has repudiated Arnold and returned to a position more like that which prevailed before him, as represented principally by Leslie Stephen, a warm admirer of Wordsworth's philosophy. The great landmarks of present-day Wordsworth scholarship are Professor Beatty's *William Wordsworth: His Doctrine and Art in Their Historical Relations* and Ernest De Selincourt's *The Prelude.* Since the appearance of these books, academic criticism has concerned itself mainly with *The Prelude* and with Wordsworth's philosophy, and a steady succession of essays and studies has indicated a widespread interest. In short, attention has shifted to the long poems. *The Excursion* is again being read with lively interest by many people, thus far mainly academics.

However, although much work has been done on *The Prelude,* little so far has been done on *The Excursion.* Up to the present time there has been no extended study of that work. Those studies which have devoted space to *The Excursion,* like Professor Beatty's book, E. A. Sneath's *Wordsworth,* and G. M. Harper's *William Wordsworth: His Life, Works, and Influence,* have treated the poem only incidentally, using it

as a source from which to extract isolated quotations which throw light
on the doctrines or the biography of the poet, and dismissing it after a
brief summary and an indication of some of its chief virtues and defects.
The Excursion has still been very little *studied.*

Since it seems clear that the next area of interest to students of Wordsworth is going to be *The Excursion,* this book has been written with the
intention of providing a general introduction for the serious reader who
wishes to tackle *The Excursion* as a poem rather than as a source for
biographical data or for quotations to be used in some other connection.
The need for such a study should be clear to anyone who has sought
scholarly aid in approaching *The Excursion* and has found how fragmentary and scattered the work on the poem has been. My study is necessarily very largely spadework, for the foundations have never been
adequately laid. I have tried to assemble for the first time all available
material on the poem and to study the poem in some detail as an independent literary work. I have done so in the belief that *The Excursion,*
despite its many flaws, is an important focal point in Wordsworth's
poetical development, deserving much closer attention than it has had in
the past; that it is the most complete and honest statement that has come
down to us of the psychological problems posed for an Englishman by
the failure of the French Revolution; and that a better grasp of the facts
about the poem, a fuller understanding of its meaning, and a more
thorough familiarity with the qualities of its poetic style than have hitherto been possible will make it easier to evaluate and more enjoyable
to read.

Since this book left my hand, the new Oxford edition of *The Excursion* has appeared (*The Poetical Works of William Wordsworth,* v,
E. De Selincourt and H. Darbishire, eds. [Oxford, Clarendon Press,
1949]), making available for the first time complete information on the
surviving manuscripts of *The Excursion.* Chapter II of the present study,
which deals extensively with the textual history of the poem, should
therefore be read in the light of Appendix III, which has been added to
make use of the new material.

In its original form this study was submitted as a dissertation to Yale
University in candidacy for the degree of Doctor of Philosophy. The
subject was suggested by Professor Frederick A. Pottle and the study
was pursued under his direction. To him I am deeply indebted for his
valuable counsel and criticism and for his generous donation of time and
assistance. No such acknowledgment as this can express my gratitude
for the privilege of having been associated with him.

I am also very grateful to my wife for her occasional assistance and
for her long patience and encouragement. Professor Benjamin C. Nangle
and Mrs. Frank McMullan have also been very kind and helpful in the
latter stages of my work.

I also wish to thank Professor Alan L. Strout of Texas Technical College and Professor Kenneth MacLean of Victoria College for help in the initial stages of my work. An unpublished Yale dissertation by Robert W. Daniel, "The Reviews of Wordsworth's *Excursion*," has been of great assistance to me, and I am grateful for the author's permission to make use of his findings.

Thomas Hutchinson's edition of *The Poetical Works of Wordsworth* (London, Oxford University Press, 1932) has been adopted as the standard text for all references to Wordsworth's poetry, A. B. Grosart's edition of *The Prose Works of William Wordsworth* (London, E. Moxon, Son, 1876) has been used for the prose, and Ernest De Selincourt's edition of the *Journals of Dorothy Wordsworth* (London and New York, Macmillan, 1941) has been adopted. The following standard abbreviations have been used for references to the letters.

EL	*The Early Letters of William and Dorothy Wordsworth.* Ernest De Selincourt, ed. Oxford, Clarendon Press, 1935.
MY	*The Letters of William and Dorothy Wordsworth, The Middle Years.* Ernest De Selincourt, ed. Oxford, Clarendon Press, 1939.
LY	*The Letters of William and Dorothy Wordsworth, The Later Years.* Ernest De Selincourt, ed. Oxford, Clarendon Press, 1939.

Other abbreviations used in this book are as follows.

Coleridge, *Letters*	*The Letters of Samuel Taylor Coleridge.* E. H. Coleridge, ed. London, William Heinemann, 1895.
Dorothy, *Journals*	*Journals of Dorothy Wordsworth.* Ernest De Selincourt, ed. London and New York, Macmillan, 1941.
Keats, *Letters*	*The Letters of John Keats.* M. B. Forman, ed. London, Oxford University Press, 1935.
Lamb, *Works*	*The Works of Charles and Mary Lamb.* E. V. Lucas, ed. London, Methuen, 1905.
"Rydal Mount Library"	"Catalogue of the Sale of the Rydal Mount Library," *Transactions of the Wordsworth Society,* No. 6. Edinburgh, T. & A. Constable, 1884.
Table Talk	*Table Talk and Omniana of Samuel Taylor Coleridge.* C. Patmore, ed. London, Oxford University Press, 1917.

Wordsworth, *Poems*   *The Poetical Works of William Words-*
                         worth. W. Knight, ed. London, Macmillan,
                         1896.

Wordsworth, *Prose*   *The Prose Works of William Wordsworth.*
                         A. B. Grosart, ed. London, E. Moxon, Son,
                         1876.

Wordsworth, *Works*   *The Poetical Works of William Words-*
                         worth. E. Dowden, ed. London, G. Bell &
                         Sons, 1893.

Dartmouth College
July, 1949

CONTENTS

If an Author, by any single composition, has impressed us with respect for his talents, it is useful to consider this as affording a presumption, that on other occasions where we have been displeased, he, nevertheless, may not have written ill or absurdly; and further, to give him so much credit for this one composition as may induce us to review what has displeased us, with more care than we should otherwise have bestowed upon it.

—Preface to *Lyrical Ballads* (1800)

THE EXCURSION

I

Introduction: The Reputation of The Excursion

WORDSWORTH'S longest poem, *The Excursion*,[1] has come to be almost a synonym for poetic dullness and difficulty, particularly among those who have never given it the careful and sympathetic study it requires. In fact, it has been generally felt that *The Excursion* is a work which can be safely neglected. In studies of Wordsworth's thought it has been customary to extract passages from *The Excursion* which lend support to theories based primarily on *The Prelude* and the shorter poems, while the development of ideas in their context in the longer poem has been left almost unexplored.

This state of affairs is particularly surprising in the light of Wordsworth's own emphatic statement that *The Excursion* is a principal part of the main structure of his poetical achievement, to which *The Prelude* is a mere introduction and all his shorter pieces only minor commentaries.[2] This *magnum opus* Wordsworth called *The Recluse,* and *The Excursion* was the second of its projected three main parts. *The Recluse* was to be his "Philosophic Poem"[3] *par excellence,* containing his "most interesting feelings concerning Man, Nature, and Society."[4] Coleridge shared this expansive confidence and enthusiasm for the plan: ". . . I prophesy immortality to his *Recluse* as the first and finest philosophical poem . . . ."[5]

When Wordsworth had completed *The Excursion,* he felt well satisfied with the result and considered the poem worthy of its intended position as a major portion of his chief monument. Just before publishing it, he wrote to Poole:

My poetical Labours have often suffered long interruptions; but I have at last resolved to send to the Press a portion of a poem which, if I live to finish it, I hope future times will "not willingly let die." These you know are the words of my great predecessor, and the depth of my feelings upon some

1. In the first edition (1814) *The Excursion* was 9,035 lines long, or 1,152 lines longer than *The Prelude* (1850). After all revisions *The Excursion* was reduced to its present length of 8,850 lines, 967 longer than *The Prelude*.
2. See the Preface to the edition of 1814.
3. Wordsworth to Wrangham, early in 1804, *EL*, p. 355.
4. Wordsworth to Sir George Beaumont, December 25, 1804, *ibid.,* p. 424.
5. Coleridge to Richard Sharp, January 15, 1804, *The Letters of Samuel Taylor Coleridge,* E. H. Coleridge, ed. (London, William Heinemann, 1895), II, 450 (hereafter referred to as Coleridge, *Letters*).

subjects seems to justify me in the act of applying them to myself, while speaking to a Friend . . . .[6]

After Francis Jeffrey's slashing review of *The Excursion,* Wordsworth's confidence was still unwavering: "I am delighted to learn that your Edinburgh Aristarch has declared against *The Excursion,* as he will have the mortification of seeing a book enjoy a high reputation, to which he has not contributed."[7] Wordsworth had tempered his confidence a little by the middle of March, 1815, when he wrote the following prediction, which is doubly important because it also shows that the poet was well aware of those characteristics of *The Excursion* which were to prove the greatest stumblingblock to its popularity: ". . . as it is in some places a little abstruse, and in all, serious, without any of the modern attractions of glittering style, or incident to provoke curiosity, it cannot be expected to make its way without difficulty."[8] When *The Excursion* failed to win the immediate acclaim he had expected, Wordsworth was probably forced to place his trust in posterity for a just estimate of the poem. Dorothy, whose ideas were often a faithful reflection of William's, wrote:

As to the permanent fate of that poem or of my Brother's collected Works I have not the shadow of a doubt. I know that the good and pure and noble-minded will in [*seal*] days and when we sleep in the grave be elevated delighted and better by what he has performed in solitude for the delight of his own Soul independent of lofty hopes of being of service to his fellow-creatures.[9]

The reception given to *The Excursion* by the most influential critics was distinctly unfavorable. One of the most famous book reviews ever written is Francis Jeffrey's review of *The Excursion.*[1] It is commonly held that Jeffrey's review is not so thoroughly condemnatory as it seems at first. This opinion is almost baseless. The review is overwhelmingly adverse. The final impression it leaves with a reader is that *The Excursion* is definitely not worth reading, and Wordsworth is condemned outright as incorrigible. The passages quoted with approval serve only to enforce the decision by lending credit to the reviewer's honesty. It is unfortunate that this review probably has had more sympathetic readers than *The Excursion* itself—unfortunate because it can be fairly definitely established that Jeffrey's critical judgment of Wordsworth was largely dishonest. For example, Coleridge wrote, "I give you my honour that Jeffrey himself told me that *he* was himself an enthusiastic admirer of

6. Wordsworth to Poole, April 28, 1814, *MY,* p. 596.
7. Wordsworth to R. P. Gillies, December 22, 1814, *ibid.,* p. 615. Wordsworth applies the name "Aristarch" to Jeffrey at some length in a footnote to his discussion of that critic in *A Letter to a Friend of Robert Burns* (London, 1816), pp. 30–4.
8. Wordsworth to Poole, March 13, 1815, *MY,* p. 646.
9. Dorothy to C. Clarkson, December 31, 1814, *ibid.,* p. 625.
1. *The Edinburgh Review,* xxiv (1814), 1–30.

Wordsworth's poetry, but it was necessary that a Review should have a character."[2] Scott adds the following evidence: "I don't know what turn the Edinr. Reviewers will take—Jeffrey is said in private to talk very highly but that is no rule for his public criticism for I['ve] seen him weep warm tears over Wordsworth's poetry & you know how he treats the poor Balladmaker when he is mounted into the Scorner's chair."[3] Jeffrey's review set the tone for most of the subsequent reviews, and they all bear its mark in one form or another, either in imitation or in opposition. It has unquestionably had a permanently injurious effect on the fortunes of *The Excursion*.[4]

It was to be expected that Coleridge would come out promptly with a favorable review, for he had praised very highly among his friends those parts of the poem which he had seen, and it was known that he had assisted in its conception. There is some evidence that he intended to write a review. Lamb wrote to Wordsworth: "Coleridge swore in a letter to me he would review the Exc[n]. in the Quarterly."[5] But Coleridge never wrote the review[6] and he let it be known that he was sorely disappointed in *The Excursion*.[7] This must have been a severe blow to the reputation of the poem.

Lamb's favorable review, which appeared in the *Quarterly* for November, 1814,[8] was so mangled by Gifford[9] that Dorothy Wordsworth could write that she was convinced the *Quarterly's* treatment of *The Excursion* would do more harm than the *Edinburgh's*.[1]

Hazlitt's review,[2a] while it was not particularly adverse on the whole, contained a very brilliant attack on rural manners as poetic subject matter, which was by far the most striking part of the article.[3a] Furthermore, by the time he collected his essays for publication as *The Round Table* in

2. S. T. Coleridge to Daniel Stuart, 1825, Coleridge, *Letters*, p. 742.
3. Scott to George Ellis, July 6, 1810, *The Letters of Sir Walter Scott*, H. J. C. Grierson, ed. (London, Constable, 1932–37), XII, 324.
4. For a detailed consideration of the Wordsworth-Jeffrey affair, see Russell Noyes, *Wordsworth and Jeffrey in Controversy*, Indiana University Publications, Humanities Series No. 5 (Bloomington, 1941); and Robert W. Daniel, "Jeffrey and Wordsworth: the Shape of Persecution," *Sewanee Review*, L (1942), 195–212.
5. Lamb to Wordsworth, September 19, 1814, *The Works of Charles and Mary Lamb*, E. V. Lucas, ed. (London, Methuen, 1905), VI, 444 (hereafter referred to as Lamb, *Works*).
6. Wordsworth wrote to Catherine Clarkson, December 31, 1814, rather sadly: "I smiled at your notion of Coleridge reviewing the Ex. in the Ed. I much doubt whether he has read three pages of the poem . . . ." *MY*, p. 662.
7. See letter to Lady Beaumont of April 3, 1815; letter to Wordsworth of May 30, 1815; Henry Crabb Robinson's diary for January 29, 1817, and December 21, 1822; *Biographia Literaria*, J. Shawcross, ed. (Oxford, Clarendon Press, 1907), II, 102.
8. *The Quarterly Review*, XII (1814), 100–11.
9. See letter from Lamb to Wordsworth, January, 1815, Lamb, *Works*, VI, 452.
1. Dorothy to Mrs. Christopher Wordsworth, February 27, 1815, *MY*, p. 642.
2a. *The Examiner*, CCCXLVII (1814), 541–2, 555–8, 636–8.
3a. On January 29, 1817, Crabb Robinson recorded that Lamb told him Hazlitt wept when he sat down to review *The Excursion*, because he was disappointed in it and

1817, Hazlitt, like some others, had developed a deep personal and political dislike for Wordsworth, with the result that he omitted some of the most encomiastic parts of the essay and altered others to give the whole a more unfavorable tone. He also disparaged *The Excursion* in brief digressions in essays on other subjects. For instance:

. . . a single letter from the pen of Gray, is worth all the pedlar-reasoning of Mr. Wordsworth's Eternal Recluse, from the hour he first squats himself down in the sun to the end of his preaching. In the first we have the light unstudied pleasantries of a wit, and a man of feeling ;—in the last we are talked to death by an arrogant old proser, and buried in a heap of the most perilous stuff and the most dusty philosophy.[4]

Another severe blow to the prestige of the poem was Byron's famous couplet in *Don Juan:*

> A drowsy, frowsy poem called *The Excursion,*
> Writ in a manner which is my aversion.[5]

James Hogg's parodies of Wordsworth in *The Poetic Mirror* are directed primarily at *The Excursion*. Hogg made use of the clever and devastating trick of permitting *The Excursion* to be its own parodist, by quoting *verbatim* several passages from different parts of the poem, carefully selected to illustrate the stylistic weaknesses, and placing them in a haphazard sequence which stripped them of all poetic semblance.[6]

The Excursion also fared ill at the hands of Wordsworth's erratic "champion" John Wilson, in the popular "Noctes Ambrosianae" in *Blackwood's*. Wilson even went so far as to say, "I confess that the 'Excursion' is the worst poem, of any character, in the English language."[7]

The newly launched *Fraser's Magazine* hastened to announce ". . . that the *Excursion* is not in strict language a poem, but a rambling

---

could not praise it as it deserved. Robinson comments somewhat acidly that he does not believe Hazlitt wept. *Henry Crabb Robinson on Books and Their Writers,* E. J. Morley, ed. (Oxford, Clarendon Press, 1927), p. 202.

4. "The Letters of Horace Walpole," *The Edinburgh Review,* xxxi (1818), 83–4.

5. Canto iii, 847–8.

6. James Hogg, *The Poetic Mirror* (London, Longman, Hurst, Rees, Orme, & Brown; and John Ballantyne, Edinburgh, 1816), pp. 133–87. There are three parodies of Wordsworth. The first, "The Stranger," contains a climactic speech by the poet which is a patchwork of quotations from *The Excursion*, iv, 1126–32, 1204, 1264; v, 959–60, 978–1010. The second, "The Flying Tailor," has a churchyard setting and a digression on the blessings of the tailor's trade, a parody of the praise of peddlers in *The Excursion*. The third, "James Rigg," is a tale of a blinded quarryman and insists on the continuance of lost senses, a parody of the similar stories in *The Excursion*. All three poems are said to be further extracts from *The Recluse.*

7. "Noctes Ambrosianae," No. 21, *Blackwood's Edinburgh Magazine,* xviii (September, 1825), 381. See also *ibid.,* xxix (April, 1831), 695–6.

series of poetic thoughts and pathetic pictures, unfinished and without obvious construction."[8]

Matthew Arnold added the crowning touch to this ignominy when, in his essay on Wordsworth (1888),[9] he gave his specific approval to Jeffrey's statement, "This will never do."[1] He also said, *"The Excursion* abounds with philosophy, and therefore *The Excursion* is to the Wordsworthian what it never can be to the disinterested lover of poetry—a satisfactory work . . . . [It is] a tissue of elevated but abstract verbiage, alien to the very nature of poetry."[2] It has recently been pointed out[3] that the direction of Arnold's attack on Wordsworth as a philosopher was determined at least in part by his animosity for what he calls "Wordsworthians." Leslie Stephen, in his essay praising Wordsworth's philosophy,[4] was the most conspicuous of these "Wordsworthians," and Arnold attacks Stephen specifically in the section of his essay in which he ridicules the passage on education in Book IX of *The Excursion.*[5] He imagines a social science congress, with a bald, bespectacled orator declaiming these lines from *The Excursion,* while a poor child of nature who has chanced to wander in is overwhelmed with woe. The orator is Leslie Stephen and the child of nature is presumably Arnold himself. Whatever motivated Arnold's attack, it was most damaging to *The Excursion,* as any disparagement of Wordsworth's philosophy must be, for *The Excursion* is primarily a philosophical poem.

It is not to be thought that *The Excursion* received only unfavorable reviews.[6] Only two, those of Jeffrey and Merivale, were distinctly hostile, while some were completely eulogistic and the remainder at least partly so. However, the most favorable reviews appeared in the least influential journals.

Thus the influence of the critics on the fortunes of *The Excursion* has been predominantly adverse. In the light of this fact, it is interesting to find that many of Wordsworth's most respectable contemporaries rated the poem very high and that it was apparently for many years widely read. Charles Lamb called *The Excursion* ". . . the noblest conversa-

8. *Fraser's Magazine,* III (June, 1831), 557–66. See also *ibid.,* VI (November, 1832), 607–25.

9. *Essays in Criticism* Ser. II, (London, Macmillan, 1888), pp. 122–62.

1. *Ibid.,* p. 156.

2. *Ibid.,* pp. 149–50. Compare the wording of the last phrase to Jeffrey's ". . . a tissue of moral and devotional ravings . . . ."

3. J. D. Wilson, *Leslie Stephen and Matthew Arnold as Critics of Wordsworth* (Cambridge, Cambridge University Press, 1939), pp. 36–9 (the Leslie Stephen Lecture delivered before the University of Cambridge on May 2, 1939).

4. "Wordsworth's Ethics," *Hours in a Library* (London, Smith, Elder, 1879), Ser. III, pp. 178–229.

5. *The Excursion,* IX, 239 ff.

6. For a complete chronological list of the reviews, with brief descriptive notes, see Appendix I of this book.

tional poem I ever read. A day in heaven . . . ."[7] John Keats, despite
his dislike for Wordsworth's overt didacticism, called *The Excursion* one
of the "three things to rejoice at in this Age."[8] Aubrey de Vere in 1839
echoed Keats's phrase in describing *The Excursion* as one of "the three
great poems of the age."[9] Robert Southey, after reading *The Excursion,*
proclaimed that posterity would place Wordsworth by the side of Milton.[1] John Gibson Lockhart recorded that he "was most highly delighted"[2] with *The Excursion* and "enjoyed" it "deeply."[3] In America,
Emerson found it a revelation,[4] and young Edwin Arlington Robinson
called it "a magnificent thing," saying that "A man must read that poem
before he knows Wordsworth; it is the man himself done over into
words, and magnificent words, too."[5]

Wordsworth probably felt that his confidence in *The Excursion* was
justified before his death, for he lived to see it go through at least seven
editions[6] and was still receiving letters of praise for it in his last years.
Nevertheless it was a mistaken sense of security, for within a decade after
his death the poem had fallen into the state of almost total neglect from
which it has not recovered to this day.

7. Lamb to Wordsworth, August 9, 1814, Lamb, *Works,* VI, 434–8.

8. Keats to B. R. Haydon, January 10, 1818, *The Letters of John Keats,* M. B. For-
man, ed. (London, Oxford University Press, 1935), p. 79 (hereafter referred to as
Keats, *Letters*). Keats repeated the assertion in a letter to George and Thomas Keats
of January 13, 1818, using the words "three things superior in the modern world." *Ibid.,*
p. 80.

9. Wilfred Ward, *Aubrey de Vere* (London, Longmans, 1904), p. 34.

1. Southey to Bernard Barton, December 19, 1814, repeated in slightly different words
in Southey to Chauncey Hare Townshend, August 17, 1816. C. C. Southey, *The Life
and Correspondence of Robert Southey* (London, Longman, Brown, Green & Longmans,
1849–50), IV, pp. 91, 195.

2. A. Lang, *The Life and Letters of John Gibson Lockhart* (London, John C. Nimmo,
1897), I, 70.

3. *Ibid.,* I, 102.

4. See "Thoughts on Modern Literature," in *Emerson's Complete Works,* J. E. Cabot,
ed. (Boston and New York, Houghton, Mifflin, 1893), XII, 187.

5. *Untriangulated Stars* (Cambridge, Harvard University Press, 1947), pp. 221–2.

6. For a list of the editions of *The Excursion,* see Appendix II of this book.

II

The History of The Excursion

THE EXCURSION was composed during a period of at least eighteen years. It was begun at the time when Wordsworth was entering his most productive period and was finished in what is usually considered the last year before his alleged anticlimax, 1814. Thus the composition of the entire poem falls within the poet's greatest years. *The Excursion* as a poem sufficiently independent to be published alone, however, was not conceived until 1813. A great portion of it had been written by that time, but the various parts had not been knitted into the unified whole which was finally published. They were scattered among Wordsworth's manuscripts as miscellaneous drafts for *The Recluse,* independent poems, and rejected drafts for *The Prelude.* The most natural way to study the composition of *The Excursion* is to take up each separate organism independently and to show how it grew and was finally included in the larger scheme. Wordsworth himself has given us an account of the composition of *The Excursion* in the Fenwick Note[1] to the poem, but this account is incomplete and, in some respects, inaccurate.

I

The first part of *The Excursion* to be written was "Margaret" or "The Ruined Cottage," which now constitutes Book I.

Wordsworth tells us in the Fenwick Note[2] that lines 871–916 of Book I were the first lines composed and that they were written at Racedown in 1795. William and Dorothy did not move into Racedown until September of 1795. For some time Wordsworth was occupied in getting settled, and he was tutoring young Basil Montagu. He was also attempting to dispose of "Guilt and Sorrow." On March 21, 1796, he wrote to William Mathews,[3] giving an account of his reading and gardening, and saying, "As to writing, it is out of the question." He added that he had been writing satires, in a tone which would indicate that he had been writing nothing else. Although the subject matter of these forty-five lines is similar to that of "Guilt and Sorrow" (1791–94), the style resembles more closely that of the poems written in 1797–98. The sharp

1. Isabella Fenwick Note to *The Excursion, The Prose Works of William Wordsworth,* A. B. Grosart, ed. (London, E. Moxon, Son, 1876), III, 195–6 (hereafter referred to as Wordsworth, *Prose*). 2. *Ibid.*
3. Wordsworth to William Mathews, March 21, 1796, *EL,* pp. 154–6.

cleavage between Wordsworth's juvenilia and his mature work is usually dated 1797. I consider it highly improbable that Wordsworth wrote these early lines of "The Ruined Cottage" before the middle of 1796, and I suspect they were written even later. Dorothy Wordsworth, in a letter of June, 1797, which was almost certainly addressed to Mary Hutchinson,[4] said that the first thing read after Coleridge's arrival on his first visit to Racedown (June 6, 1797) "was William's new poem *The Ruined Cottage* with which he was much delighted." Now, Mary had left Racedown just before Coleridge arrived,[5] and it is probably safe to say that she saw as much of the poem as was then written. Either she took a copy home with her or Dorothy sent it to her, for in a later letter we find definite evidence that she had lines 871–916 and no more.[6] It seems highly probable that if any other part of the poem had been written when Mary received this copy, it would have been included, and the fact that Dorothy, writing to Mary, called it "William's new poem" in June, 1797, seems to me to point very strongly to the possibility that lines 871–916, which Mary either had already copied or was going to receive, were all that had been written in June, 1797, and that they had been written quite recently. It is perhaps also of some significance that Coleridge, writing to the Rev. J. P. Estlin during the same month of June, 1797, included a transcript of these same lines, made for him by Dorothy.[7] This date agrees with Wordsworth's statements in the Fenwick Note that that passage was written first, and at Racedown. The only change is in the year, and it is generally acknowledged that the dates in these notes are untrustworthy.

Lamb visited Coleridge during the second week in July (1797), and "Margaret" was read to him at that time.[8]

It is not known when Wordsworth began his expansion of "The Ruined Cottage." He was probably engaged in it during the autumn of 1797 and had written a great deal by the time he appropriated the *Alfoxden Notebook* from Dorothy and continued the composition in that. Evidently that notebook contains upward of 450 lines, and all of them can be dated between January 20 and March 5, 1798. They deal particularly with the character of the Wanderer.[9] The expansion was almost complete by March 5, when Dorothy, in response to a request of Mary Hutchinson, transcribed for her a great part of what had been added to "The Ruined Cottage" since Mary had received her transcrip-

4. *Ibid.*, pp. 168–9. See editor's footnote.　　　　5. *Ibid.*, p. 167, n.

6. Dorothy to Mary Hutchinson, March 5, 1798, *ibid.*, pp. 176–87, especially: "You have the rest to the end of Margaret's story," p. 187.

7. Coleridge to Estlin, June, 1797, *Unpublished Letters of Samuel Taylor Coleridge*, E. L. Griggs, ed. (London, Constable, 1932), I, 76–7.

8. Lamb to Wordsworth, August 9, 1814, Lamb, *Works*, VI, 434.

9. *The Prelude*, E. De Selincourt, ed. (London, Oxford University Press, 1926), pp. xxxiii, xxi, 502.

tion of lines 871–916.[1] Probably Dorothy had written Mary that the poem was being expanded, and Mary replied by asking for a copy of the additions. In response Dorothy wrote that she could not send them all, for the poem had now grown to the length of 900 lines. This is most important, for it enables us to reconstruct almost the whole poem as it then existed. Of these 900 lines she transcribed only 379. However, her acknowledged omissions made it clear that the poem then corresponded in scope almost exactly to what is now Book I of *The Excursion,* which is 970 lines long but only 916 to the end of the story of Margaret. The poem was considerably revised before it was published as a part of *The Excursion.*[2] In the final version, only 65 lines of *The Excursion,* Book I, are identical with lines in Dorothy's transcript. There are only about 30 lines in the transcript which have no resemblance to lines in *The Excursion.* The remaining lines copied by Dorothy all reappear in *The Excursion* in a slightly altered form. Since Wordsworth's practice in revision, as seen in the parts we have, was definitely to expand the original, the conclusion is inescapable that Dorothy's "900 lines" included some which were either omitted from the final form or used in a different part of *The Excursion* or in *The Prelude.* At least some of the lines originally written to describe the Wanderer were ultimately used in *The Prelude* to describe Wordsworth himself.[3] It is probably impossible to determine just when "The Ruined Cottage" was incorporated in the larger plan of *The Recluse.* De Selincourt seems to feel that it had been incorporated by March 6, 1798, the day after Dorothy transcribed it for Mary Hutchinson.[4] We shall consider this below.

2

In the Fenwick Note Wordsworth informs us that the second part of *The Excursion* to be composed after Book I, lines 871–916, was Book IV, lines 1,207–74. This crucial passage on communion with the forms of nature as a means of restoration from despondency was certainly written early; it probably dates from roughly the same time as the expansion of "The Ruined Cottage." Coleridge quotes a part of the passage in a letter of April, 1798,[5] and this is the earliest evidence we

1. Dorothy to Mary Hutchinson, March 5, 1798, *EL,* pp. 176–87.
2. See, for example, December 23, 1801, in the *Journals of Dorothy Wordsworth,* E. De Selincourt, ed. (London and New York, Macmillan, 1941), I, 95 (hereafter referred to as Dorothy, *Journals*) : "William worked at *The Ruined Cottage* and made himself very ill." I do not take this to be an erroneous reference to "The Pedlar," since it becomes evident from the succeeding entries that Wordsworth had set aside "The Pedlar" for a time. Three days later he was working on *The Prelude,* and there is no mention of his resuming work on "The Pedlar" until January 30, 1802. *Ibid.,* I, 104. The best evidence of revision is naturally a comparison of the two texts.
3. *The Prelude,* De Selincourt, ed., p. xxxiii.   4. *Ibid.*
5. Coleridge to the Rev. George Coleridge, April, 1798, Coleridge, *Letters,* I, p. 244.

have of its existence. It was certainly much revised before it reached its final form, but in its general significance it remained the same. It is important to remember that a passage written during the first flowering of Wordsworth's genius, when he and Coleridge were just becoming aware of the importance of nature to their world-views, was given one of the most climactic positions in the whole of *The Excursion,* a fact which reveals the tenacious unity of Wordsworth's thought over the years and shows his tendency to modify and strengthen his old positions with his new, rather than to substitute the new for the old.

3

Next was the conception of Wordsworth's most grandiose scheme, a philosophical poem to contain all his most interesting thoughts on man, nature, and society and to include all his poetry, either directly or by implicit parallel, in its massive design. The poem was to be entitled *The Recluse* and was to be so extensive that Wordsworth could say, "Indeed, I know not any thing which will not come within the scope of my plan."[6] The idea was clearly an outgrowth of conversation with Coleridge.

The earliest evidence we have of its conception is in a letter of Wordsworth, dated March 6, 1798,[7] in which he announced the plan and said he had already written "1,300 lines." On March 8, Coleridge wrote Cottle that Wordsworth had written "1,200 lines of a blank verse, superior, I hesitate not to aver, to anything in our language which in any way resembles it."[8] And on March 11 Wordsworth told Losh that the 1,300 lines had been written in the past few weeks.[9] These letters tell us a great deal about what had been done—that it was in blank verse, that it had been composed in the past few weeks, that it was 1,300 lines long, and that its subject matter was philosophical, "views of Nature, Man, and Society"[1]—but they furnish us with almost no clue as to the exact identity of the lines written. De Selincourt, working on the clues we do have, identifies them as follows :[2]

Later printed as Prospectus to *The Excursion*	107 lines
Meeting with the discharged soldier, *The Prelude,* Bk. IV, 373–504	141 lines
"The Old Cumberland Beggar"	197 lines
"The Ruined Cottage"	900 lines
Total	1,345 lines

The earlier versions of the first three were probably shorter. This di-

6. Wordsworth to James Tobin, March 6, 1798, *EL,* pp. 187–9.   7. *Ibid.*
8. Coleridge to Cottle, March 8, 1798, Coleridge, *Letters,* 1, 239.
9. Wordsworth to James Losh, March 11, 1798, *EL,* p. 190.   1. *Ibid.*
2. *The Prelude,* E. De Selincourt, ed., p. xxxiii.

vision of the 1,300 lines is based on the facts that the *Alfoxden Note-book* shows that Wordsworth had been working on most of these poems in the past few weeks and that this is presumably all the blank verse Wordsworth had written at the time. But it is dangerous to make such assumptions. For example, lines 1,207–74 of *The Excursion,* Book IV, were almost certainly written by then, and they would clearly have formed a part of the 1,300 lines. Furthermore, it is far from certain that "The Ruined Cottage" had been incorporated in the larger scheme by this time. At least it seems suspicious that on one day (March 5) Dorothy should treat it as a totally independent narrative poem and that on the very next day (March 6) Wordsworth should treat it as the major part of a speculative fragment. Coleridge's enthusiasm at this time is also hard to explain if "The Ruined Cottage" had been incorporated, for as late as 1832 we find him lamenting that "The Ruined Cottage" had not been printed separately.[3] On the other hand, Coleridge often applied to "The Ruined Cottage" the same words that he used in speaking of *The Recluse:* "superior, I hesitate not to aver, to anything in our language which in any way resembles it."[4] Dorothy, in her journal for December 23, 1801, seems still to have regarded "The Ruined Cottage" as a separate poem.[5] It is dangerous to assume that there was no other blank verse written by March, 1798, simply because no manuscript containing it has come down to us. Perhaps the only safe assumption is that some form of the 107 lines subsequently printed as Prospectus to *The Excursion* was a part of the 1,300 lines, for the words "On Man, on Nature, and on Human Life," as well as the broad, confident tone of the whole passage, seem to bear a close relation to the letters of this time.

After the composition of these original 1,300 lines, *The Recluse* was neglected for some time. In the summer of 1799 Coleridge was urging Wordsworth to go on with it.[6] In a letter of October 12, 1799, it becomes evident that Wordsworth had decided to dedicate *The Recluse* to Coleridge, evidently in a "tailpiece" to be appended to *The Recluse.*[7] Wordsworth, it eventually proved, had a pressing need to review the development of his own mind before he could feel justified in recording his philosophy. In this spirit the tailpiece was developed into the long poem published after Wordsworth's death as *The Prelude.* In 1804, when

3. "Table Talk," July 21, 1832, *Table Talk and Omniana of Samuel Taylor Coleridge,* C. Patmore, ed. (London, Oxford University Press, 1917), pp. 188–9 (hereafter referred to as *Table Talk*).
4. These words are applied to the "1,200 lines" of *The Recluse* in the letter to Cottle of March 8, 1798, quoted above. They are applied to "The Ruined Cottage" in a letter to Lady Beaumont of April 3, 1815 and in *Table Talk,* p. 188.
5. Dorothy, *Journals,* I, 95. See p. 9, n. 2, *supra.*
6. Coleridge to Wordsworth, summer of 1799, in C. Wordsworth, *Memoirs of William Wordsworth* (London, Moxon, 1851), I, 159.
7. Coleridge to Wordsworth, October 12, 1799, *ibid.*

The Prelude was well under way, Dorothy described it as "an appendix to *The Recluse*."⁸ It was soon decided, however, that it would serve better as an introduction,⁹ and such Wordsworth considered it for the rest of his life. In fact, his great reason for not publishing *The Prelude* during his life was that its only justification was in its relationship to *The Recluse*.¹ It was "tributary" to *The Recluse,* and less important.²

After the composition of the original 1,300 lines of *The Recluse* Wordsworth evidently did no more with it, apart from *The Prelude,* until he wrote Part I, Book I, "Home at Grasmere," sometime between the end of January and April 11, 1800. This date is definitely deducible from internal evidence. Passages in the poem make it clear that Wordsworth and Dorothy had been at Grasmere for two months of winter weather before it was written,³ and they did not reach Grasmere until December 20, 1799. Another passage proves that Coleridge had not yet visited them,⁴ while it is known he was there by April 11.⁵ The last 107 lines of this poem are those which were printed as Prospectus to *The Excursion* in 1814, and I have already suggested that they may have been written early in 1798. Wordsworth printed three other passages from "Home at Grasmere" during his life,⁶ and two more appeared in the *Memoirs* in 1851,⁷ but the poem was not published as a whole until 1888.⁸ᵃ It is probably the only part of *The Recluse* written by 1814 that was not included in *The Excursion.*

After writing this opening book of *The Recluse* in early 1800, Wordsworth neglected his great work for several years. In 1801, 1802, and 1803 he devoted himself to "The Pedlar" (an independent poem), to parts of *The Prelude,* and to shorter poems. In November, 1803, Dorothy wrote, "William has not yet done anything of importance at his great work."⁹ᵃ Coleridge's enthusiasm for Wordsworth and *The Recluse* was

---

8. Dorothy to Mrs. Clarkson, February 13, 1804, *EL,* p. 361.

9. Wordsworth to Sotheby, March 12, 1804, *ibid.,* p. 372. The first evidence of the famous figure in the Preface to *The Excursion,* in which *The Prelude* is described as an antechapel and *The Recluse* as a cathedral, occurs in a letter, Wordsworth to Sir G. Beaumont, June 3, 1805, in which Wordsworth calls *The Prelude* "a sort of portico to *The Recluse." Ibid.,* p. 497.

1. Wordsworth to R. Sharp, April 29, 1804, *ibid.,* p. 386.

2. Wordsworth to De Quincey, March 6, 1804, *ibid.,* p. 370. See also p. 372.

3. See "Home at Grasmere," ll. 181, 244.

4. See *ibid.,* ll. 657–61.   5. See *EL,* p. 242.

6. "Water-Fowl" (203–29) in 1827 and subsequent editions, and two passages in *Guide to the Lake District:* "Water-Fowl" again and ll. 122–5 (Wordsworth, *Prose,* II, 246–7, 264).

7. Lines 152–67, *Memoirs of William Wordsworth,* I, 155–6; ll. 71–97, 110–25, *ibid.,* I, 157–8.

8a. William Wordsworth, *The Recluse* (London, Macmillan, 1888). Reviews: *Athenaeum,* LXII, 109–10; *Academy,* XXXV (1889), 17–18 (Dowden); *The Edinburgh Review,* CLIX (1889), 415–47 (Smith); *Saturday Review,* LXVII (January 12, 1889), 43–4. Second ed.: 1891.

9a. Dorothy to Mrs. Clarkson, November 13, 1803, *EL,* p. 351.

more ardent than ever in January, 1804,[1] and Wordsworth himself was still confident about his great poem.[2] On March 6, 1804, he described it to De Quincey in specific terms, saying, "I have written one book and several scattered fragments."[3] Possibly the one book was "Home at Grasmere" and the scattered fragments the 1,300 lines of 1798. However, it is also possible that "Home at Grasmere" had not yet been included in the plan for *The Recluse* and that the "one book" was "The Ruined Cottage" or something else. When Coleridge left for Malta in April, 1804, there was no longer an important stimulus to Wordsworth's composition of *The Recluse*.[4] Nevertheless, in December the plan was still very much in his mind, when he wrote to Sir George Beaumont, "I may have written of it altogether about 2,000 lines. It will consist, I hope, of about 10 or 12 thousand."[5] In this same letter he mentioned that "The Pedlar" had been made a part of *The Recluse*. This would add 280 lines more to the total and, if we include "Home at Grasmere" as well as the original 1,300 lines, the sum is well over 2,000 lines, but Wordsworth was obviously speaking in round numbers. Once again we cannot be sure.

Early in 1805 Wordsworth began to wish he could finish *The Prelude,* in order to fall to work on *The Recluse*.[6] But the death of John on February 5 brought all composition to a standstill. For a time Wordsworth had a plan for unburdening his heart of sorrow in a poem about John, to be included in *The Recluse*. Although he composed much, he was unable to finish it, and it was all lost.[7] In the depth of his sorrow he began to despair of ever finishing *The Recluse*.[8] Shortly afterward, however, having finished *The Prelude,* Wordsworth went on a short trip, supposedly to rest before beginning in earnest on *The Recluse*.[9] Two months later, although he was "anxious" to begin, he had not yet "resumed his great work," and the same was true through October and November.[1a] In December he was "reading for the nourishment of his mind preparatory to beginning,"[2a] and in January, 1806, his "thoughts were employed upon *The Recluse*."[3a] By the end of July he was finally at work, and going on rapidly.[4a] He had added 700 lines to the poem by August 1,[5a] and he continued until he had completed a book of 1,000

1. Coleridge to R. Sharp, January 15, 1804, Coleridge, *Letters,* II, 450.
2. Wordsworth to Wrangham, early in 1804, *EL,* p. 355.
3. Wordsworth to De Quincey, March 6, 1804, *ibid.,* p. 364.
4. See p. 61 of this book.
5. Wordsworth to Sir G. Beaumont, December 25, 1804, *EL,* p. 424.
6. Wordsworth to R. Sharp, February, 1805, *ibid.,* p. 441.
7. See *ibid.,* pp. 480, 488, 495.
8. Wordsworth to Sir G. Beaumont, June 3, 1805, *ibid.,* p. 497.
9. Dorothy to Lady Beaumont, June 11, 1805, *ibid.,* pp. 501–2.
1a. See *ibid.,* pp. 517, 528, 535, 547.   2a. *Ibid.,* p. 561.
3a. Dorothy to Lady Beaumont, January 19, 1806, *MY,* p. 2.
4a. See *ibid.,* pp. 47, 50.   5a. *Ibid.,* p. 51.

lines. Then, after a short rest, he wrote 300 lines more, "I hope all tolerably well, and certainly with good views."[6] After this burst of composition, he again set the poem aside and again began to fear that he would never finish it.[7] There is no evidence that he wrote any more of it for well over a year. In fact, not until September, 1808, did he write that he had added 500 lines.[8] Then there was another long lapse, until February, 1810, when he was once again deeply engaged in composition. Dorothy wrote, "Before he turns to any other labour, I hope he will have finished three books of *The Recluse*."[9] But he set it aside once more and did not take it up again until May, 1811.[1] He was soon interrupted anew,[2] however, and we do not find him back at work until late in December.[3] On February 6, 1812, Wordsworth wrote that *The Recluse* could not be published for many years because of the comprehensiveness of the subject.[4] 1812 was a year first of travel and then of the tragic death of Wordsworth's little daughter Catherine (June 4). The poet had hardly recovered from this blow when his son Thomas also died (December 1). Naturally, the great poem was neglected during these trying months.

On January 5, 1813, Dorothy wrote: "William has begun to look into his poem the Recluse within the last two days and I hope he will be the better for it."[5] Evidently from this time on Wordsworth made rapid progress, for on October 18 Henry Crabb Robinson recorded that *The Recluse* was to be published during the winter and that Southey had predicted it would establish Wordsworth as the first poet of his age and country.[6a] Nothing was published during the winter, but in April (1814) Dorothy wrote:

William is actually printing 9 books of his long poem. It has been copied in my absence, and great alterations have been made some of which indeed I had an opportunity of seeing during my week's visit. But the printing has since been going on briskly, and not one proofsheet has yet met my eyes. We are all most thankful that William has brought his mind to consent to printing so much of this work, for the MSS. were in such a state that, if it had pleased Heaven to take him from this world, they would have been almost useless. I do not think the book will be published before next winter.[7a]

6. Wordsworth to Sir G. Beaumont, September 8, 1806, *ibid.*, p. 62. In *EL*, p. 410, De Selincourt erroneously assigns this letter to the year 1804. The error is corrected in *MY*, p. 62.

7. Wordsworth to Sir Walter Scott, November 10, 1806, *MY*, p. 74.

8. Wordsworth to Samuel Rogers, September 29, 1808, *ibid.*, pp. 244–5.

9. Dorothy to Lady Beaumont, February 28, 1810, *ibid.*, p. 359.

1. Dorothy to C. Clarkson, May 12, 1811, *ibid.*, pp. 449–50.

2. Dorothy to C. Clarkson, August 14, 1811, *ibid.*, p. 463.

3. Dorothy to C. Clarkson, December 27, 1811, *ibid.*, p. 484.

4. Wordsworth to Lord Lonsdale, February 6, 1812, *ibid.*, p. 485.

5. Dorothy to C. Clarkson, January 5, 1813, *ibid.*, p. 535.

6a. *Henry Crabb Robinson on Books and Their Writers*, p. 132.

7a. Dorothy to C. Clarkson, April 24, 1814, *MY*, pp. 589–90.

Wordsworth described it to Wrangham—"It is serious, and has been written with great labour"[8]—and likewise to Poole.[9] In May he wrote that it was to be 8,000 lines long.[1] He must have added to it while it was in press, for when it finally appeared it was over 9,000 lines long.

In the Preface to *The Excursion* Wordsworth announced that this poem was the second of the three parts of which *The Recluse* was to have been composed and that here the ideas were presented through a dramatic medium, while in the first and third parts they were to be presented directly in meditative verse. He also implied that the composition of the first part was considerably advanced. This is unquestionably false. All that had been written of the first part was "Home at Grasmere." The rest had not even been planned (1815): "As he intends completely to plan the first part of the Recluse before he begins the composition, he must read many Books before he will fairly set to labour again."[2] Wordsworth wrote very little more of *The Recluse* before his death. There is evidence, however, that he did some work on it. For instance, in July, 1832, Sir William Hamilton wrote Aubrey de Vere that he had heard that Wordsworth had been so occupied with *The Recluse* during the previous winter "as to forget his meals and even his politics."[3] Likewise Robinson recorded that Wordsworth had read him a passage of poetry "containing a poetical view of water as an *element* in the composition of our globe," "which is to be an introduction to a portion of his great poem."[4] He always intended to finish it[5] but he never really settled down to work on it. Perhaps his final attitude is best summed up in these words of Dorothy (1824): "My Brother has not yet looked at the Recluse; he seems to feel the task so weighty that he shrinks from beginning with it . . . yet he knows that he has now no time to loiter if another great work is to be accomplished by him."[6] Years later he was apparently resigned to leaving it incomplete when he told Aubrey de Vere "that the 'Recluse' has never been written except a few passages—and probably never will."[7]

There are probably two main reasons why *The Recluse* was never finished. One reason is that the poet exhausted his material in *The Prelude* and *The Excursion*. The 1850 editor of *The Prelude* tells us in the Advertisement that the third part of *The Recluse* was only planned

8. Wordsworth to Wrangham, April 26, 1814, *ibid.*, p. 594.

9. Quoted on p. 1 of this book.

1. Wordsworth to Rogers, May 5, 1814, *MY*, pp. 597-8.

2. Dorothy to Sara Hutchinson, February 18, 1815, *ibid.*, p. 635.

3. Sir W. R. Hamilton to Aubrey de Vere, July 3, 1832, in R. P. Graves, *The Life of Sir William Rowan Hamilton* (London, Longmans, 1882), 1, 585.

4. *Henry Crabb Robinson on Books and Their Writers*, pp. 339-40.

5. See *MY*, p. 801; *LY*, pp. 28, 44, 71.

6. Dorothy to Henry Crabb Robinson, December 13, 1824, *The Correspondence of Henry Crabb Robinson with the Wordsworth Circle*, E. J. Morley, ed. (Oxford, Clarendon Press, 1927), p. 132.   7. Ward, *Aubrey de Vere*, p. 66.

and that practically all of what had been written of *The Recluse* apart from *The Excursion* and "Home at Grasmere" had been incorporated in the author's other publications. This seems to confirm the suspicion that Wordsworth had used up all his ideas. He had simply left himself nothing of pressing importance to say in the other two parts. The second reason is that Coleridge had lost interest in the scheme. After their misunderstanding in 1810, Wordsworth probably never again felt the great stimulus which Coleridge's ideas had provided in the past. When *The Excursion* appeared, Coleridge spoke at first of reviewing it, but this, like so many other things, he never did. Neither did he write Wordsworth any word of approbation. He merely kept a painful silence. Finally he let some words of adverse criticism drop in a letter to Lady Beaumont,[8] and she promptly relayed them to Wordsworth. This evidently caused Wordsworth considerable pain, for he wrote directly to Coleridge and asked him outright for a detailed, specific critique.[9] Coleridge replied frankly and kindly, reviewing the plan which he and Wordsworth had made for *The Recluse* in conversation and pointing out that the poem had failed to fulfill the purpose that had been planned for it.[1] As I have already indicated,[2] Coleridge was subsequently unsparing in his criticism of *The Excursion,* both in print and in conversation. However, he never ceased to accord the first two books of it the highest possible praise. But his frank disapprobation of the whole must have taken the joy out of the large scheme for Wordsworth. I doubt that the abuse of Jeffrey and his imitators was a primary influence in deterring Wordsworth from completing *The Recluse.* Wordsworth's confidence in his ability to complete the poem remained unshaken to the end, but the need and the burning desire to do so were gone.

4

The next separate part of what was to become *The Excursion* is "The Pedlar." This poem was evidently an independent organism, coeval with "The Ruined Cottage," into which was poured the overflow of the character of the Wanderer. It is difficult to ascertain just when it was separated from "The Ruined Cottage," for there is always the possibility (accepted by Dowden)[3] that "The Pedlar" was for a time

8. Coleridge to Lady Beaumont, April 3, 1815, Coleridge, *Letters,* II, 641–2.
9. Wordsworth to Coleridge, May 22, 1815, *MY,* pp. 669–70.
1. Coleridge to Wordsworth, May 30, 1815, Coleridge, *Letters,* II, 643–50.
2. See p. 3 of this book.
3. *The Poetical Works of William Wordsworth,* E. Dowden, ed. (London, G. Bell & Sons, 1893), VI, 347 (hereafter referred to as Wordsworth, *Works*). Dowden's claim that "The Pedlar" was at one time 2,000 lines long and equal to *The Excursion,* Books I and II, is unsound. It is based on a misreading of a letter to Sir G. Beaumont (December 25, 1804, *EL,* p. 424), in which Wordsworth really says that *The Recluse* is about 2,000 lines long and that "The Pedlar" is to be a part of it.

used as an alternative name for "The Ruined Cottage." However, I consider this possibility small. If one adds the lines Dorothy transcribed in 1798[4] (379) to those she omitted with acknowledgment (287), one gets a total of only 666 lines, which is 234 lines less than 900, which she gave as the total. The explanation of this discrepancy lies, I believe, in her words at the end of the transcription, "There is much more about the Pedlar." I believe that this "much more" was some 200 lines of independent poetry on the Wanderer and that it later came to be considered a separate poem, known as "The Pedlar." It is to be noticed that Wordsworth's subsequent work on "The Pedlar" was usually spoken of as revision and that the addition of 80 lines to the original 200 is thoroughly consistent with the descriptions of this later work in Dorothy's journals.

If one holds, with De Selincourt, that "The Ruined Cottage" was incorporated in *The Recluse* in 1798, then "The Pedlar" must be considered a separate poem from the first, for almost the first reference to it we have speaks of a plan for publishing it separately, evidently with no thought of its having ever been dependent on any other work. The first allusion to "The Pedlar" by that name comes when Dorothy speaks of reading it after tea on October 6, 1800.[5] The almost inescapable inference at this juncture is that she is speaking of an independent poem based on the Wanderer and that the poem is considered complete. Three days later Coleridge indicates that "Christabel" has been withheld from the second edition of *Lyrical Ballads* in order that it may be published with "The Pedlar," which he calls "a long blank-verse poem."[6] Evidently this plan was abortive, and "The Pedlar" was untouched for over a year. Then, in December (1801) Wordsworth read it over. "He was in good spirits, and full of hope of what he should do with it."[7] On the following day he added a few lines to the poem.[8] After setting it aside for over a month, Wordsworth resumed work on it in late January (1802)[9] and devoted himself to it exclusively during the first week of February.[1] On February 7 Dorothy wrote: "William had had a bad night and was working at his poem. We sate by the fire, and did not walk, but read *The Pedlar,* thinking it done; but lo! though Wm. could find fault with no one part of it, it was uninteresting, and must be altered.

4. Dorothy to Mary Hutchinson, March 5, 1798, *EL,* pp. 176–87.
5. October 6, 1800, Dorothy, *Journals,* 1, 64.
6. Coleridge to H. Davy, October 9, 1800, Coleridge, *Letters,* 1, 337. In the same letter Coleridge says "the *Christabel* was running up to 1,300 lines," and in a letter to Poole postmarked October 14, 1800, he says *Christabel* "has swelled into a Poem of 1400 lines . . . ." Since the two parts of *Christabel* contain only 677 lines, these passages are suspect. *Unpublished Letters of Samuel Taylor Coleridge,* 1, 156.
7. December 21, 1801, Dorothy, *Journals,* 1, 93.
8. December 22, 1801, *ibid.,* p. 93.
9. January 30, 1802, *ibid.,* p. 104.
1. February 1, 2, 4, 5, 1802, *ibid.,* pp. 105–7.

Poor Wm. !"[2] On the next day Wordsworth was back at work on the poem[3] and two days later Dorothy wrote it out for what, it was hoped, would be the last time. However, on reading it over, Wordsworth discovered "an ugly place"[4] and was forced to spend the next few days altering and refitting it.[5] But he was still dissatisfied with it, and on February 28 he returned to it, with such unfortunate results that Dorothy wrote in the margin of her journal the eloquent words, "Disaster Pedlar."[6] On March 3 she suggested rewriting the poem, to her subsequent regret, for the poet exhausted himself.[7] She copied it again on March 6, stitched it up on March 7, and William read it on March 9, altering it in a few places.[8] On March 10 he spoke of publishing it with the "Yorkshire Wolds Poem,"[9] and on March 20 he read it to Coleridge.[1] During the following months Wordsworth evidently altered it still more. On July 8 Dorothy wrote it out in its final form, which was 280 lines long.[2a] Two years later it was still considered a separate poem, when Dorothy was copying it for Coleridge to take with him to Malta.[3a] Evidently Coleridge read it to Sir George Beaumont. By the end of 1804 it was decided that "The Pedlar" should form a part of *The Recluse*.[4a]

It is impossible to discover from internal evidence in *The Excursion* exactly what "The Pedlar" was. It was written over a comparatively long time, and with great effort. It was frequently expanded and revised, always at the cost of painful labor. In Dorothy's transcription of "The Ruined Cottage" of 1798,[5a] when she came to the part which deals with the life of the Wanderer she omitted a long passage, with the comment, "The poem then goes on describing his character and habits and way of life for above 200 lines." In the final version it goes on thus for 315 lines.[6a] Dowden has taken this discrepancy to indicate that "The Pedlar" was inserted here,[7a] but such can hardly be the case, for the discrepancy is one of less than 115 lines, while "The Pedlar" was 280 lines long. No more than half of "The Pedlar" could have been inserted here, and of course this is possibly what was done, the remainder being included elsewhere. On the other hand, it seems very unlikely that a poem of sufficient unity to stand alone would be broken in two and the

2. February 7, 1802, *ibid.*, p. 107.   3. February 8, 1802, *ibid.*

4. February 10, 1802, *ibid.*, p. 110.

5. February 11, 12, 13, 14, 16, 1802, *ibid.*, pp. 110–15.

6. February 28, 1802, *ibid.*, p. 118.   7. March 3, 1802, *ibid.*, p. 119.

8. March 6, 7, 9, 1802, *ibid.*, pp. 120–1.

9. March 10, 1802, *ibid.*, pp. 121–2. I take the "Yorkshire Wolds Poem" to be *Peter Bell*.

1. March 20, 1802, *ibid.*, p. 127.   2a. July 8, 1802, *ibid.*, p. 168.

3a. Dorothy to Coleridge, March 6, 1804, *EL*, p. 364.

4a. Wordsworth to Sir G. Beaumont, December 25, 1804, *ibid.*, p. 424.

5a. Dorothy to Mary Hutchinson, March 5, 1798, *ibid.*, pp. 176–87.

6a. *The Excursion*, I, 125–440.   7a. Wordsworth, *Works*, VI, 347.

halves distributed into different parts of a longer poem. This would have left no room for expansion, and Wordsworth's tendency in revising "The Ruined Cottage" for inclusion in *The Excursion* was definitely to expand. Dorothy was clearly speaking in round numbers when she wrote "above 200 lines," and I think it much more likely that this omitted passage of "The Ruined Cottage" was expanded to its final form in *The Excursion* with at most only minor borrowings from "The Pedlar." I strongly suspect that the bulk of "The Pedlar" was included in Book II of *The Excursion*.[8] But I must also mention the remote possibility that it was worked into what became Books VIII and IX.

5

When Wordsworth came finally to write *The Excursion,* he also made use of poetry originally written for *The Prelude* but ultimately not used in that poem. There are six main examples:

a) The Excursion, Book II, lines 1–25. These lines were used (in "MS Y") to open Book VIII of *The Prelude*. They compare the rich and varied life of the ancient minstrel with that of the Wanderer. They were soon (in "Notebook X") removed from *The Prelude* and placed in their present position in *The Excursion*.[9]

b) The Excursion, Book II, lines 741 ff. The tragic story of the poor pensioner first appears among drafts for *The Prelude* in "Notebook X."[1]

c) The Excursion, Book III, lines 928–40. This ideal description of the savage Indian's communion with nature occurs in a much shorter form in a cancelled draft for *The Prelude,* Book VIII, lines 208–13.[2]

d) The Excursion, Book IV, lines 402–12. A passage describing the mystical effect of a lamb's cry on the mountainside, these lines occur in a cancelled draft for *The Prelude,* Book VII, between lines 497 and 498 in "MS Y."[3]

e) The Excursion, Book IV, lines 763–5. These important lines occur in a cancelled draft for *The Prelude,* Book VIII, lines 159–72.[4]

f) The Excursion, Book IX, lines 437–48. In "MS Y" these beautiful descriptive lines are deleted from between lines 497 and 498 of a draft for Book VIII of *The Prelude*.[5]

The close textual interrelationship of the two poems is further em-

8. There is a draft of Book II of *The Excursion* in "Notebook X," and the rest of the material in this notebook is dated April and October or November, 1804, by De Selincourt. *The Prelude,* De Selincourt, ed., p. xxiii. This might put the draft of Book II just before the letter of December 25, 1804, to Sir G. Beaumont, announcing that "The Pedlar" had been incorporated in *The Recluse*.

9. *The Prelude,* De Selincourt, ed., pp. xxiii–xxiv.

1. *Ibid.,* p. xxiii.   2. *Ibid.,* p. 558.

3. *Ibid.,* p. 562.

4. *Ibid.,* p. 553. For a prose paraphrase, see *MY,* p. 126.

5. *The Prelude,* De Selincourt, ed., pp. 562–3.

phasized by the fact that Wordsworth used some lines originally drafted for a description of the Wanderer to describe himself in *The Prelude.*[6] All the lines borrowed from *The Prelude* for *The Excursion* can be dated about 1804.

6

There were undoubtedly numerous other parts of *The Excursion* existing in manuscript in 1813, either as independent poems or as miscellaneous drafts for *The Recluse,* when Wordsworth set about collecting them and amalgamating them into a unit. He always felt that a strong oneness of purpose united all his works, and so it was only natural that he should slightly alter existing poems to fit them into the larger scheme.

Perhaps we have a good example of Wordsworth's method in the story of the deaf man in Book VII of *The Excursion.*[7] This tale appeared at the end of the "Essay upon Epitaphs" as it existed in manuscript at Wordsworth's death.[8] The first part of this essay had appeared on February 22, 1810, in *The Friend.* It is probable that the remaining two parts, which were never published during Wordsworth's lifetime, were designed as subsequent installments to appear in successive issues of *The Friend* and therefore were written at the same time as the first part, about 1809–10. Therefore this poem on the deaf man can be dated 1809–10. Comparing the two versions, we find that the revision is very slight but just such as might be made to fit the earlier independent poem into its position in the larger poem. The only noteworthy change is at the beginning:

"Essay upon Epitaphs"	*The Excursion,* VII, 395–481
Beneath that pine which rears its dusky head	Almost at the root
Aloft, and covered by a plain blue stone	Of that tall pine, the shadow of whose bare
Briefly inscribed, a gentle Dalesman lies, etc.	And slender stem, while here I sit at eve,
	Oft stretches toward me, like a long straight path
	Traced faintly in the greensward, there beneath
	A plain blue stone, a gentle Dalesman lies, etc.

Other than this, there are only minor verbal changes in four lines. Many others of the stories in *The Excursion* may originally have been independent poems like "Margaret," "The Pedlar," and this story. It is

6. *Ibid.,* pp. xxi, xxxiii, 513–14, 548, 549. 7. *The Excursion,* VII, 395–481.
8. Wordsworth, *Prose,* II, 73–5.

truly astonishing that a poem made up of so many ingredients could have so great a unity of idea and texture as *The Excursion*. It speaks very highly for the work Wordsworth did on the poem in 1813 and in early 1814, when he was molding the fragments into a whole. One may estimate that as much as two thirds of *The Excursion* had already been written by January 5, 1813, when Wordsworth began the amalgamation, revision, and expansion which were to culminate in the publication of *The Excursion* a year and a half later. It can be demonstrated that over one third of the poem had been written by the end of 1808, and it is even possible that one half had been written by that time.[9] We can witness the deftness and sureness of touch with which Wordsworth drew these many fragments and short poems together by studying the revisions he made in those parts which we do have in their earlier forms, such as "The Ruined Cottage," the drafts for *The Prelude,* and the story of the deaf man. He added many lines, struck out some, and altered others; fitting, refitting, polishing, rejecting, composing, and unifying, he must have been fired with sudden inspiration and awareness of purpose.

7

It has been customary to set the date for the publication of *The Excursion* in the month of July, 1814. This error has arisen from a letter Wordsworth wrote on July 16, in which he said, ". . . it will be out I hope in ten days from this time at the latest."[1] However, on August 9, when Charles Lamb wrote to thank Wordsworth for his presentation copy, the poem had evidently not yet been released.[2] On August 10 the *Times* carried the first advertisement: "This day is published, in 4to price 2£.2s boards, The Excursion; being a portion of the Recluse, a Poem. By WILLIAM WORDSWORTH. Printed for Longman, Hurst, Rees, Orme, and Brown, Paternoster-row."[3] Beclouding the issue somewhat, the *Morning Chronicle* announced on August 11: "In a few days will be published, THE EXCURSION . . . ,"[4] and it was not until August 17 that this paper carried its first advertisement. Evi-

---

9. "The Ruined Cottage" (1798)—900 lines; *The Excursion,* Bk. IV, 1207-74 (1798) —67 lines; "The Pedlar" (1802)—at least 80 lines, and possibly all 280, were separate from the 900 of "The Ruined Cottage"; *The Recluse* (September 8, 1806)—1,300 lines; *The Recluse* (September 29, 1808)—500 lines; drafts for *The Prelude* (1804)—about 212 lines: total, at least 3,059, possibly 3,259. If it be granted that any of the 1,300 *Recluse* lines of 1798 are different from "The Ruined Cottage," the Prospectus, etc., the additional lines may possibly be added to this total; and these in addition to other lines possibly written at this time, but of which we have no record, may conceivably swell the total of lines written for *The Excursion* by the end of 1808 to well over half of the poem in its published form, which was originally (1814) 9,035 lines long.
1. Wordsworth to Wrangham, July 16, 1814, *MY*, pp. 598-9.
2. Lamb, *Works,* VI, 434-8.   3. *The Times,* August 10, 1814, p. 2.
4. *The Morning Chronicle,* August 11, 1814, p. 2.

dently the *Morning Chronicle* was simply tardy, for the poem was definitely out by August 12. On that day Byron wrote to Moore, "Wordsworth . . . has just spawned a quarto of metaphysical blank verse,
which is nevertheless only a part of a poem,"[5] and on the following day
Henry Crabb Robinson wrote: "I stole out of the theatre to call on
Madge, at whose apartments I found the new great poem of Wordsworth, *The Excursion.*"[6] *The Excursion* certainly appeared between
August 10 and 12, 1814, and it is probably safe to accept the date of the
Times, August 10. Longman continued to advertise "This day is published . . ." into January of 1815.[7]

The Excursion was published as a beautiful quarto, with large print
and fine paper,[8] selling for the exorbitant price of two guineas. This price
seemed particularly high when it was remembered that it was for only
a part of a poem.[9] The first edition did not sell rapidly. The letters of
William and Dorothy betray great anxiety for a long time after the
publication.[1] Only 500 copies were printed, and it was hoped that they
would soon be sold to the wealthy, so that a cheaper edition could be
brought out in octavo. But the sale went slowly, and soon the note of
hopefulness disappeared from the letters.[2] By February 18, 1815, only
269 copies had been sold.[3] Then Wordsworth and his sister began writing to their friends in a frank effort to promote the sale.[4] Knowing the
connection of Mr. Clarkson with the editors of the *Philanthropist,* they
wrote and urged him to exercise his influence toward having a favorable
review appear in that magazine. They hoped thus to reach the Quakers,
"who are wealthy and fond of *instructive* Books."[5a] Despite all efforts,
the book continued to sell slowly, and the octavo could not appear until
1820. Wordsworth was sorely disappointed, and the occasional praise
from high places[6a] could not compensate for the general indifference
to the book. He and Dorothy came to consider appreciation of *The Excursion* as a measure for a man's moral stature.[7a]

Perhaps nothing need be added to what has been said in Chapter 1
about the reviews of *The Excursion.* In Appendix 1 will be found a
complete list of the reviews with a brief note on each.[8a] It is important
to remember that only two of the eleven notices were distinctly hostile

5. Byron to Moore, August 12, 1814, *The Works of Lord Byron,* "Letters and Journals," R. E. Prothero, ed. (London, Murray, 1904), III, 125.

6. *Henry Crabb Robinson on Books and Their Writers,* p. 147.

7. See *The Times,* January 26, 1815, p. 2.

8. For information on this edition and for a complete list of all subsequent editions,
see Appendix II, p. 143 of this book.

9. See the quotation from Byron above, and *MY,* pp. 625, 652.

1. See *MY,* pp. 602–3, 606–7, 612, 615–16, 621–7, 637–8, 642, 646, 651–2, 655–6, 665, 668.

2. *Ibid.,* pp. 632–3, 665.   3. *Ibid.,* pp. 637–8.

4. *Ibid.,* pp. 622, 630.   5a. *Ibid.,* p. 622.

6a. *Ibid.,* pp. 606, 612, 622.   7a. *Ibid.,* pp. 612, 626.

8a. See p. 141 of this book.

and that some were distinctly favorable. Furthermore, the private comments of Lamb,[9] Keats,[1] Southey,[2] and Robinson[3] show that the poem was received with great interest and enthusiasm in literary circles and that not everyone was, like Coleridge, disappointed. It makes a most interesting study to follow the reactions of Robinson as he sees the poem for the first time, reads the reviews, reads the poem, discusses it with friends, rereads it, and finally discusses it with Wordsworth himself. Following are some of his most interesting comments:

August 13, 1814:

It is a poem of formidable size, and I fear too mystical to be popular. But it will, however, put an end to the sneers of those who consider him or affect to consider him as a puerile writer [who] attempts only little things. But it will draw on him the imputation of dullness possibly. Still it will, I trust, strengthen the zeal of his few friends. My anxiety is great to read it.[4]

October 15, 1814:

. . . the *Examiners* for the last three months . . . contain an excellent review of Wordsworth's poem by Hazlitt, excepting from this praise some very coarse and cynical remarks on a country life, in which the poor inhabitants of the Lakes are designated as more ignorant, selfish, and worthless than the lower classes elsewhere.[5]

November 2, 1814:

I have yet read but little of this exquisite work.[6]

November 4, 1814:

The fourth book I found by no means dull or uninteresting, though purely reasoning, and the book has hitherto had in my mind greater beauties and fewer faults that [*sic*] I anticipated.[7]

November 11, 1814:

I also read part of the fifth book of *The Excursion,* but it is far inferior to the fourth, perhaps to any preceding book. It is the first part of the work that I found heavy.[8]

November 23, 1814:

Finished this week Wordsworth's poem. It has afforded me less intense pleasure on the whole perhaps than I expected, but it will be a source of

9. Lamb, *Works*, vi, 434–8, 443–6, 449–52.
1. Keats, *Letters*, pp. 79–80.
2. *Life and Correspondence of Robert Southey*, iv, 97. Southey repeated this in at least two other places.
3. *Henry Crabb Robinson on Books and Their Writers, passim.*
4. *Ibid.*, p. 147.   5. *Ibid.*, p. 151.   6. *Ibid.*, p. 152.
7. *Ibid.*   8. *Ibid.*, p. 153.

frequent gratification. The wisdom and high moral character are beyond anything similar that I am acquainted with, and the spirit of the poem flags much less frequently than might be apprehended. . . . Wordsworth has succeeded better in light and elegant painting in this poem than in any other.[9]

December 25, 1814:

The first book I found so much more delightful on perusal loud [*sic*], than I feared it might appear to a listener, that I lost my apprehensions.[1]

January 3, 1815:

The Excursion on the second perusal gratified me still more than the first, . . . [Jeffrey's review] will do little mischief among those who are already acquainted with the *Edinburgh Review* articles; but it will close up the eyes of many who might have otherwise recovered their sight.

Perhaps, after all, *The Excursion* will leave Mr. Wordsworth's admirers and contemners where they were. Each will be furnished with instances of excellence and deformity to strengthen his own persuasions. Certainly I could wish for a somewhat clearer development of the author's opinions, for the retrenchment of some of the uninteresting interlocutory matter . . . . But with these deductions from the worth of the poem, I do not hesitate to place the poem among the noblest works of the human intellect, and to me it is one of the most delightful. . . . Passages are not few which place the author on a level with Milton.[2]

There are many other opinions and anecdotes about *The Excursion* in Robinson's writings.[3] Most interesting is his account of Blake's reactions. Blake took umbrage at certain lines in the Prospectus, as did another friend of Robinson.[4] But, on the whole, the reception of *The Excursion* cannot be said to have been disappointing except for the sale, which Wordsworth always professed was his chief interest in publication.

When in 1820 *The Excursion* appeared in octavo it was noticed by only one review, which was favorable.[5] The poem was only slightly revised, the changes unimportant. 500 copies were printed and they were exhausted within four years.[6] The poem next appeared when Wordsworth's collected poems were published in 1827. It was then for the first time incorporated in the "Complete Works." *The Excursion* was printed as Volume v, although it was also furnished with a separate title page in order that it might be sold separately. Of this edition Wordsworth wrote to Robinson: "I have revised the poems carefully particu-

---

9. *Ibid.*, pp. 154–5.   1. *Ibid.*, p. 157.   2. *Ibid.*, pp. 158–9.
3. *Ibid.*, pp. 160, 212, 275, 153, 507, 780, 832; *The Correspondence of Henry Crabb Robinson with the Wordsworth Circle*, pp. 300–1, 421, 474, 532, 718.
4. *Henry Crabb Robinson on Books and Their Writers*, pp. 156–7, 327, 490.
5. *The Literary Gazette* (1820), p. 837.
6. *The Correspondence of Henry Crabb Robinson with the Wordsworth Circle*, pp. 164, 168.

larly the excursion—and I trust with considerable improvement; but you shall judge—"[7] The revision of which Wordsworth was speaking is predominantly condensation. Wordsworth shortened *The Excursion* in 1827 by 106 omissions, varying in length from one line to 73 lines. He cut 12 lines out of the passage in Book I that Coleridge had criticized for excessive minute detail.[8] At the end of Book VI he omitted the story of a widower's happy second marriage, which was 73 lines long. Evidently he had developed a prejudice against second marriages, for he also removed all references to the Wanderer's stepfather in Book I. A passage of 28 lines was excised from the story of the unfaithful husband, Wilfred Armathwaite, in Book VI.[9] The remaining omissions are shorter and less important and seem to have been designed simply to remove unessential lines. Wordsworth also exercised economy by shortening the Arguments. Only six passages in the poem were expanded. In 49 instances Wordsworth substantially altered the phrasing or wording, evidently in an effort to smooth and harmonize the verse. There is a puzzling manipulation of "which" and "that" and of the verb "to frame." On the whole the 1827 revision was directed toward condensation and mechanical improvement of the poem. There are no important changes in the doctrines.

In subsequent editions the revisions were less extensive. Wordsworth gave the poem another thorough overhauling for the fifth collected edition of his poems in 1837. Here again there are several omissions and some manipulation.

By far the most interesting alterations were made in 1845. At that time he made some further contractions and small expansions in a few places, as well as doing a great deal of technical refitting and alteration of diction. But the most striking fact is that Wordsworth made an effort to cast a more specifically Christian light over the whole poem. Since this is a most important matter, I will present all the chief examples.

Original	1845
	The Excursion, I, 934–40
	Nor more would she have craved as due to One
	Who, in her worst distress, had ofttimes felt
Be wise and chearful; and no longer read	The unbounded might of prayer;

7. In 1830 Wordsworth wrote: "In the edition of 27 it was diligently revized; and the sense in several instances got into less room, yet still it is a long Poem for these feeble and fastidious times." *LY,* pp. 472–3. In 1802 Wordsworth had written: "I am for the most part uncertain about my success in *altering* Poems." *EL,* p. 305. The above quotation is from *The Correspondence of Henry Crabb Robinson with the Wordsworth Circle,* p. 178.

8. *The Excursion,* I, 111 ff. Coleridge quotes the original version with disfavor in *Biographia Literaria,* II, 108.   9. *The Excursion,* VI, 1080–1114.

Original	1845
The forms of things with an unworthy eye.	and learned, with soul Fixed on the Cross, that consolation springs, From sources deeper far than deepest pain, For the meek sufferer. Why then should we read The forms of things with an unworthy eye?

The Excursion, I, 952–5

Appeared an idle dream, that could not live Where meditation was. I turned away,	Appeared an idle dream that could maintain, Nowhere, dominion o'er the enlightened spirit Whose meditative sympathies repose Upon the breast of Faith. I turned away,

The Excursion, II, 436–7

"Gracious Heaven!" The Wanderer cried, "it cannot but be his,"	"His it must be!" The Wanderer cried, "cannot but he his,"

The Excursion, III, 403

the human Soul	the immortal Soul

The Excursion, V, 824–6

[Absent]	My comfort:—would that they were oftener fixed On what for guidance in the way that leads To heaven, I know, by my Redeemer taught.

The Excursion, VI, 766–74

And safe from all our sorrows? She is safe,	'And safe from all our sorrows.' With a sigh She spake, yet, I believe, not unsustained By faith in glory that shall far transcend Aught by those perishable heavens disclosed To sight or mind. Nor less than care divine Is divine mercy. She, who had rebelled,

Original	1845
	Was into meekness softened and subdued;
	Did, after trials not in vain prolonged,
	With resignation sink into the grave;
	The Excursion, IX, 225–8
	Foretasted, immortality conceived
Foretasted, immortality conceived.	By all,—a blissful immortality,
Strange, etc.	To them whose holiness on earth shall make
	The Spirit capable of heaven, assured.
	Strange, etc.
	The Excursion, IX, 469–73
	Cannot be lasting in a world like ours,
Like those reflected in yon quiet Pool,	Whose highest beauty, beautiful as it is,
Cannot be lasting in a world like ours,	Like that reflected in yon quiet pool,
To great and small disturbances exposed.	Seems but a fleeting sunbeam's gift, whose peace
	The sufferance only of a breath of air![1]

In these alterations Wordsworth was clearly attempting to give a more orthodox Christian tone to *The Excursion* than it had had in its original form. The poem is incapable of assimilating some of this theological diction, for the prevalent tone is not theological, and in some instances the resultant passages are conspicuous misfits. Both the diction and the theology of the poem will be discussed in their proper places below.

I shall not encumber the text of this book with a detailed bibliographical record of *The Excursion.* That will be found in Appendix II.[2] However, it may be well to indicate the main trends. *The Excursion* reached its ninth edition[3] in the year of Wordsworth's death (1850). Up to the present there has been a total of at least 22 separate editions. The increasing neglect which the poem has suffered is best indicated by the fact that in 1870, 56 years after the publication of *The Excursion,* it had gone through at least 18 editions, and there had never been an interval of more than 7 years between editions, while in the 78 years from 1870

1. For additional examples of the same tendency in the 1845 revision, see the alterations made at that time in *The Excursion,* II, 204–5; V, 157–64, 360.

2. P. 143 of this book.

3. All these figures refer to editions of *The Excursion* separate from the collected works.

to the present there have been only about 4 editions, with one interval of over 30 years. Shortly after Wordsworth's death there began a long succession of editions of selections from *The Excursion,* reaching a total of at least 15 between 1858 and 1897, since when there have been none. These books usually contained Book I of *The Excursion,* sometimes Books I and II, and, in at least one instance, Book IX.[4] These were often in students' series.

Wordsworth, in his later years, was much given to quoting and discussing *The Excursion* in letters and conversations, and naturally it was often in his mind in connection with revisions and new editions.[5] In his last years he became dissatisfied with the versification of *The Excursion* and made a few "last-ditch" efforts to rectify it.[6] Nevertheless he learned, to his great satisfaction, that the poem had given aid and comfort to many people in trying circumstances,[7] and he probably felt that his most sanguine hopes for it had been fulfilled before his death, for not only was it having a good sale but it was also indisputably doing great good. Wordsworth probably felt completely victorious in his struggle against "that ignorant coxcomb Jeffrey," for he could not have foreseen the eclipse which *The Excursion* was destined to suffer only 20 years after his death.

4. A complete list of these books will also be found in Appendix II, p. 144.

5. See *MY,* pp. 663–4, 695–6, 747, 768, 833; *LY,* pp. 71, 312–13, 472–3, 810–11, 987, 1062, 1072, 1233; *Henry Crabb Robinson on Books and Their Writers,* pp. 339–40; *The Correspondence of Henry Crabb Robinson with the Wordsworth Circle,* pp. 200–1, 630; *Dorothy, Journals,* II, 30, 404.

6. *The Correspondence of Henry Crabb Robinson with the Wordsworth Circle,* pp. 548, 551.   7. *LY,* pp. 642, 921.

III

Sources and Analogues

I

THE preliminary design for *The Excursion,* as it was evolved by Wordsworth and Coleridge in the Quantock Hills, was completely original. As it was first conceived, *The Recluse* was to have marked the creation of a new literary genre, that of the philosophical poem. Wordsworth and Coleridge were thoroughly dissatisfied with every previous effort to embody a system of thought in poetry, yet they felt certain that the ideas they exchanged in their daily conversations were important enough to be disseminated, and they both were confident of Wordsworth's ability to set them forth in a truly poetical form. Wordsworth's unwavering confidence has already been discussed[1] but Coleridge's more articulate anticipation over a long period of time will perhaps throw greater light on the bold originality of the scheme.

1804:

. . . I dare affirm that, he will hereafter be admitted as the first and greatest philosophical poet, the only man who has effected a complete and constant synthesis of thought and feeling and combined them with poetic forms . . . . I prophesy immortality to his "Recluse," as the first and finest philosophical poem . . . .[2]

1815:

Whatever in Lucretius is poetry is not philosophical, whatever is philosophical is not poetry; and in the very pride of confident hope I looked forward to "The Recluse" as the *first* and *only* true philosophical poem in existence. Of course, I expected the colours, music, imaginative life, and passion of *poetry;* but the matter and arrangement of *philosophy;* not doubting from the advantages of the subject that the totality of a system was not only capable of being harmonised with, but even calculated to aid, the unity (beginning, middle, and end) of a poem.[3]

The philosophical system which Wordsworth was to provide with poetical garb in this way was probably delineated in some detail during

1. See chap. ii, sec. 3, of this book.
2. Coleridge to R. Sharp, January 15, 1804, Coleridge, *Letters,* II, 450.
3. Coleridge to Wordsworth, May 30, 1815, *ibid.,* II, 648. The remainder of this letter is very important. It gives further details of the original plan and Coleridge's criticisms of *The Excursion* in the light of that plan. For other comments of Coleridge on *The Recluse,* see C. Wordsworth, *Memoirs of William Wordsworth,* I, 159; *Biographia Literaria,* J. Shawcross, ed., II, 129; *Table Talk,* pp. 188–9, July 21, 1832.

the famous conversations in Somersetshire, and it was undoubtedly altered and expanded in subsequent discussions at Dove Cottage, Coleorton, and Allan Bank.

While Wordsworth proved himself a fearless literary pioneer in *Lyrical Ballads* and the famous *Preface* (1800), he was utterly incapable of executing such an ambitious, grandiose, speculative design as that for *The Recluse* without the constant stimulation and nourishment of his intellectual faculties which Coleridge had supplied during the Quantock period but was never to supply again in the same degree and kind.[4] From the hour of their separation at Hamburg in 1798, when Coleridge went to Ratzeburg and Göttingen and became imbued with German transcendentalism and Wordsworth went to Goslar to shiver through a lonely winter of reminiscence, they probably never again enjoyed the perfect intellectual rapport which had given birth to the first grand outline of *The Recluse*. The mercurial mind of Coleridge often moved quickly from one position to another, while the steadier, tougher mind of Wordsworth moved slowly from point to point, building each new position on the solid foundation of his past beliefs. Coleridge had the intellectual fire to strike off plans of great originality but he lacked the persevering industry of Wordsworth to put them into effect. Conversely, Wordsworth was incapable of sustaining himself for long in the rarefied atmosphere of original metaphysical speculation but he could make poetry of his occasional brief soarings by long sessions of honest industry. The gradual fracture of their early intimacy left Wordsworth incapable of carrying out the original plan. Wordsworth had to make the most of the limited metaphysical material at his command. His decision to divide *The Recluse* into three parts—two speculative and one "dramatic"—was the first retreat. Its inevitable result was the composition first of the "dramatic" part, which was obviously best suited to his powers and habits of composition. The fact that the two parts which were to "consist chiefly of meditations in the Author's own person"[5] were never written speaks for itself. All the principal products of his private speculation had been exploited in the conversations of *The Excursion,* and he had nothing of importance left to say.

The Excursion, then, is not of the highly original design first projected for *The Recluse*. Failing to initiate a new literary genre, it falls well within established forms. There is even something creaky and archaic about the towering and intricate structure of the poem. In short, it is most nearly akin to the long, blank-verse didactic poem of the eighteenth century. Wordsworth was a keen student of the poetry of the eighteenth century. Despite his critical disapproval of many of the poets of that age,

4. Wordsworth himself described the period of their closest intimacy as of only two years' duration. See Wordsworth, *Prose,* III, 469–70.
5. Preface to *The Excursion,* edition of 1814.

expressed so directly in the Preface to the second edition of *Lyrical Ballads,* the Appendix to the Preface, and the Essay Supplementary to the Preface, he gradually came to appreciate more fully the high moral purpose which supports their massive poetical structures, and when he came to organize and complete *The Excursion,* he inadvertently dropped into the structural habits of the eighteenth century. It is interesting to speculate on the reception which would have been accorded *The Excursion* had it been published during the second quarter of the eighteenth century. It would probably have been much more favorably received by that age which was nourished on *The Seasons* and *An Essay on Man.* However, coming as it did nearly a century later, *The Excursion* met somewhat of a rebuff, for its form and content were archaic. Paradoxical though it may seem, Wordsworth himself, in his critical pronouncements and to some extent in his poetic practice, probably contributed inadvertently to the very shift in sensibility which was ultimately to relegate *The Excursion* to the realm of forgotten books.

There are really four principal streams of eighteenth-century literature which meet in the structure of *The Excursion.* These are the long blank-verse didactic poem; the philosophical dialogue; the short verse narrative of humble life, separate or in framework; and the funeral elegy.

In *The Seasons* (1726–30) of James Thomson we have the very fountainhead of long blank-verse didactic poems in English. The poet's rich imagery and the pastoral-idyllic tone he gives to the whole poem tend to cloak from our direct gaze his primarily didactic purpose. Furthermore, his teaching is diffused through so great a variety of subjects that it fails to give the reader any distinct impression of having been instructed. Nevertheless, the didactic element, though not systematic, bulks large in the poem, covering science, history, religion, political and domestic morals, commerce, and philosophy. There can be little doubt that Thomson considered the instruction of the poem as its true *raison d'être,* while all the delightful natural descriptions and rustic anecdotes were decoration.

There are many passages in *The Seasons* which closely resemble that fusion of religion and appreciation of nature which informs so much of Wordsworth's poetry, particularly *The Excursion.*[6] Thomson also felt a strong interest in the mind of man and the manner in which it is developed,[7] as did Wordsworth. It is also important to keep in mind the interspersed anecdotes from rustic life when comparing *The Seasons* with *The Excursion.* In the former they are less frequent but they are used to much the same purpose in some cases. Thomson's poem lacks the strong sense of passionate struggle against difficult personal problems that we find in *The Excursion*—his whole presentation is more de-

6. See, for example, "Spring," 853–5, 902; "Autumn," 670–2.
7. See particularly "Summer," 792–9.

tached than that of Wordsworth—but, with their rambling didactic digressions on a multitude of subjects interspersed with descriptions of natural scenery and with their many illustrative tales set in a long blank-verse framework, the two poems have much in common. The arguments of the two poems are cast in the same form and those of Thomson give some hints of his didactic purpose.

In 1728 David Mallet published a long blank-verse poem in two books, entitled *The Excursion*.[8] It is tempting to infer that this is the source of Wordsworth's title, particularly when we find that he pointed out the similarity himself.[9] There is no evidence that Wordsworth had ever considered the title *The Excursion* before the poem actually appeared, and he left no record of his reason for this choice. It has a double aptness, for not only do the characters make a physical excursion through the lake country but they also make a metaphysical excursion into the realm of the "pure imagination." That this double application was intended by Wordsworth becomes almost certain when we notice that in one of the most crucial passages of the whole poem he italicizes the word "excursive" in speaking of "the mind's *excursive* power."[1] "Excursive," a word of rather infrequent usage, enjoyed considerable currency in the eighteenth century. For example, it occurs in *The Seasons*[2] and in Cowper's *The Task*.[3] Whether Wordsworth took his title from Mallet or from the nature of his own subject matter, it was well chosen.

Mallet's poem has some further resemblances to Wordsworth's. The title of the earlier poem also has a double significance. The trip through the wonders of nature has its counterpart in an intellectual journey among the most interesting ideas of the age. There is a panegyric on Newton, a discussion of the deity "infus'd" through nature, and an expression of the popular idea of a graduated scale or chain of beings, with innumerable orders and degrees, which was also mentioned by Thomson[4] and which was to reach its fullest poetic expression in Pope's *Essay on Man*. In Mallet's poem the nature poetry is rather too ecstatic to be compared to Wordsworth's controlled raptures in *The Excursion*, but again the use of nature as the vehicle and even as the object of didacticism presents a parallel.

A more forthright effort to present philosophy in poetry was made by Akenside, whose *Pleasures of Imagination* appeared in 1744. This first edition was in Wordsworth's library at his death.[5] Akenside was very directly concerned with the mind of man in this poem. Wordsworth

8. London, J. Walthoe, 1728.
9. *The Correspondence of Henry Crabb Robinson with the Wordsworth Circle*, p. 630.
1. *The Excursion*, IV, 1263.   2. "Summer," 198.
3. *The Task*, IV, 242.   4. "Summer," 334.
5. Lot 451, "Catalogue of the Sale of the Rydal Mount Library," *Transactions of the Wordsworth Society*, No. 6 (Edinburgh, T. & A. Constable, 1884), p. 237 (hereafter referred to as "Rydal Mount Library").

announced in the Prospectus to *The Excursion* that the mind of man was likewise his poetical province. Some of the more specific similarities are as follows. Both poets assert that man alone has the power to consult eternal measures of moral truth supplied by the creative wisdom.[6] Both poets are concerned for the humble laborers, who have no opportunity to develop the faculties by which moral truth is to be apprehended.[7] Both poets suggest communion with the forms of nature as a means of conversing with God.[8] Both seek to show the connections between the mind of man and natural objects,[9] and both are interested in the association of ideas.[1] There is also an interesting parallel between the famous lines (62–8) in the Prospectus, which tell how well the individual mind and the external world are fitted to each other, and these lines of Akenside:

> . . . even so did Nature's hand
> To certain species of external things
> Attune the finer organs of the mind:
> . . . till now the soul
> At length discloses ev'ry tuneful spring,
> To that harmonious movement from without
> Responsive.[2]

This passage as a whole could be included in *The Excursion* at any of several points without the slightest incongruity; indeed, there are passages in *The Excursion* which say the same thing.[3] *Pleasures of Imagination* resembles most closely the parts of *The Excursion* that are given to forthright speculation (i.e., Books IV, V, VIII, and IX) rather than those in which the narrative element prevails.

In the same year (1744) John Armstrong published his curious poem, *The Art of Preserving Health,* in blank verse. A copy of this poem was also in Wordsworth's library[4] and Wordsworth mentions Armstrong in his notes to *The River Duddon.* Armstrong's theme is somewhat more worldly than those of Thomson, Akenside, and Mallet, but there is an occasional touch of neoplatonic mysticism which is quite suggestive of Wordsworth.[5] He treats a wide range of subjects in his numerous digressions; three principal interests which he shares with Wordsworth are nature, religion, and the mind of man.

Edward Young's *Night Thoughts* (1742–45) must also be men-

6. *Pleasures of Imagination* (original version), I, 537–43; *The Excursion,* IV, 71–6, and IX, 229–40.
7. *Pleasures of Imagination,* III, 265–77; *The Excursion,* VIII, 297–433, and IX, 161 ff.
8. *Pleasures of Imagination,* III, 599–633; *The Excursion,* IV, 1204 ff.
9. *Pleasures of Imagination,* III, 282–6; *The Excursion,* IX, 19–20.
1. *Pleasures of Imagination,* III, 342; *The Excursion,* IV, 1247–9, 1265 ff.
2. *Pleasures of Imagination,* I, 113–24. This parallel was first pointed out in *Blackwood's Edinburgh Magazine,* XXVI (November, 1829), 774–88.
3. See, for example, *The Excursion,* II, 708–22.
4. Lot 451, "Rydal Mount Library," p. 237.
5. See, for example, *The Art of Preserving Health,* IV, 11–13, 21.

tioned as falling within the same tradition of long, blank-verse didactic poems. This poem is of roughly the same length as *The Excursion* and, like *The Excursion,* is divided into nine books. The most noteworthy parallel is the long argumentative effort to reclaim a skeptic, which appears in both. The argument in *Night Thoughts* is partly in dialogue form; the skeptic is treated as a sick man to be cured, as in *The Excursion.* Young adduces nature as evidence and as a means of cure, he cites the piety of the Greeks, he points to the "chain of being" as design in nature, and he criticizes science, all of which are points of similarity with *The Excursion.* But Young's chafing impetuosity and vehement religiosity have little in common with the quiet, meditative tone of *The Excursion.*

William Cowper's *The Task* (1784) is the next obvious parallel.[6] Here we find the same intermingling of personal struggle, philosophical speculation, natural description, illustrative story, and frequent digressions on a wide variety of subjects. Both poets teach the transience of worldly affairs[7] and both find extensions of deity diffused through all things.[8] There are also a few more specific similarities, which, while they may well be fortuitous, are worth noticing.

The Task, I ("The Sofa"), 389 stretch their lazy length	*The Excursion,* VII, 175 though no soft and costly sofa there Insidiously stretched out its lazy length,
The Task, VI, 244–6: [God] includes, In grains as countless as the sea-side sands, The forms with which he sprinkles all the earth.	*The Excursion,* IV, 92–3 the blessed Spirits, Which thou includest, as the sea her waves.

Perhaps the closest resemblance between these two poems is intangible and is to be found in the atmosphere created by the poets' frames of mind. Both poems have a warm meditative glow, which gives them an atmosphere of peaceful repose and optimism, even while they are facing boldly up to the full sordidness and asperity of life.

In none of these long blank-verse poems is the philosophizing predominantly in the form of dialogue, as it is in *The Excursion.* The eighteenth century also supplies this deficiency.

Richard Savage's *The Wanderer* (1729) is composed largely of

6. A comparison was made between *The Excursion* and *The Task* in "Noctes Ambrosianae," No. 56, *Blackwood's Edinburgh Magazine,* XXIX (April, 1831), 695–6.
7. *The Task,* V, 531 ff.; and *The Excursion,* IV, 69–71, 140 ff., and VII, 976 ff.
8. *The Task,* VI, 185, 221–2; and *The Excursion,* IX, 1 ff.

peripatetic dialogue between the Wanderer and a Hermit. The latter has retired from the world as a result of bereavement, and much of the discussion between the two men concerns fortitude in time of sorrow. Like *The Excursion, The Wanderer* includes a church scene; later the Hermit recounts the lives of three men over their graves. Some of the speculation touches on subjects to be found in *The Excursion*. Nature is adduced as evidence of deity, and in the concluding passage the Hermit exhorts the Wanderer to commune with nature as the highest religious act. The dialogue is interspersed with varied natural descriptions. However, apart from these general similarities and the specific parallel in the name of the central character, *The Excursion* has, perhaps fortunately, little in common with *The Wanderer*.

In 1733 Bishop Berkeley published his *Alciphron or The Minute Philosopher,* a series of seven prose dialogues in which two Christians, Euphranor and Crito, try to overthrow the skeptical philosophy of two freethinkers, Alciphron and Lysicles. There is some effort made to characterize the four disputants, and a continuity is maintained throughout the seven dialogues. The characters ramble about between their arguments, indulging in some communion with nature, and there are even a few events which take place apart from the conversations. The discussions are temporarily ended with each day, to be resumed on the next. The speeches vary between rapturous outbursts and closely argued Platonic dialogue. Plato is clearly the model for the greater part of the conversations. A Platonic element is also perceptible in the dialogues of *The Excursion,* for the truth is not spoken exclusively by one character but is divided among them all, so that even the defeated Solitary makes some very telling points. The skeptics in *Alciphron* are not drawn with much sympathy by Berkeley. They are made to uphold all the least defensible absurdities of Shaftesbury, Mandeville, Spinoza, and the mechanists, and to do so with such arrogance and cynicism that they defeat themselves even before Crito and Euphranor demolish their positions step by step, with smug relish. There are obviously many similarities between this plan and that of *The Excursion*. There is no evidence that Wordsworth knew *Alciphron* but there can be little doubt that Coleridge knew it, for he was long an enthusiastic admirer of Berkeley.[9]

A much more convincing source[1] is a work by John Thelwall, entitled *The Peripatetic; or Sketches of the Heart, of Nature and Society; in a Series of Politico-sentimental Journals, in Verse and Prose, of the*

9. He named one of his sons after Berkeley, and the records show that he was reading Berkeley in 1796. Paul Kaufman, "The Reading of Southey and Coleridge: The Record of Their Borrowings from the Bristol Library, 1793–98," *Modern Philology,* xxi (1923–24), 317–20.

1. This parallel was first pointed out by Charles Cestre in *John Thelwall* (London, Sonnenschein, 1906), pp. 27–9, and was subsequently confirmed by B. Sprague Allen in "William Godwin's Influence upon John Thelwall," *PMLA,* xxxvii (1922), 662–82.

Eccentric Excursions of Sylvanus Theophrastus; etc.[2] In the first place
it is to be noticed that this title suggests both the title of *The Excursion* and Wordsworth's description of the subject matter of *The Recluse,* "Man, Nature and Society."[3] This lengthy work by Thelwall
is in the form of a miscellany describing a series of rambles in the en-
virons of London, partly in prose and partly in verse. There is more
prose than verse, and the verse is written in a great variety of meters
and rhyme-schemes, although there is some blank verse. The author's
manner is frankly fashioned after that of Sterne, but Thelwall is much
more serious than his predecessor. As the author travels about, he
meets several interesting people and engages them in conversation.
Several stories are interspersed among the conversations, poems, and
essays. The characters are mere mouthpieces for Thelwall's views on a
wide variety of subjects, particularly politics. One of the characters is
alluded to as "The Wanderer,"[4] which may have suggested that name
to Wordsworth. Theophrastus in *The Peripatetic* represents Thelwall
himself and corresponds to the Poet of *The Excursion.* Thelwall's Ambulator resembles Wordsworth's Wanderer, for he is a wise antiquarian
with a great love for humble life. Arisor in *The Peripatetic* corresponds
to the misanthropic Solitary. Both works present philosophical and social views through dialogue; both show great interest in local topography.
The poet of *The Peripatetic* speaks of Armstrong's *The Art of Preserving Health* as his favorite poem,[5] and *The Peripatetic* has a passage on
the observation of regular living habits as a key to health,[6] much as
The Excursion does.[7] There is a long passage on the advantages and
disadvantages of commerce in *The Peripatetic,* just as in *The Excursion.*[8]
There is also a strikingly similar graveyard scene in *The Peripatetic,*
in which the characters moralize over selected graves somewhat as they
do in *The Excursion,* Books vi and vii. Thelwall's acute social consciousness colors much of *The Peripatetic,* and in several other points, such
as the occasional touches of humor, the urban setting, and the extensive
use of prose, this work differs vastly from *The Excursion.*

However, there is some contemporary confirmation of Wordsworth's
borrowing from Thelwall. On February 12, 1815, after paying a visit
to Thelwall, Henry Crabb Robinson made the following record in his
diary: "He [Thelwall] talked of 'The Excursion' as containing finer
verses than there are in Milton, and as being in versification most ad-
mirable; but then Wordsworth borrows without acknowledgment from
Thelwall himself!!"[9] Thelwall also had in manuscript a record of his

---

2. "Printed for the Author, and Sold by him, No. 2, Maze Pond, Southwark"; 1793,
3 vols.   3. *EL,* p. 424.
4. *The Peripatetic,* I, 59, 221.   5. *Ibid.,* I, 95.
6. *Ibid.,* I, 5 ff.   7. *The Excursion,* IV, 491–504.
8. *The Peripatetic,* I, 37–43; *The Excursion,* VIII, 117–47.
9. *Diary, Reminiscences, and Correspondence of Henry Crabb Robinson,* T. Sadler,
ed. (London, Macmillan, 1869), I, 473.

summer walking tours, which he called "Notes of Pedestrian Excursion."[1] This also may have had some suggestions for Wordsworth, if we may assume that he knew it. Wordsworth had known Thelwall personally for many years and had read at least some of his literary productions, enough to develop a great respect for Thelwall's ability to write blank verse.[2]

The illustrative tales of humble life which appear in such abundance in *The Excursion* are really part of a separate tradition of eighteenth-century poetry. There were a few tales in Thomson's *The Seasons,* but the first striking examples are to be found in Shenstone's *Schoolmistress* (1737), always a favorite with Wordsworth. Langhorne developed the idea in his *Country Justice* (1774–77) by using his central character as a frame for several smaller pictures. Of these two poems Wordsworth once wrote:

I do not wonder that you are struck with his [Langhorne's] Poem of the Country Justice—You praise it, and with discrimination—but you might have said still more in its favour. As far as I know, it is the first Poem, unless perhaps Shenstone's Schoolmistress be excepted, that fairly brought the Muse into the Company of common life, to which it comes nearer than Goldsmith . . . .[3]

Despite this comment on Goldsmith, we must also acknowledge certain echoes of *The Deserted Village* in *The Excursion,* particularly in Book I, "The Ruined Cottage" story, and in the awareness of social maladjustments which actuates so much of Wordsworth's poem. Gray's "Elegy Written in a Country Churchyard" first gave a popular impulse to the graveyard setting for speculations on the humble life. Cowper's *The Task* has several stories of country life interspersed throughout, which have much the same meditative, sympathetic tone as Wordsworth's stories in *The Excursion.* Montgomery, in his review of *The Excursion,* was the first to notice the similarities and differences between Cowper's and Wordsworth's stories. He also suggested that both be compared with the works of George Crabbe: "Crabbe gives low life with all its meanness and misery; Cowper paints it with sprightly freedom as the familiar friend of the Poor; Wordsworth casts over it a pensive hue of thought, that softens its asperities, and heightens its charms, without diminishing its verisimilitude."[4]

The comparison of *The Excursion* to the poetry of Crabbe is very apt. It was noticed not only by Montgomery but also by Merivale, who called *The Excursion* a "poetical parish-register";[5] by the author of the notice in the *British Critic,* who wrote that Wordsworth tells his stories

1. Cestre, *op. cit.,* p. 35, n.
2. For Wordsworth's own description of his acquaintance with Thelwall, see his letter to Thelwall's widow, *LY,* p. 959. 3. *Ibid.,* p. 829.
4. *The Eclectic Review,* New Ser., III (January, 1815), 37.
5. *The Monthly Review,* Ser. II, LXXVI (January, 1815), 134.

with "all the truth of Crabbe's descriptive pencil, and with all the deli-
cacy of Goldsmith's";[6] and by John Wilson in the "Noctes Ambrosianae."[7] There is probably more in the resemblance of *The Excursion*
to Crabbe's poetry than mere coincidence.

In 1807 George Crabbe published a volume of verse that included
"The Village," which had first appeared in 1783, and, for the first
time, "The Parish Register." Francis Jeffrey reviewed the volume in
the *Edinburgh Review*[8] and took the opportunity to draw a detailed
comparison between Crabbe and Wordsworth, highly uncomplimentary
to the latter, as might be expected. In fact, Jeffrey so warmed to his subject as he struck out at Wordsworth that he was quite carried away and
devoted a very substantial part of the essay to an invective against
the poor "lake poet," almost forgetting Crabbe in his heat. However,
Jeffrey's main point is that Crabbe "shows us something which we
have all seen, or may see, in real life" and thus "delights us by the
truth . . . of his representations," while "Mr. Wordsworth and his
associates show us something that mere observation never yet suggested
to anyone." In other words, Jeffrey much prefers the stark realism of
Crabbe's pictures to the sympathetic warmth of Wordsworth's. Wordsworth evidently read both the volume of Crabbe and the review of
Jeffrey. The following quotation from a letter written a few months
later reveals his reaction to both.

I am happy to find that we coincide in opinion about Crabbe's *verses;* for
poetry in no sense can they be called. . . . After all, if the Picture were
true to nature, what claim would it have to be called Poetry? At the best, it
is the meanest kind of satire, except the merely personal. The sum of it all
is, that nineteen out of 20 of Crabbe's Pictures are mere matters of fact;
with which the Muses have just about as much to do as they have with a
Collection of medical reports, or of Law cases.[9]

This passage in its entirety seems to be a point-by-point rebuttal of
Jeffrey's praise for Crabbe at the expense of Wordsworth. The inference
is that Wordsworth was stung by Jeffrey's article and wished to defend
himself. His adverse criticism of Crabbe was an instinctive critical reaction, for he was well aware of the qualities which distinguished
Crabbe's poetry from his own. He continued to criticize Crabbe as
"misanthropic"[1] and "far removed from beauty and refinement"[2] later

6. *The British Critic,* New Ser., III (May, 1815), 462.
7. No. 21, *Blackwood's Edinburgh Magazine,* XVIII (September, 1825), 381.
8. *The Edinburgh Review,* XII (April, 1808), 131–51.
9. Wordsworth to S. Rogers, September 29, 1808, *MY,* p. 244.
1. *Henry Crabb Robinson on Books and Their Writers* (January 3, 1839), p. 562.
2. From a tea-time conversation at Rydal Mount, July 31, 1840, recorded by Lady
Richardson in her notebook for that year and reproduced in *The Autobiography of
Mrs. Fletcher* (London, Hamilton, 1876), pp. 248–9.

in life. It is my belief, furthermore, that Wordsworth attempted, in Books VI and VII of *The Excursion,* to meet Crabbe on the latter's own ground and to vindicate himself from the charges of Jeffrey. The most striking parallel is with "The Parish Register." In both poems the narrator is a country parson telling stories about his parishioners, living and dead. In both poems the stories tend to be tragic, and many of them have identical subjects: death, seduction, and prodigality. It is almost as if Wordsworth had deliberately chosen his stories to parallel those of Crabbe, in order that he might demonstrate the advantages of his style and in order that he might offset the rather unfavorable picture Crabbe draws of country life. Wordsworth felt, as Crabbe did not, that even the most penurious and painful country life has compensations which far outweigh the disadvantages. Both poets tell their stories with a moral purpose, but Crabbe is a bit more outspoken in his moralizing than Wordsworth. Crabbe simply adds a moral exhortation to the end of each story or group of stories, unlike Wordsworth, who weaves his moralizing into the very fabric of each tale. Crabbe seems to be disinterested, with his candid, matter-of-fact narration, while Wordsworth is emotionally involved in every story he tells, never for a moment losing sight of his purpose in telling it. The most striking difference between the two is exactly in their treatment of the subject matter. Crabbe, using the closed couplet, is utterly realistic. He does not soften the blows of sordid fact at all. His style is clear and swift, so that he really makes much easier reading than Wordsworth. Wordsworth spreads a veil of nostalgic sentiment over his tales, so that even the most sordid have a pleasant meditative warmth. He does this because his avowed purpose is to show that whatever is human, regardless of its faults, commands our love and respect. He is partially successful, although his purpose occasionally leads him into sententiousness from which the clean, rapid style of Crabbe is a welcome relief.

Apart from their identity of general framework and choice of subject matter, the similarities between Crabbe's work and *The Excursion* are not striking. The story of Lucy, the miller's daughter, in "The Parish Register"[3] corresponds in some details to Wordsworth's Ellen,[4] but it is not difficult to point out several other stories of seduction which fall into the same pattern. For instance, Ruskin suggests a comparison between Wordsworth's Ellen and Shenstone's Jessy,[5] and Southey has an "English Eclogue" (III) entitled "Hannah" which tells a roughly similar story. In each case there are resemblances but none of them is very striking. Parallels could be drawn between several others of the

3. "The Parish Register," I, 277–402.   4. *The Excursion,* VI, 787–1052.
5. Shenstone's Jessy is in Elegy XXVI; Ruskin's suggestion occurs in "On the Pathetic Fallacy," *Modern Painters,* III, chap. xii, 4–15.

stories in Crabbe's poems and those in *The Excursion*. For instance, one might compare Crabbe's "frugal couple" with Wordsworth's,[6] or Crabbe's "prodigal" with Wordsworth's.[7] But such comparisons are not very fruitful, because there is such a wide difference in detail and treatment. The really important analogy is that between their frameworks and the stories of humble life contained within them.

The fourth main stream of eighteenth-century literature which flowed into *The Excursion* was that of the funeral elegy. This mingled to some extent with each of the three elements discussed above, but there is reason to believe that it also exerted an independent influence on *The Excursion*.

The funeral elegy enjoyed considerable vogue during the first half of the eighteenth century; one of its characteristic forms was what has been called the generalized elegy.[8] This type of elegy departed from the customary elegiac concentration on a specific death and the sorrows it occasioned, and turned to more general speculation, usually starting with a horrible parade of the conventional graveyard death symbols and proceeding by way of meditations on bereavement to melancholy philosophizing on life and death. The chief works in this tradition are Thomas Parnell's "Night-Piece on Death" (1722), William Broome's "Poem on Death" (1727), Edward Young's *Night Thoughts* (1742), and Robert Blair's *The Grave* (1743). Purged of its crudities, the generalized elegy culminated in Gray's "Elegy."

Wordsworth had even less use than Gray for the conventional horror symbols, but nearly all the melancholy speculative themes of the generalized elegy appear in *The Excursion,* where they do much toward establishing the tone of the whole poem. The most obvious example in *The Excursion* is a passage near the end of Book VII (976–99) which states the inevitability of death and the consequent vanity of worldly wealth, position, and power. Death viewed as a leveller, or the inevitable common lot of proud and humble, is a frequent theme in the generalized elegy. Numerous passages in *The Excursion* mention the transience of possessions, passions, life, and the universe.[9] The answering of a complaint against death occurs in *The Excursion;*[1] death is praised as a peaceful refuge from worldly toil and tumult;[2] and different views of death are compared.[3] These devices are all characteristic of the generalized elegy. Gray's lines on the humble rustic gravestones, the invariable tribute of sorrow paid at death, and the oral record of the dead are

6. "The Parish Register," I, 403–47; *The Excursion*, v, 670–837.

7. "The Borough" (1810), Letter XIV; *The Excursion*, VI, 275–375.

8. J. W. Draper, *The Funeral Elegy and the Rise of English Romanticism* (New York, New York University Press, 1929).

9. *The Excursion*, IV, 69–70, 100–3.

1. *Ibid.*, III, 209–32.

2. *Ibid.*, III, 275–81.

3. *Ibid.*, III, 253–324; v, 552–7.

echoed in the Pastor's long speech on his churchyard in *The Excursion*.[4] Likewise there is a suggestion of Gray's "mute inglorious Milton" in Wordsworth's "Oh! many are the Poets that are sown By Nature. . . ."[5] Death and attitudes toward death are a constantly recurring theme in *The Excursion;* indeed, *The Excursion* as a whole can be viewed as an effort to "fix A satisfying view upon" death and to find the "power An agonizing sorrow to transmute."[6]

There have been other suggestions of indebtedness on Wordsworth's part for the general plan of *The Excursion*. One scholar has indicated several analogies between the framework of Bernardin de St. Pierre's *Paul et Virginie* and that of *The Excursion*,[7] but these apply primarily to Book I of Wordsworth's poem and even there can be considered no more than remote analogies. The only close parallel is at the beginning, where the ancient sage seats himself before the ruined cottages to recount the tale connected with them for the author, just as the Wanderer in *The Excursion* tells the story of Margaret to the Poet, while seated before the ruins of her cottage. Beyond this there is no striking parallel.

Several scholars have seen a relationship between Schiller's "Der Spaziergang" and the general material of *The Excursion*.[8] It is true that the poet in this work is walking and that his mind is led from nature through a strange succession of thoughts and visions, finally returning from his oppressive thoughts to nature, with great relief. But this is all that the two poems have in common. It is a most tenuous relationship, and our understanding of neither poem is improved by the comparison.

A more useful parallel exists between *The Prelude* and *The Excursion*. "Imagination and Taste, How Impaired and Restored,"[9] perhaps the crucial book of *The Prelude,* is suggestive of "Despondency" and "Despondency Corrected,"[1] which are certainly the most important books of *The Excursion*. In each case Wordsworth is treating the same personal problem, in *The Prelude* through the direct autobiographical method, and in *The Excursion* through the indirect method of metaphysical discourse and narrative illustration.

Perhaps enough has now been said to show that when Wordsworth was unable to carry out the highly original design first conceived in conversation with Coleridge, he fell back into the established forms of

---

4. *Ibid.*, v, 903–1016.   5. *Ibid.*, i, 77 ff.   6. *Ibid.*, iv, 157–68.
7. N. F. Adkins, "Wordsworth's *Margaret; or The Ruined Cottage*," *Modern Language Notes*, xxxviii (1923), 460–6.
8. Theodor Zeiger, *Beiträge zur Geschichte des Einflusses der neueren deutschen Litteratur auf die englische* (Berlin, A. Duncker, 1901), p. 41 and note. This parallel is criticized by Max J. Herzberg in a valuable article, "William Wordsworth and German Literature," *PMLA*, xl (1925), 302–45, esp. p. 342.
9. *The Prelude*, Bk. xii.   1. *The Excursion*, Bks. iii, iv.

the eighteenth century, such as the long blank-verse didactic or philosophical poem, the dialogue, the versified tales of humble life, particularly as combined in a framework by Crabbe, and the funeral elegy.
Something of the originality of the initial scheme is perhaps to be
found in Wordsworth's combination and synthesis of these various
elements into one unified whole. Certainly no poem had ever been written with a plan corresponding to the whole of *The Excursion*. But an
undeniable atmosphere of archaism arises from the length of the poem,
its didacticism, and the sentimental morality of the framework stories,
which takes us back into the middle of the eighteenth century.

2

Wordsworth left a detailed account of his sources or models for the
setting of *The Excursion* in the Fenwick Note.[2] There he recorded that
the scene of Book I is set in the country in which it was written, that
is, on a common in Somersetshire or Dorsetshire. The scene is carefully drawn, particularly in the opening passage of that book. Then in
Book II the Poet and the Wanderer leave the plain country and ascend
into the beautiful mountains and valleys which provide the setting for
the remainder of the poem and which, Wordsworth tells us, are fashioned after the Furness Fells in the Lake Country. This inconsistency
of scene should occasion no discomfort and would probably never have
been noticed had not Wordsworth himself called attention to it. There is
no reason why a common such as that described in Book I could not be
within walking distance of mountainous terrain such as that which
adorns the rest of the poem. The transition is clearly marked,[3] and none
of the locations is so easily identified that the change seems questionable.
The inconsistency exists only in the Fenwick Note, not in *The Excursion*.

In Book II the Poet and the Wanderer are visualized as starting from
the vicinity of Grasmere and walking up the Vale of Langdale to the
west. Having ascended the hill at the end of the vale, they look down
into the circular recess which is the abode of the Solitary and which
is actually known as Blea Tarn. This was a favorite objective for Wordsworth on his numerous walks. He took Robinson there in 1816, and
the diarist's comments make a valuable supplement to Wordsworth's
own description.[4] From the Solitary's retreat the characters descend
into Little Langdale, which lies just to the south of Langdale; this
Wordsworth makes into the parish of the Pastor. Then, "as by the wav-
ing of a magic wand," we are transported back to the Vale of Grasmere
for the description of the parish church and its graveyard, the row upon

2. Isabella Fenwick Note to *The Excursion*, Wordsworth, *Prose*, III, 199.
3. *The Excursion*, II, 85–96.
4. *Henry Crabb Robinson on Books and Their Writers*, p. 195.

the lake, and the closing scene of the Pastor's prayer, which is set on the side of Loughrigg Fell, at the foot of the lake.

This localizing of the scene by Wordsworth is unfortunate, because not only are there the inconsistencies which he points out himself in the Fenwick Note but there are other difficulties, such, for instance, as the facts that the Grasmere island is not fringed with birch trees, there are no lilies of the vale at Grasmere, there are no goats or waterfalls near Grasmere, and no spotted deer, all of which Wordsworth describes.[5] There are details drawn from Rydal Water and Windermere included in the description of Grasmere, which in turn has been transplanted to Little Langdale. Graves are moved from all parts of the Lake Country into the Grasmere churchyard. Wordsworth really drew his scenery from wherever he wished, and it is a hopeless and useless task to identify all the details or to try to bring them into consistency. The geography of the poem by itself is so clearly drawn that no reader would have any difficulty describing the course followed by the characters. The only difficulty arises when one attempts to use *The Excursion* as a guidebook for a tour through the Lake Country. Wordsworth called this criticism down upon his own head when he made the identifications in the Fenwick Note. The setting of the poem is best considered as an imaginative creation from the scenery of the Lake Country, resembling the Lake Country very closely in general atmosphere, but not in detail. From this viewpoint the scenery of the poem becomes a real asset and presents no difficulties.

3

Wordsworth described his models for the characters of *The Excursion* in some detail in the Fenwick Note.[6] Like the setting, they are made up of elements drawn from several different models, with additions from Wordsworth's imagination.

The Wanderer, as the central character, is most carefully drawn. Wordsworth became very intimate with a traveling packman during his boyhood school days at Hawkshead. This man entertained the future poet with stories of his nomadic life and accounts of the philosophy he had built up in the course of his travels. It may well be imagined that few details of this man's character were lost from Wordsworth's retentive mind during the years which intervened between his Hawkshead school days and the composition of those parts of *The Excursion* which deal primarily with the character of the Wanderer. There was also another model for the Wanderer. Sara Hutchinson, during her childhood, lived for some

---

5. See the footnote to Knight's edition of *The Excursion,* where the geographical difficulties are pointed out in great detail, particularly in a note on p. 371. *The Poetical Works of William Wordsworth,* W. Knight, ed. (London, Macmillan, 1896), v (hereafter referred to as Wordsworth, *Poems*).   6. Wordsworth, *Prose,* III, 196–8.

time under the care of her cousin Margaret Patrick at Kendal. Her cousin-in-law was one David Patrick, who was famous throughout the north of England as an intellectual peddler. He acted as a sort of tutor to Sara and they developed a great mutual admiration and affection.[7] From Sara's letters to Wordsworth describing Patrick, Wordsworth drew many details of the character of the Wanderer.[8] And finally, as Wordsworth himself acknowledges, there is much of himself in the character of the Wanderer. Always a great foot traveler, Wordsworth fancied that, if he had been born into different circumstances, he would have chosen the life of a peddler; the Wanderer is a picture of the sort of man he would have hoped to become. There are also literary parallels to this character: the narrator in St. Pierre's *Paul et Virginie,* Ambulator in Thelwall's *The Peripatetic,* and Euphranor in Berkeley's *Alciphron.*

The character of the Solitary also derives from several different models. A Scotchman who had once been chaplain to a Highland regiment and subsequently settled at Grasmere, evidently having been shattered in fortune, gave Wordsworth some suggestions. The poet also drew many of the Solitary's characteristics from different persons he had observed in London during the high tide of revolutionary fervor in the early 1790's. One may well suspect that Wordsworth himself had shared the wild enthusiasms of those days; at least a part of the Solitary's mental history is that of Wordsworth himself. But the most noteworthy single model was Joseph Fawcett.

Joseph Fawcett was a preacher at a Dissenting meeting-house in the Old Jewry during Wordsworth's early residence in London. He was of very radical views, as is best indicated by the fact that he had a conscious part in the production of William Godwin's *Political Justice.* He was a very popular preacher, attracting large audiences which often included Mrs. Siddons, the Kembles, Holcroft, and young William Wordsworth. Since his greatest mission was a crusade against war, one can well imagine the influence he would exert over the young poet, who was at this time probably a fervent disciple of Godwin. Fawcett retired from the Old Jewry in 1795 and withdrew to a farm at Hedge Grove, near Walford, Hertfordshire, where he remained until his death in 1804. In his retirement he was not a shattered and intemperate man as Wordsworth paints him in *The Excursion* and specifically describes him in the Fenwick Note. Wordsworth's false report probably grew out of malicious gossip which reached him at Grasmere. Fawcett evidently passed his last years in peace and happiness. The flux of radical ideas entertained by the Solitary, and

7. This account of David Patrick is drawn from E. De Selincourt, *Dorothy Wordsworth* (Oxford, Clarendon Press, 1933), p. 56. I assume that there is some error in the identification of Patrick as James Patrick in Wordsworth, *Poems,* v, Appendix, Note A, p. 391.

8. One of these letters was received by Wordsworth on January 27, 1802. See Dorothy, *Journals,* I, 102 and note.

his ensuing despondency when the French Revolution failed, can probably be attributed to Wordsworth almost as readily as to Fawcett. When Wordsworth wrote the Fenwick Notes, he wished to conceal his early radicalism; when he wrote *The Excursion* he wanted to show why he had abandoned it. The Solitary is a picture of the typical Godwinian as seen by the more sober, partly disillusioned Wordsworth of 1800–14. If one remembers that Wordsworth had once been a Godwinian himself, it will become evident that the Solitary is not merely a calumny on Joseph Fawcett but also a criticism directed by the mature Wordsworth at his own earlier self.[9] There is perhaps also something of Thelwall's Arisor and Berkeley's Alciphron in the Solitary.

One of the most specific shortcomings in the character of the Solitary is his inability to absorb the shock occasioned by the deaths of his two children.[1] It is well known that Wordsworth himself had lost two children less than two years before the publication of *The Excursion*. The parallel seems obvious, but there is a qualification. The uncontrolled grief of the Solitary is exactly what Wordsworth was contrasting with his own Christian fortitude. The Solitary was not a Christian, and therefore he lacked what Wordsworth had:

> One adequate support
> For the calamities of mortal life
> Exists—one only; . . . Faith absolute in God . . . .[2]

I think the following quotation from a letter of Wordsworth will show what may have suggested this contrast to his mind.

Thelwall the Politician many years ago lost a Daughter about the age of Scott's child. I knew her she was a charming creature. Thelwall's were the agonies of an unbeliever, and he expressed them vigorously in several copies of harmonious blank verse, . . . but though they have great merit, one cannot read them but with much more pain than pleasure.

You probably know how much I have suffered in this way myself; having lost within the short space of half a year two delightful creatures a girl and a boy of the several ages of four and six and a half. . . . I do not mourn for them; yet I am sometimes weak enough to wish that I had them again.[3]

The Solitary's are also "the agonies of an unbeliever."

The character of the Pastor is not founded on a living model, according to the Fenwick Note. Wordsworth wished to embody the idea of a

9. A complete account of Fawcett and his relation to Wordsworth's Solitary can be found in an excellent article by M. Ray Adams, "Joseph Fawcett and Wordsworth's Solitary," *PMLA*, XLVIII (1933), 508–28. See also Arthur Beatty, *Joseph Fawcett: The Art of War, Its Relation to the Early Development of William Wordsworth*, University of Wisconsin Studies by the Department of English, No. 2 (September, 1918), pp. 224–69.

1. *The Excursion*, III, 638–705.   2. *Ibid.*, IV, 10–12, 22.
3. Wordsworth to B. R. Haydon, January 20, 1817, *LY*, p. 1368.

cultured man from the upper ranks of society who has been brought to a love of rural life by his pastoral office. It is, however, difficult to ignore what seems almost a careful antithesis between Crabbe's somewhat hard-bitten, unfeeling clergyman in "The Parish Register" and Wordsworth's more kindly, tolerant Pastor in *The Excursion.*

Nothing need be said about the Poet of *The Excursion,* for he is really a mere foil to the other characters, swaying with the conversation in just the best manner to draw the proper comments from his companions. It is, however, dangerous to assume that the Poet is Wordsworth himself. In some cases he is a mere mouthpiece for the sentiments of Wordsworth, but so are all the other characters, and, like them, the Poet says many things which we can hardly attribute to Wordsworth. One of the most difficult problems of *The Excursion* is to determine just when the characters are Wordsworth and when they are independent creations of his pen.

4

There are 22 short stories within the framework of *The Excursion,* 7 about the living and 15 about the dead. One is related by the Poet, 2 by the Wanderer, 2 by the Solitary, and 17 by the Pastor. The stories occupy about 3,480 lines, which is between one third and one half (roughly two fifths) of the entire poem in its final form. There are specific sources known for all but three of them. Most of the sources are to be found in real life, but several of the stories have literary analogues.

a) The life of the Wanderer.[4] This story is related by the Poet. The sources in real life and the literary analogues have been indicated in the previous section of this chapter. Many of the incidents in the Wanderer's childhood are closely analogous to the incidents of Wordsworth's own childhood, as related in *The Prelude.* This is particularly true of the mystical experiences, or "spots of time." For example, compare *The Excursion,* I, 198–221, to *The Prelude,* IV, 323–38.

b) "Margaret, or The Ruined Cottage."[5] The Wanderer tells this story to the Poet. It was written largely in 1797–98 and is probably the outgrowth of the powerful antiwar sentiments impressed alike on Wordsworth, Southey, and Coleridge by Godwin and Fawcett. Fawcett's long blank-verse poem, "The Art of War," published in 1795, influenced Wordsworth a great deal, as he acknowledged in the Fenwick Note to *The Excursion.* In the course of his blistering indictment of war, Fawcett draws a picture of the desolation at home during a foreign war, in which he mentions the "ruin'd houses," "female woe," and "pale afflictions."[6] I believe that this passage, with the impetus given by Godwin

---

4. *The Excursion,* I, 108–433.　　　　5. *Ibid.,* I, 497–916.
6. Beatty, *op. cit.,* pp. 257–8, ll. 847–910.

to the sentiments it expresses, exercised a great influence over Wordsworth and Southey. In Southey's *Commonplace Book*[7] there appears a series of notes with the heading "Subjects for Idylls." Among these notes is a description of a ruined mansion-house. Below this is a suggestion for an idyll on "a ruined cottage," "not to be told in dialogue." Further on Southey recurs to this note, writing: "The ruined cottage has matter for a best poem. The path overgrown—the holyhock blooming amid weeds. It shall be related to a friend whom I have purposely led there in an evening walk."[8] The striking parallels between these specifications and Wordsworth's story in *The Excursion* lead one to suspect that there was either a common source or some exchange of ideas. In 1799 Southey wrote an "English Eclogue" which he entitled "The Ruined Cottage,"[9] and, although the story told is different from Wordsworth's, the frameworks are the same, and the ruined cottages are very similar.

In the Fenwick Note[1] Wordsworth tells us that everything which pertains to Margaret was taken from actual observations made during his residence in the southwest of England. The people after whom he fashioned Margaret were some of them known to him, and some not. In St. Pierre's *Paul et Virginie,* the mother of Paul is named Margaret, while the character and circumstances of the mother of Virginie closely resemble those of Wordsworth's Margaret. However, this similarity is not very convincing. The despair of Robert, Margaret's husband, is representative of something which Wordsworth had much opportunity to observe while in London at the time of England's rupture with France in 1793, as he relates in the Fenwick Note.[2]

Wordsworth used a few lines from previously composed poetry when he wrote "The Ruined Cottage." He used line 9 of a rejected version of "Guilt and Sorrow," now line 888 of Book I of *The Excursion;* he also used a few passages from a fragmentary poem entitled "Incipient Madness," probably begun in 1795.[3]

c) The story of the Solitary is really related twice, once by the Wanderer[4] and once by the Solitary himself.[5] The sources of this story have

7. *Southey's Commonplace-Book,* J. W. Warter, ed. (Ser. IV. London, Longman, 1850), p. 95.   8. *Ibid.*

9. Robert Southey, "English Eclogues," VI: "The Ruined Cottage"; Westbury, 1799. This comparison was first suggested by Arthur Beatty, *William Wordsworth: His Doctrine and Art in Their Historical Relations,* University of Wisconsin Studies in Language and Literature, No. 17 (Madison, 1922), p. 254, n.

1. Isabella Fenwick Note to *The Excursion,* Wordsworth, *Prose,* III, pp. 198–200. I reproduce the material in the Fenwick Notes for the sake of completeness, to supplement them with additional information, to separate the important information they contain from the great burden of gratuitous, irrelevant information and *ex-post-facto* moralizing, and to correct a few errors.   2. *Ibid.,* p. 200.

3. See *The Poetical Works of William Wordsworth: Early Poems,* E. De Selincourt, ed. (Oxford, Clarendon Press, 1940), pp. 336, 375.

4. *The Excursion,* II, 164–315.   5. *Ibid.,* III, 480–955.

probably been sufficiently indicated in the discussion of the Solitary in the previous section of this chapter.

d) The story of the poor pensioner.[6] According to the Fenwick Note,[7] this story is compounded of two ingredients. The character of the pitiful old man is fashioned after a pauper who was boarded in a house in the Vale of Grasmere. Dorothy Wordsworth gives an account of the death of a man who answers to this description, whom she calls "Poor old Willy" in her *Grasmere Journal*.[8] With this character are combined the character of a woman in Patterdale and a sequence of events which actually took place in that village. The story was told to Wordsworth by his friend Luff, and much of the scenery which adorns it was also described for him by Luff. On November 9, 1805, when Wordsworth and his sister were making an excursion on the banks of Ullswater under the guidance of Luff, he took them aside to show them the ruined chapel in which the poor old man was found. Dorothy recorded the entire story in her journal, and it corresponds very closely to the version in *The Excursion*.[9] It was Wordsworth's practice to have Dorothy record incidents which he hoped to use later in his poetry. Wordsworth supplemented Luff's account of the scenery with his own observations on a subsequent trip through that region.[1] The Solitary uses this story as an example of the human ingratitude and cruelty which have destroyed his faith in mankind. He recurs to it later in the discussion.[2]

e) The story of the Pastor.[3] The source of the Pastor's story has been discussed in the preceding section of this chapter.

f) The quarryman and his wife.[4] This story is told partly by the Wanderer and partly by the Pastor. It was drawn from real life. The models were Jonathan and Betty Yewdale, who lived on the ridge between the two Langdales and of whom Wordsworth gives some account in the Fenwick Note.[5] They were close friends of the Wordsworth family. Dorothy identifies them in a letter and mentions that she is going to pay a visit to the "good woman" on the following day "with a party of young ones."[6a]

g) The story of unrequited love and despair overcome.[7a] This account begins the series of graveyard tales related by the Pastor. The man whom it concerns is not yet buried there but his grave is open to receive him. Wordsworth's model was a Hawkshead schoolmate. The

6. *Ibid.*, II, 732–895.   7. Wordsworth, *Prose*, III, 200.

8. Dorothy, *Journals*, I, 160, where the editor transcribes a note of Gordon G. Wordsworth suggesting the identity, but the reference given is to a later allusion to the Poor Pensioner, not to his story proper.   9. *Ibid.*, pp. 417–18.

1. Fenwick Note to *The Excursion*, Wordsworth, *Prose*, III, 200.

2. *The Excursion*, V, 880–90.   3. *Ibid.*, V, 98–132.

4. *Ibid.*, V, 670–837.

5. Fenwick Note to *The Excursion*, Wordsworth, *Prose*, III, 200–1.

6a. Dorothy to Catherine Clarkson, January 12, 1819, *MY*, p. 833.

7a. *The Excursion*, VI, 88–211.

story is thoroughly based on fact, except that Wordsworth knew nothing of the man's death, and he was not buried in the Grasmere churchyard.[8]

h) The persevering miner.[9] The man after whom Wordsworth fashioned this story was an inhabitant of Patterdale, and the story is based on fact in every detail.[1]

i) The prodigal.[2] Wordsworth evidently got this story from the lips of the Grasmere townspeople, for the young man was dead when Wordsworth arrived at Grasmere. The prodigal's name was Dawson[3] and he was probably the brother of the young volunteer who is the subject of one of the subsequent stories in *The Excursion.*[4]

j) The Jacobite and the Hanoverian Whig.[5] Dame Tyson, in whose home Wordsworth lived while attending school at Hawkshead, told this story to Wordsworth. It is based on real characters and events. The Jacobite was named Drummond and the Whig Vandeput. Their place of retirement was Hawkshead, not Grasmere or Little Langdale.[6]

k) The story of the miserly woman.[7] It is probably a safe conjecture that this woman was Agnes Fisher. Wordsworth describes her merely as a near neighbor in the Fenwick Note,[8a] but the inference is inevitable that he refers to Agnes Fisher and her son John. Dorothy Wordsworth's *Grasmere Journal* mentions Agnes Fisher's powers of conversation and her thrift; it also mentions John Fisher's "intake," which may correspond to the description of his restored fortune in *The Excursion.* He was often employed by the Wordsworths as a gardener, and the description of his wild youth in *The Excursion* is borne out by the facts.[9a]

l) The story of Ellen.[1a] In the Fenwick Note[2a] Wordsworth recorded that this story is true in detail. He learned it from Mary and Dorothy, to whom it was related by the sister of "Ellen." "Ellen" had lived in Hawkshead. Stories of seduction were of such common currency in the century preceding *The Excursion* that even when based on true events it was almost inevitable that they should fall into a pattern of sentimental morality which made them all much alike. The parallels between the stories of Ellen, Shenstone's Jessy, various characters in Crabbe's works, and Southey's Hannah have already been mentioned.[3a] It must

---

8. Fenwick Note to *The Excursion,* Wordsworth, *Prose,* III, 202–3.
9. *The Excursion,* VI, 212–55.
1. Fenwick Note to *The Excursion,* Wordsworth, *Prose,* III, 204.
2. *The Excursion,* VI, 275–375.
3. Fenwick Note to *The Excursion,* Wordsworth, *Prose,* III, 204–5.
4. *The Excursion,* VII, 695–890.   5. *Ibid.,* VI, 392–521.
6. Fenwick Note to *The Excursion,* Wordsworth, *Prose,* III, 205.
7. *The Excursion,* VI, 675–777.   8a. Wordsworth, *Prose,* III, 205–6.
9a. Dorothy, *Journals,* I, Appendix I, pp. 434–5.
1a. *The Excursion,* VI, 787–1052.   2a. Wordsworth, *Prose,* III, 206.
3a. In sec. I of this chapter.

be said, nevertheless, that Wordsworth's treatment of the subject is particularly skillful and that the story of Ellen vies with that of Margaret
for the highest critical approbation of any part of *The Excursion.*

m) Wilfred Armathwaite.[4] This story of a man who broke the marriage vow was told more fully in the original version, where the family
circumstances were related and where there was also a description of
the object of the man's lawless passion, a blooming servant-girl. In the
1827 edition, Wordsworth struck out most of the detail and added lines
1085–92, which describe the story as unworthy of being recounted and
give a slightly more religious turn to the whole. There is no known
source for this tale. Wordsworth gives no account of it in the Fenwick
Note.

n) Story of the widower with six daughters.[5] No account of this
family was given by Wordsworth, but it seems probable that the models
were Thomas Ashburner of Grasmere and his daughters. Ashburner's
first wife died in 1791, leaving him with five daughters. He remarried
in the same year. His second wife was a woman of delicate health. The
family enjoyed intimate friendship with the Wordsworths.[6] The fact
that Wordsworth gives his widower six daughters instead of five and
makes no mention of the second marriage may be attributed to the growing prejudice of Wordsworth against second marriages, or merely to
poetic license, since Wordsworth followed this story in the first edition with one describing a widower who did remarry, and he undoubtedly wished to draw a contrast between the two. Perhaps he converted
Ashburner's second wife into a sixth daughter for his purposes. Another
possibility is that the story was written during a temporary absence of
Ashburner's second wife in 1802.[7]

The story of the widower whose second marriage was prudential and
successful, which originally concluded Book VI and which was removed
by Wordsworth in 1827, may be found in the notes to any of the com-
parative editions of the poem. It was 73 lines long.

o) The courtier-parson.[8] Wordsworth describes this family in such
detail both in the poem and in the Fenwick Note[9] that it is easy to
identify it as that of the Reverend Joseph Sympson, Vicar of Wythburne.
They were very close friends of the Wordsworths, as Dorothy's *Grasmere Journal* shows by its almost daily allusions to the Sympsons. All
that is said of them in *The Excursion* is true, except for the description
of their journey to Grasmere (which was drawn from life in another
instance) and the description of their graves.[1]

4. *The Excursion*, VI, 1079–1114.   5. *Ibid.*, VI, 1115–91.
6. See Dorothy, *Journals*, and *EL, MY*, and *LY, passim.*
7. Dorothy, *Journals*, I, Appendix I, p. 433.
8. *The Excursion*, VII, 31–291.   9. Wordsworth, *Prose*, III, 206–7.
1. For an account of this family and its association with the Wordsworths, see
Dorothy, *Journals*, I, Appendix I, pp. 437–8.

p) The story of "Wonderful" Walker.[2] The Reverend Robert Walker (1709–1802), Vicar of Seathwaite, was Wordsworth's model for this character. The poet also sings his praises in "The River Duddon," Sonnet XVIII, and in a long note to that sonnet he gives a memoir of Walker which contains all that is required for an understanding of his model in this part of *The Excursion*. The memoir has some merit of its own.

q) The deaf man.[3] The grave of this man is in the churchyard at the head of Haweswater. Wordsworth heard his story from relatives of the man on the spot.[4]

r) The blind man.[5] This character is drawn from an inhabitant of Kendal, named John Gough. Strangely enough, he was not dead when the description of his grave in *The Excursion* was published. He died in 1825. Wordsworth knew him personally, and the account of his skill as a botanist (by touch) and mathematician as given in *The Excursion* is not exaggerated.[6]

s) The woodsman.[7] This man passes by the four men in the churchyard dragging a huge tree to the sawmill. He requires no model but simply reflects Wordsworth's lifelong abhorrence of all lumbering among his native hills.

t) The infant girl.[8] This is an exact picture of a sequence of events which Wordsworth himself had observed.[9] The family was named Green and had long been located at Grasmere.[1]

u) The young volunteer.[2a] This young man was George Dawson, brother to the prodigal of Book VI.[3a] Wordsworth knew the father well and attended the funeral of this son.[4a] The afternoon of the funeral was extremely beautiful as Wordsworth describes it in *The Excursion* and as he often recurred to it later.[5a]

There is a curious garbling of the accounts given by Wordsworth of this story and the next in the Fenwick Note, both in Grosart's edition of *The Prose Works of William Wordsworth*[6a] and in Christopher Wordsworth's *Memoirs of William Wordsworth*,[7a] from which it may be concluded that the error was made by Miss Fenwick in taking down the dictation of Wordsworth. Evidently Wordsworth concluded his discussion of the young volunteer with the words, "as described in the

2. *The Excursion*, VII, 316–95.   3. *Ibid.*, VII, 395–481.
4. Fenwick Note to *The Excursion*, Wordsworth, *Prose*, III, 207.
5. *The Excursion*, VII, 482–515.
6. For additional information on John Gough, see Coleridge's essay on "The Soul and Its Organs of Sense"; *LY*, p. 1233; and Note E in the Appendix to Knight's edition of *The Excursion*, Wordsworth, *Poems*, V, 398–9.
7. *The Excursion*, VII, 536–651.   8. *Ibid.*, VII, 632–94.
9. Fenwick Note to *The Excursion*, Wordsworth, *Prose*, III, 207.
1. See Wordsworth, *Poems*, V, 309, n.   2a. *The Excursion*, VII, 695–890.
3a. Lines 275–375.
4a. See *The Excursion*, VII, 695–875 ff.; *MY*, p. 138; and *LY*, p. 1122.
5a. Fenwick Note to *The Excursion*, Wordsworth, *Prose*, III, 207–8.
6a. Vol. III, p. 208.   7a. Vol. II, p. 46.

poem," and then quoted a few lines from the following tale as an introduction to his remarks on the man who served as its model. Miss Fenwick apparently understood Wordsworth to say, "as described in the poem*s*," and therefore she took the quotations from the following tale to be the titles of separate poems. Thus the reader of the Fenwick Notes finds no separation between the notes on the two tales and must provide it for himself. One will search in vain for a poem by Wordsworth entitled "The house is gone," but one can find these words at the beginning of the last framework story in *The Excursion*.[8]

v) Sir Alfred Erthing.[9] These traditions survived about a gentleman, the ruins of whose mansion and a few of whose cottages were still standing in Wordsworth's day. They were called "Nott Houses," since he was the progenitor of the Knott family.[1] The title is Wordsworth's invention. The following quotation will explain itself.

William and Mary and little Willy paid a visit to old Mrs. Knott yesterday with the Excursion in hand, William intending to read to the old Lady the history of the Grasmere Knight. She could not hear his loud voice; but understood the story very well when her Niece read it, and was greatly delighted. Today they have returned the Book and poor Miss K has written a . . . note . . . saying in plain words that she had written to Kendal to order the Book. . . . I tell William that the family made a trading voyage of it.[2]

5

The present study does not undertake to indicate all possible sources for every line of *The Excursion*. That is the work of a critical editor, and a good beginning has been made in the critical editions already available.[3] Wordsworth himself provided the poem with several notes, including the "Essay upon Epitaphs." Some of the more important sources of specific passages do call for our attention here.

The most important single source for isolated specific passages is Wordsworth's own life. It is self-evident that each of the main characters in *The Excursion* bears at least some resemblance to Wordsworth himself, and the whole poem is in one sense a thinly veiled account of how Wordsworth solved a difficult and important personal problem. The similarity of *The Excursion* to *The Prelude* in this respect is patent. The close textual interrelation of the two poems has also been pointed out in the previous chapter of this study. In addition there are several details in the narrative parts of *The Excursion* which seem clearly to have

---

8. *The Excursion*, vii, 958.   9. *Ibid.*, vii, 921–75.
1. Fenwick Note to *The Excursion*, Wordsworth, *Prose*, iii, 208.
2. Dorothy to Sara Hutchinson, February 12, 1815, *MY*, p. 638.
3. That of Knight is still the most useful, pending the long-awaited new Oxford edition.

been suggested to Wordsworth by events in his own life. Some have parallels in *The Prelude;* others do not.

In Book IX of *The Excursion,* lines 484–8, when the Poet tells how the act of rowing recalls to his mind the days of his childhood, when he rowed with friends on Lake Windermere, it is unmistakably Wordsworth who is speaking, recalling his days as a schoolboy at Hawkshead. The account of the schoolboy's association with the Wanderer in Book I, lines 52–76, is clearly a description of Wordsworth's own acquaintance with the Hawkshead packman mentioned in the Fenwick Notes. The description of the Wanderer's studies is probably an account of Wordsworth's own studies, and the mention of mathematics is definitely reminiscent of a passage in *The Prelude.*[4] Likewise there can be little doubt that the Wanderer's mystical experiences in childhood are those of Wordsworth himself.[5] There is even some verbal similarity:

The Prelude (1850), I, 418, 422	*The Excursion,* I, 219–20
A lonely scene more lonesome, . . .	on the lonely mountain-tops,
In solitude such intercourse was mine.	Such intercourse was his,

The first 30 lines of Book VII of *The Excursion* are devoted to a description by the Poet of his youthful experience of listening to aged harpists while on a walking tour among the mountains. Here Wordsworth is recalling the spring of 1791, when he went on a walking tour in Wales with his friend Robert Jones. The long account in *The Excursion* of the Solitary's state of mind during the flood tide of the French Revolution is in general probably a faithful description of Wordsworth's own reactions to the same events, which may best be ascertained by a comparison with the corresponding passage in *The Prelude.*[6] When the Solitary tells of his retirement with his bride to Devonshire and when he describes their walks upon the downs, we may hear Wordsworth describing his residence in the Quantock Hills with Dorothy.[7]

In 1803, when England was in fear of invasion, Wordsworth and many others of the able-bodied men of Grasmere marched off to volunteer their services for the home defense.[8] The little company became known as the Grasmere Volunteers, and it is easy to see an account of them in the description which introduces the story of the young volunteer in *The Excursion.*[9] The deaths of Wordsworth's two children in 1812 have an obvious parallel in the Solitary's losses of a daughter and a son in that order, and both within the course of one year.[1] An effort

---

4. *The Excursion,* I, 252–7; *The Prelude* (1850), VI, 142–67.
5. *The Excursion,* I, 198–221; *The Prelude* (1850), IV, 323–38.
6. *The Excursion,* III, 680–991; *The Prelude* (1850), IX–X (*passim*), XI, 286–320.
7. *The Excursion,* III, 513–49.
8. See letter, Dorothy to Catherine Clarkson, October 9, 1803, *EL,* pp. 335–6.
9. *The Excursion,* VII, 757–71.   1. *Ibid.,* II, 198–200; III, 638–49.

has been made to show that Wordsworth was afraid of losing his sight, and *The Excursion* is brought to the support of this theory.[2] There may be some truth in such a suspicion, but the passage from *The Excursion* which is offered as confirmation[3] really bears little weight, especially in the light of Wordsworth's comments on blindness after the story of John Gough, where he shows that blindness would be no deterrent to his work, but even an aid.

> And know we not that from the blind have flowed
> The highest, holiest, raptures of the lyre:
> And wisdom married to immortal verse?[4]

It was Wordsworth's habit to use the journals of Dorothy as a sort of storage place for the raw materials of poetry. The most famous examples of this process are "Resolution and Independence," "Alice Fell," and "Beggars," each of which has a prose model in Dorothy's journals.[5] There are a few passages in *The Excursion* which also seem to be based on Dorothy's prose. We have already noticed that Dorothy gives an account of the old man who was to become the poor pensioner of *The Excursion*,[6] and the two versions correspond very closely. On September 3, 1800, Wordsworth, his brother John, and Mr. Sympson left home to climb Helvellyn. While they were gone Dorothy attended the funeral of a village pauper. She wrote a very moving description of the funeral in her journal for that day. Wordsworth, when he came to write the passages in *The Excursion* which describe the funeral of the poor pensioner, took several suggestions from this entry.

Dorothy's journal	*The Excursion*
I went to a funeral at John Dawson's. . . . They talked sensibly and chearfully about common things. . . . The coffin was neatly lettered and painted black, and covered with a decent cloth. They set the corpse down at the door; and, while we stood within the threshold, the men with their hats off sang with decent and solemn countenances a verse of a funeral psalm. The corpse was then borne down the hill, and they sang till	several voices in one solemn sound, Was heard ascending; mournful, deep, and slow The cadence, as of psalms—a funeral dirge! . . . forth appeared in view a band Of rustic persons, from behind the hut Bearing a coffin in the midst, with which They shaped their course along the sloping side

2. E. C. Batho, *The Later Wordsworth* (New York, Macmillan, 1933), pp. 319–20.
3. *The Excursion*, IV, 103–12.   4. *Ibid.*, VII, 534–6.
5. For "Resolution and Independence," see entry for October 3, 1800, Dorothy, *Journals*, I, 63. For "Alice Fell," see entry for February 16, 1802, *ibid.*, I, 114–15. For "Beggars," see entry for June 10, 1800, *ibid.*, I, 47–8.
6. See the previous section of this chapter. Dorothy's entry (November 9, 1805) is to be found in Dorothy, *Journals*, I, 417–18; the story in *The Excursion* is in Bk. II, 730–895.

they had passed the Town-End. . . .
I thought she was going to a quiet
spot, and I could not help weeping
very much. When we came to the
bridge, they began to sing again, and
stopped during four lines before they
entered the Churchyard.[7]

Of that small valley, singing as they
  moved;
A sober company and few, the men
Bare-headed, and all decently at-
  tired!
Some steps when they had thus ad-
  vanced, the dirge
Ended; . . .
We heard the hymn they sang—a
  solemn sound
Heard anywhere; . . . a hush of de-
  cency;
Then from the threshold moves with
  song of peace,
And confidential yearnings, tow'rds
  its home,
Its final home on earth. . . .
A mute procession on the houseless
  road;
Or passing by some single tenement
Or clustered dwellings, where again
  they raise
The monitory voice.[8]

On July 27, 1800, William, Dorothy, and John Wordsworth went for
an evening row on the lake. Dorothy made the following record in her
journal, which Wordsworth found useful in composing *The Excursion*.

Dorothy's journal

We heard a strange sound in the
Bainriggs wood, as we were floating
on the water; it *seemed* in the wood,
but it must have been above it, for
presently we saw a raven very high
above us. It called out, and the dome
of the sky seemed to echo the sound.
It called again and again as it flew
onwards, and the mountains gave
back the sound, seeming as if from
their center; a musical bell-like answering to the bird's hoarse voice.
We heard both the call of the bird,
and the echo, after we could see him
no longer.[9]

The Excursion

  and often, at the hour
When issue forth the first pale stars,
  is heard
Within the circuit of this fabric huge,
One voice—the solitary raven flying
Athwart the concave of the dark blue
  dome,
Unseen, perchance above all power of
  sight—
An iron knell! with echoes from afar
Faint—and still fainter—as the cry,
  with which
The wanderer accompanies her flight
Through the calm region, fades upon
  the ear,
Diminishing by distance till it seemed

7. Dorothy, *Journals*, i, 59.
9. Dorothy, *Journals*, i, 52.

8. *The Excursion*, ii, 374–94, 548–66.

> To expire; yet from the abyss is
> caught again,
> And yet again recovered !¹

Another member of Wordsworth's family contributed a few ideas to *The Excursion*. In 1810 Christopher Wordsworth, the poet's brother, published his *Ecclesiastical Biography*. This was a ponderous collection of the best biographies of all the most important leaders and martyrs of the English Church, from Becket to Tillotson. The poet read his brother's anthology, at least in part, with great care. There can be little doubt that this collection of studies of the great men of the Established Church provided the inspiration for the glowing panegyric delivered by the Poet near the beginning of Book VI of *The Excursion*.² Wordsworth's intimate knowledge of his brother's work is also indicated by the fact that he quotes from the life of Latimer which Christopher used and refers the reader to Christopher's footnote on the quoted passage. In a note to *The Excursion*, Wordsworth also refers the reader to a passage in his brother's work, but he does not specifically acknowledge the close verbal indebtedness involved. This is an important parallel because it concerns one of the most specifically Christian passages in *The Excursion*, which has been used as evidence of Wordsworth's complete orthodoxy at that time.

Ecclesiastical Biography	*The Excursion*
. . . my fear of dying was wont to tell me that I was not sufficiently loosened from this world. But I find that it is comparatively very easy to me to be loose from this world, but hard to live by faith above. To despise earth is easy to me; but not so easy to be acquainted and conversant in heaven. I have nothing in this world which I could not easily let go; but to get satisfying apprehensions of the other world is the great and grievous difficulty.³	'Tis, by comparison, an easy task Earth to despise; but to converse with heaven— This is not easy :—to relinquish all We have, or hope, of happiness and joy, And stand in freedom loosened from this world, I deem not arduous; . . . if he could fix A satisfying view upon that state etc.⁴

In his later years Wordsworth became an intimate friend of Dr. Andrew Bell, a famous educator of the day.⁵ Born in Scotland, Dr. Bell had taught for a time in America and in 1789 had been made the superintendent of an orphan asylum in Madras. A shortage of teachers led him to develop a system of proctorship and mutual tuition by the stu-

---

1. *The Excursion*, IV, 1175–87.   2. *Ibid.*, VI, 42–74.
3. "Richard Baxter" (autobiography), *Ecclesiastical Biography* (London, F. & J. Rivington, 1853), IV, 512.   4. *The Excursion*, IV, 130–5, 157–8.
5. See *MY, passim*.

dents themselves. In 1797, when he had returned to London, he published a pamphlet, *An Experiment in Education,* which attracted very little attention. Nevertheless, his system was put into practice in several places and gradually it became famous. Therefore in 1808 Dr. Bell published a more detailed exposition of his method, entitled *The Madras School, or Elements of Tuition: Comprising the Analysis of an Experiment in Education, Made at the Male Asylum, Madras; with Its Facts, Proofs, and Illustrations; to Which Are Added, Extracts of Sermons Preached at Lambeth; a Sketch for Training up the Children of the Poor; and a Specimen of the Mode of Religious Instruction at the Royal Military Asylum, Chelsea.*[6] In October of the same year Wordsworth wrote as follows.

I have read Dr. Bell's Book upon education which no doubt you must have seen, it is a most interesting work and entitles him to the fervent gratitude of all good men: but I cannot say [? it has made] any material change in my views of [.] [I] would however strenuously recommend [? the system] wherever it can be adopted.[7]

Wordsworth came to entertain a still higher opinion of the Madras system, and soon he was having his own children educated "on Dr. Bell's plan."[8] Subsequently he could not praise it too highly: "If you have read my Poem, *The Excursion,* you will there see what importance I attach to the Madras System. Next to the Art of Printing it is the noblest invention for the improvement of the human species."[9] The influence of Dr. Bell's book on *The Excursion* is considerable. The peculiarities of the administrative method which came to be known as the Madras system do not appear in the poem; but Wordsworth renders them high praise in the last note to Book ix of *The Excursion.* The parts of Dr. Bell's book which are not primarily concerned with his system had the greatest influence over Wordsworth when he was composing Books viii and ix of *The Excursion.* Part iii, Chapter ii, of *The Madras School* consists of extracts from a sermon originally preached at Lambeth on the subject of the education of the poor; and Part vi, Chapter iv, contains an appeal for the establishment of compulsory universal education. These two chapters probably provided Wordsworth with many suggestions and a few specific details for the last two books of *The Excursion.*

Dr. Bell approaches the subject of the education of the poor by contrasting the tremendous advances in science, manufacture, and commerce under the stimulus of material gain with the great lack of advances in moral and intellectual education.[1] Wordsworth approaches

6. London, printed by T. Bensley, Bolt Court, for J. Murray; Cadell and Davies; Rivingtons; Hatchard; and A. Constable; 1808.

7. Wordsworth to Wrangham, October 2, 1808, *MY,* pp. 245–6.

8. *Ibid.,* p. 605.   9. Wordsworth to Poole, March 13, 1815, *ibid.,* p. 646.

1. Bell, *op. cit.,* pp. 108–12.

it in practically the same way, by painting the advances in science, manufacture, and commerce in strong colors and then by showing how human beings now apply themselves to industry and its idol—gain— as zealously as their forefathers applied themselves to the worship of God, with the result that the domestic affections and virtues which have in the past always been England's greatest asset are now disappearing.[2] Dr. Bell points out that industry has become an obstruction to the moral education of the poor, so that they no longer are able to reach the full moral stature to which their innate spiritual equality entitles them.[3] In a similar manner Wordsworth paints a dismal picture of the modern child, whose spirit is smothered by early confinement in factories, and then points to the lack of equal educational opportunities as the source of all other inequalities, for the moral truths are available to all alike.[4] Man's injustice in the dispensation of moral and literary education is all "that hath made So wide a difference between man and man."[5] In the same way, both writers deplore the fact that so many young minds are left in total ignorance, and even caused to turn into evil ways, by the lack of the rudiments of education.[6] And, finally, both conclude their arguments with an appeal to the English legislators to assure the education of all the poor children in the nation, instead of leaving such an important matter to the precarious subsistence provided by charity.[7]

It should be mentioned that Wordsworth later changed his mind about both the Madras system and universal compulsory free education. He came to feel that the Madras system fostered envy and overemphasized purely intellectual attainments, and that overeducation of the masses created industrial unrest and threatened the collapse of the family.[8]

Coleridge mentions Dr. Bell and praises the Madras system very liberally in *The Friend,* much of which was written while Coleridge was visiting Wordsworth at Allan Bank.[9] There is some further relationship between *The Friend* and *The Excursion.* For instance, Coleridge quotes from *The Excursion* and praises Wordsworth highly as his fellow laborer in the same cause.[1] There are also many similarities of doctrine, which will be discussed in the next chapter. The "Essay upon Epitaphs," which was originally printed in *The Friend,* later appeared as a note to *The Excursion.* Finally, one passage in *The Friend* which resembles some lines in *The Excursion* has been pointed out, but the similarity is not close.[2a]

There has been a great deal of discussion of the extent of Words-

2. *The Excursion,* VIII, 180–95.   3. Bell, *op. cit.,* p. 105.
4. *The Excursion,* VIII, 297 ff.; IX, 206–54.   5. *Ibid.,* IX, 253–4.
6. Bell, *op. cit.,* p. 104; *The Excursion,* IX, 304–10, 314–20, 359–62.
7. Bell, *op. cit.,* pp. 315–31; *The Excursion,* IX, 293 ff., 299–345.
8. See *LY,* 326–35.   9. *The Friend* (September 14, 1809), p. 71.
1. Coleridge quotes *The Excursion,* I, 626–34, in *The Friend,* (November 16, 1809), and praises Wordsworth on p. 112 (September 23, 1809).
2a. See Wordsworth, *Poems,* v, 41, n.

worth's indebtedness to German literature in *The Excursion.*[3] The parallels between Schiller's "Der Spaziergang" and *The Excursion* have already been mentioned.[4] They are negligible. The famous passages on the Greek myths in *The Excursion,*[5] while very original, bear some resemblances to two passages in the works of Schiller. There is a speech by Max in Act II, scene 4, of *The Piccolomini* which tells of the origin and power of Greek myths in a manner similar to that of the passages in *The Excursion.*[6] This play was translated by Coleridge in 1799. In "Die Götter Greichenland" there is an even more impressive and explicit resemblance to Wordsworth's passages. But in both cases the idea is put to an entirely different use from that which Wordsworth makes of it, and nowhere is there an unmistakable instance of borrowing on Wordsworth's part. If he took the original suggestion from Schiller—which is quite possible—he made it entirely his own in developing it. There have been some who have seen a resemblance between the glorious sunset at the end of *The Excursion* and that in Schiller's *Die Räuber,*[7] but it seems strange that one should look for a literary source for a sunset in Wordsworth, of all poets, and since the passage in Schiller bears no specific resemblance to that in *The Excursion,* the only similarity being in the solemn effect of the sunset on the characters, the parallel can be dismissed.

A few verbal reminiscences of Bürger, possibly coincidental, can be found in *The Excursion.*[8] Parallels have also been indicated between Goethe's *Faust* and *The Excursion,* but there is evidently no indebtedness involved.[9] There are also a few traces of Kant in *The Excursion,* but Wordsworth's intimacy with Coleridge is thoroughly adequate to explain these.[1] This is particularly true in the light of the following statement.

"I asked Wordsworth," says Captain Hamilton, writing from the Lakes, where he resided latterly, "about that passage in the 'Excursion' which William says contains the doctrine of Kant. Wordsworth says he is utterly ignorant of everything connected either with Kant or his philosophy. So that it could not have come from that source, but is a casual coincidence."[2]

3. For an able summary, see M. J. Herzberg, "William Wordsworth and German Literature," *PMLA,* XL (1925), 302–45.   4. See the first section of this chapter.
5. *The Excursion,* IV, 718 ff., 847–87.
6. This parallel was first suggested by R. P. Gillies, *Blackwood's Edinburgh Magazine,* XIV (1823), 395.
7. *Die Räuber,* Act III, sc. ii. T. Rea, *Schiller's Dramas and Poems in England* (London, Unwin, 1906), p. 21.
8. For instance, compare Bürger's "Drei Spannen lang," from "Pfarrer's Tochter," with Wordsworth's "three spans long," *The Excursion,* VII, (Wordsworth, *Poems,* V, 309, n.)
9. O. Heiler, "Goethe and Wordsworth," *Modern Language Notes,* XIV (1899), 262–4.
1. R. Wellek, *Kant in England* (Princeton, Princeton University Press, 1931), pp. 159–62. Mr. Wellek points out that all the definitely Kantian passages in *The Excursion* (especially IV, 66 ff., and IX, 113 ff.) have parallels in *The Friend.*
2. John Veitch, *Memoir of Sir William Hamilton, Bart.* (Edinburgh and London,

The possibility of Kant's influence will be mentioned again in connection with the doctrines of *The Excursion*, below.

Wordsworth's reading of travel-books also bore fruit in *The Excursion*. The passages on Persian myths, the Tower of Semiramis, the construction of Babylon, and the Chaldeans were apparently all drawn from Purchas, a copy of whose *Pilgrimage* (1614) was in the Rydal Mount library.[3] Carver's *Travels* and other books dealing with America evidently supplied Wordsworth with the Indian name for the whippoorwill ("Muccawiss")[4] and the myth concerning the origin of the human race ("men Leapt out together from a rocky cave").[5]

The Bible is given a prominence in *The Excursion* which it enjoys nowhere else in Wordsworth's works. There are several allusions to it[6] and several passages concerned primarily with Biblical characters and events.[7] The most striking of these is the account of the Creation taken from the Bible in Book IV.[8]

Walter Savage Landor accused Wordsworth of plagiary from *Gebir* in the famous passage on the sea shell in Book IV.[9] He was probably only half in earnest, for the suggestion was made in a flippant "Imaginary Conversation" which Landor evidently wrote originally for his own amusement. He sent a copy to Henry Crabb Robinson and succeeded in arousing his wrath.[1] Robinson asked Wordsworth about the passage and recorded that the poet "admitted no obligation."[2] The parallel is not close enough to indicate any borrowing, and the entire incident is unfortunate, particularly since the "Imaginary Conversation" which contained the accusation was subsequently published in *Blackwood's*.[3a]

William Blackwood & Sons, 1869), p. 89. For a collection of the evidence for direct and indirect influence of Kant on Wordsworth, see M. M. Rader, *Presiding Ideas in Wordsworth's Poetry* (Seattle, University of Washington Press, 1931), Appendix C. See also E. F. Carrit, "Addison, Kant, and Wordsworth," *Essays and Studies by Members of the English Association,* XXII (1937), 26–36.

3. E. K. Holmes, "Some Sources of Wordsworth's Passages on Mythology in *The Excursion*," *Modern Language Notes,* LIV (1939), 127–9. *Purchas His Pilgrimage* was item 285 on the second day of the Rydal Mount sale ("Rydal Mount Library"). The pertinent pages in that edition (1614) of *Purchas* are: 53, 55, 56, 370, 371. The passages in *The Excursion* occur in Bk. IV, 671–749, including one drawn from Francis Rous's *Archaeologiae Atticae* (1642), item 233 in the Rydal Mount sale, "Rydal Mount Library."

4. *The Excursion,* III, 947. See Wordsworth, *Poems,* v, Appendix, Note C, pp. 393–6.

5. *The Excursion,* III, 241–2. See Wordsworth, *Poems,* v, Appendix, Note B, pp. 392–3.

6. *The Excursion,* I, 223–5; III, 861–5; IV, 160; v, 992; VII, 451; IX, 637–8.

7. *Ibid.,* VII, 811–16; IV, 631–62.   8. *Ibid.,* IV, 631–62.

9. *Ibid.,* IV, 1132–47. Compare *Gebir,* I, 159 ff.

1. *Henry Crabb Robinson on Books and Their Writers,* pp. 507, 516.

2. *The Correspondence of Henry Crabb Robinson with the Wordsworth Circle,* pp. 21–2.

3a. *Blackwood's Edinburgh Magazine,* LIII (April 1843), 518 ff. The "Imaginary Conversation" is between Landor himself and Christopher North. The accusation, which is qualified by words put in the mouth of North, takes place on p. 534. The article is introduced by a letter from E. Quillinan to North, attacking Landor.

IV

The Content of The Excursion

I

WORDSWORTH'S great project of writing a philosophical poem grew out of conversations with Coleridge in 1798. The plan was developed in subsequent letters and conversations between the two poets at Dove Cottage, Coleorton, and Allan Bank. The evidence indicates that Wordsworth depended rather heavily on the ideas of Coleridge in working out the design. Coleridge later admitted that the original plan was suggested partly by himself.[1] Another striking bit of evidence is contained in the following three quotations. The first two are taken from letters written by Wordsworth to Coleridge when the latter was about to depart for Malta, and the third is Coleridge's reply.

I am very anxious to have your notes for *The Recluse*. I cannot say how much importance I attach to this; if it should please God that I survive you, I should reproach myself forever in writing the work if I had neglected to procure this help.[2]

I would gladly have given 3 fourths of my possessions for your letter on *The Recluse* at that time. I cannot say what a load it would be to me, should I survive you and you die without this memorial left behind. Do, for heaven's sake, put this out of the reach of accident immediately.[3]

my ideas respecting your Recluse were burnt as a Plague-garment.[4]

Wordsworth was rushing *The Prelude* to completion, and he looked forward to beginning serious work on *The Recluse* immediately afterward. He needed a firm foundation of Coleridgean metaphysics to work on, and these letters represent his effort to get it before Coleridge departed for Malta. However, Coleridge's "ideas" were destroyed, if he ever really wrote them down, and Wordsworth had to wait for Coleridge's return to England. It was finally December 21, 1806, when Coleridge arrived at Coleorton to stay for about two months, thus giving Wordsworth an opportunity to read *The Prelude* to him and to get his ideas on the long-projected philosophical poem. Coleridge was enrap-

1. "Table Talk" (July 21, 1832), *Table Talk*, p. 188.
2. *EL*, p. 368.　　　　　　　　　　　3. *Ibid.*, p. 380.
4. *Ibid.*, p. 508. Quoted by Wordsworth with the date May 1, 1805. Coleridge entrusted some papers to a Major Adye, who died of plague at Gibraltar and whose papers, including those of Coleridge in his custody, were burned.

tured on hearing *The Prelude,* and it may well be supposed that the conversation soon turned to the great work which was to follow. From the latter part of 1808 until late October of 1810, Coleridge lived with the Wordsworths at Allan Bank. During this time Wordsworth did some work on *The Recluse* and Coleridge was engaged on *The Friend.* There was probably a great deal of conversation on the great poem. Shortly afterward came the estrangement, and Coleridge probably offered no further suggestions to Wordsworth until he wrote his letter criticizing *The Excursion* in 1815.[5] From this letter, and from others of his recorded comments, we are able to reconstruct in some detail the suggestions which Coleridge made for the poem which was finally to appear as *The Excursion.*

Perhaps the first suggestion for *The Excursion* proper is contained in the following words of a letter from Coleridge to Wordsworth in the summer of 1799.

I do entreat you to go on with "The Recluse"; and I wish you would write a poem in blank verse, addressed to those, who, in consequence of the complete failure of the French Revolution, have thrown up all hopes of the amelioration of mankind, and are sinking into an almost epicurean selfishness, disguising the same under the soft titles of domestic attachment and contempt for visionary *philosophes.* It would do great good, and might form a part of "The Recluse", for in my present mood I am wholly against the publication of any small poems.[6]

This reads almost like a specific order for *The Excursion,* especially Books III and IV. We have definite evidence that Wordsworth was deeply impressed by the suggestion, for in *The Prelude* (II, 432–40) he paraphrased Coleridge's words unmistakably. It is also interesting to observe that Wordsworth was at great pains to make the Solitary an Epicurean.[7]

The most important mission that Coleridge wanted the philosophical poem to fulfill was antimechanistic. In 1801 Coleridge announced that he had overthrown the doctrines of Hartley—associationism and necessity[8]—and his progress into transcendentalism from this time forth was rapid. As he imbibed the doctrines of the German idealists and of the orthodox theologians, his opinion of the empirical school of philosophy stemming from Locke fell lower and lower. He became a champion of intuitional as opposed to sensational psychology. Evidently he felt that there was a pressing need for a poetical assault on "the sandy sophisms" of Locke, Hartley, Priestley, and Godwin, for the whole weight of his reasoning was thrown toward this end in the conversations on *The*

5. Coleridge, *Letters,* II, 643–50.
6. *Memoirs of William Wordsworth,* C. Wordsworth, ed., I, 159.
7. See *The Excursion,* II, 311–12, 672–84, 896–904; IV, 475–77.
8. Coleridge, *Letters,* I, 348.

Recluse.[9] Wordsworth was to remove "the mechanic dogmatists" by "demonstrating that the senses were living growths and developments of the mind and spirit, in a much juster as well as higher sense, than the mind can be said to be formed by the senses"; he was to substitute "life and intelligence . . . for the philosophy of mechanism, which, in everything that is most worthy of the human intellect, strikes *Death,* and cheats itself by mistaking clear images for distinct conceptions, and which idly demands conceptions where intuitions alone are possible or adequate to the majesty of the Truth."[1]

Coleridge's next great requirement of *The Recluse* was that it should substitute a vital Christianity for the prevalent empiricism. A fall was to be affirmed, then man in his fallen states was to be contemplated, and finally a manifest scheme of redemption was to be declared.

These are the primary influences that Coleridge exerted over Wordsworth in the conception of *The Excursion.* The fact that Coleridge was deeply disappointed with the poem when it was published shows that Wordsworth did not fulfill the great purposes to Coleridge's satisfaction. Nevertheless, a close examination of *The Excursion* shows that Wordsworth had both purposes constantly before him. It may be argued that Coleridge's speculations had no influence over Wordsworth's own determinations, but there is strong evidence that Wordsworth was much swayed by Coleridge's beliefs and that they regarded themselves as striving toward the same philosophical goals.

Mr. Wordsworth I deem a fellow-labourer in the same vineyard, actuated by the same motives and teaching the same principles, but with far greater powers of mind.[2]

[Wordsworth] called [Coleridge] wonderful for the originality of his mind, and the power he possessed of throwing off in profusion grand central truths from which might be evolved the most comprehensive systems.[3]

In the Prospectus to *The Excursion,* Wordsworth explicitly acknowledges that his own intellect is "deeply indebted" to that of Coleridge. There is, furthermore, a passage in *The Prelude* (xi, 282–93) in which Wordsworth seems to be promising Coleridge that in a future poem (*The Excursion*) he will give expression to their common convictions, which might seem out of place in *The Prelude* itself. The weight of Coleridge's influence directed Wordsworth to substitute in *The Recluse* a thoroughgoing transcendental Christian theology for the popular natural philosophy of the day.

Probably the most important single purpose of *The Excursion* re-

9. This appears both in the letter to Wordsworth on *The Excursion* and in the similar account in "Table Talk." Coleridge, *Letters,* ii, 643–50; *Table Talk,* p. 188.

1. Coleridge, *Letters,* ii, 648–9.

2. Coleridge in *The Friend* (September 23, 1809), p. 112.

3. Wordsworth, *Prose,* iii, 469.

sulted from Wordsworth's own pressing need to reconcile himself to the terrible realities of life. The joyful and self-reliant optimism which grew out of Wordsworth's early independence after the loss of his parents and the subsequent liberty he enjoyed at Hawkshead laid him open to severe shocks of adversity. Unfortunately the shocks came, and it is remarkable how long he retained his optimistic viewpoint when their severity is realized. The failure of the French Revolution and the enforced separation from Annette came as a double blow from which he never really recovered his former self. But with the assistance of Dorothy he kept his fundamental joyousness and optimism almost intact. The most staggering and insupportable catastrophe of his whole life was the death of his brother John by drowning on February 5, 1805. John had been closer to William and Dorothy than either Richard or Christopher. He had lived with them for many months since their arrival at Grasmere and had shared their excursions, their conversations, and their difficulties. The voyage on which he met his death had been undertaken primarily in the hope of earning enough money to be of some financial assistance to the beloved circle at Grasmere. This was Wordsworth's first mature experience of death,[4] and it came in a particularly cruel form. The letters of this period give a pathetic picture of Wordsworth, Dorothy, and Mary sitting together by the hour, all hopelessly and helplessly weeping and each powerless to allay the sorrow of the others. This melancholy event had more than a temporary effect on the mind of the poet. It caused him to reconsider the philosophy of joyful optimism which had led him into such a vulnerable position. If his belief in immortality had been hesitant or incomplete before that time, he found that now an active and absolute faith was necessary to his peace of mind. He also found that he needed to alter his former vague concept of some sort of universal benevolent deity, in order to reconcile this seemingly cruel blow with his faith in benevolence. Some traces of his agonized soul-searchings appeared in his letters.

Would it not be blasphemy to say that, upon the supposition of the thinking principle being destroyed by death, however inferior we may be to the great Cause and Ruler of things, we have *more of love* in our nature than He has? The thought is monstrous; and yet how to get rid of it, except upon the supposition of *another* and a *better world,* I do not see.[5]

The horrors of the Napoleonic Wars, and the grief and discomfort caused by them at home, added to the force of other catastrophes in making Wordsworth come to final grips with the problem of reconciling his world-view with "the thousand natural shocks that flesh is heir to." The deaths of his two children in 1812 gave him an unhappy oppor-

4. I except the death of Raisley Calvert, whom Wordsworth had not known for a very long time and for whose death he was well prepared.
5. Wordsworth to Sir George Beaumont, March 12, 1805, *EL,* p. 460.

tunity for testing his new intellectual equilibrium. When he had come through the trials of that disastrous year, the changes which had taken place within his mind became quite apparent to him, as did the direction in which he was moving, and since he regarded them as an advance—an adjustment that all thoughtful human beings are forced to make at some time—he believed his victory was worthy material for a part of his great philosophical poem. Looking back on the tempestuous agonies of the past twenty years, he saw the intellectual excesses he had committed, and he saw in them the cause of his vulnerability to mortal accidents. He lost no sympathy with his former self, but he realized that "years which bring the philosophic mind" were upon him and that he was a stronger and a better man for it. His lifelong habit of thoughtful introspection gave him a shrewd insight into the processes that had been working in his mind, and he felt that a poetical description of the complication, climax, and resolution which had been the dramatic story of his own mind in the past two decades would be of great value to others who were facing the same problems. He had achieved a sort of meditative calm which he realized was in some sense the goal toward which all men were striving. He felt that his success would be more complete if he could pass in review all the many steps by which he had ascended to the position in which he then found himself. And, equally important, he felt that he might make the same ascent easier for others.

Another important purpose of *The Excursion,* closely allied to the two already considered, was specifically stated by Wordsworth: "One of the main objects of *The Recluse* is to reduce the calculating understanding to its proper level among the human faculties."[6] Both Wordsworth and Coleridge felt a pressing need to combat the prevailing enthusiasm of their day for pure reason. Ever since Bacon and Locke had blazed the trail for science there had been an increasing tendency to credit nothing that cold, scientific reason could not prove. Poetry, as a passion, was regarded with suspicion, for it evidently made no contribution to scientific truth. The grotesque efforts of Erasmus Darwin to effect the marriage of poetry and scientific truth bear sad evidence to the state of affairs. The whole universe had been gradually analyzed into molecules which functioned without regard to human values, and poetry and molecules were strange bedfellows.

The climax of the gradual aggrandizement of human reason came in William Godwin's *Political Justice,* where reason was presented as the self-effecting, irresistible implement of man's perfectibility. The price of this all-powerful force was a complete denial of emotion, inspiration, and domestic affection. Godwin's near view of the pacific millennium captured the fancies and stimulated the enthusiasms of many young men, including Shelley and Wordsworth. But Wordsworth was constitution-

6. *MY,* p. 619.

ally averse to any system that denied the affections and emotions which were the very core of all his thought and being. He soon realized his mistake, and *The Borderers* is his renunciation of excessive rationalism. Many others of his poems, including several of the stories in *The Excursion,* merely assert the domestic affections and hence can be interpreted as an articulation of his revulsion from Godwin. Wordsworth realized, as did Coleridge, that the error was not Godwin's alone, but that it had been growing for over a century. He saw that science, like philosophy, had fixed its eye too firmly on the *facts* of experience, to the neglect or outright denial of the *values* of experience. Wordsworth wanted to effect a reunion between the cold categories and facts of reason and the emotional qualities of experience which had been left out by the overenthusiastic research of his predecessors and contemporaries. In short, he wanted to delimit the area in which the unassisted reason is operative.[7] The parallel that this presents to the aims of Kant is striking, especially since the two seem to have been independent. Wordsworth habitually accepted only those philosophical tenets which accorded with his own past experience, and his knowledge of Kant, as it came to him filtered through Coleridge, could hardly account for this basic intellectual need.

These three major impulses—antimechanism, personal fortitude, and antirationalism—were all operative as separate purposes while Wordsworth was composing *The Excursion,* but they may also be found fused together into one great effort: to find unity in diversity, eternity in time, infinity in space, good in evil, and "central peace subsisting at the heart of endless agitation."[8] Wordsworth's impulse toward unification of all the data of experience into one central truth that could embrace all the accidents and divergencies of mortal life was growing more imperative. His earlier optimistic half-beliefs no longer supported him because they were not sufficiently active and inclusive.

There were other specific purposes in Wordsworth's mind while he was composing *The Excursion.* One of these was to glorify Scotland, which country had always exerted a strong influence on his mind. He toured Scotland with Dorothy in 1803, visiting Scott on his return trip.

When he was in Cambridge in 1844 Archdeacon Hare asked him to call on Daniel and he paid several visits to the shop, especially one long one in which he dwelt on the influence Scotland had on him in early life and how he had sought in the *Excursion* to bring out the spiritual life of Scotland which he thought had never been adequately sung by any of her poets, who had mainly confined themselves to the humanities.[9]

7. On this subject, see A. N. Whitehead, "The Romantic Reaction," *Science and the Modern World* (Lowell Lectures, 1925; Cambridge University Press, 1926), chap. v.

8. *The Excursion,* IV, 1146–7.

9. Thomas Hughes, *Memoir of Daniel MacMillan* (London, Macmillan, 1882), p. 26 and note.

In the light of this comment it is interesting to notice that both the Wanderer and the Solitary are Scots and that some of their models were also Scots.[1]

In the first section of the preceding chapter of this book it was suggested that Wordsworth may have felt a need to combat the stark realism of George Crabbe's poems on country life, principally because they gave such an unfavorable evaluation of what Wordsworth himself valued very highly but also because Jeffrey had compared him with Crabbe and had decided in favor of the latter. Another suggestion is that Wordsworth thought it was necessary to establish his reputation with a *big* poem. It is known that Milton was the inspiration of Wordsworth's sonnets, and it was a common practice among his admirers to compare him, not unfavorably, with Milton. Evidently he was conscious of imitating Milton in his determination to leave one great work behind him, for we find him quoting Milton's famous wish that he might write one poem which the world would "not willingly let die,"[2] in discussing *The Recluse.* With Wordsworth it was more than ambition and imitation; there was a financial need for him to establish himself. Evidently a prevalent opinion was that which considered Wordsworth a writer of short, simple, trivial poems, who was incapable of anything more extensive. Such is the inference one draws from Robinson's statement that the publication of *The Excursion* would "put an end to the sneers of those who consider him or affect to consider him as a puerile writer [who] attempts only little things."[3]

2

It has long been customary to consider the characters of *The Excursion* as mere personified aspects of Wordsworth's own character and history. There is some truth in such a description, and it can be very interesting and enlightening to analyze the characters from that standpoint. The Solitary represents what Wordsworth was in the days of the Revolution—an overenthusiastic, overconfident rationalist—and what he was becoming after the failure of the Revolution (and would have become had not association with Dorothy and Coleridge rescued him)—an apathetic recluse. The deaths of the Solitary's wife and two children represent the similar catastrophes in Wordsworth's life, the deaths of John and the two children, and possibly his separation from Annette. It is dangerous, however, to pursue these parallels too far. The Solitary is given several characteristics which Wordsworth could never have attributed to himself, such as bitter cynicism, arrogance, and Epi-

---

1. Fenwick Note to *The Excursion*, Wordsworth, *Prose*, III, 196–7.
2. See *MY*, p. 596.
3. *Henry Crabb Robinson on Books and Their Writers*, p. 147.

cureanism. For similar reasons the Wanderer cannot be said to represent Wordsworth. The Wanderer is a Scotch peddler who has retired, and this position in life meant several very definite things to Wordsworth. It fixed on the Wanderer characteristics which Wordsworth himself did not and never would share. The Wanderer is represented as an old man; since Wordsworth drew this character between his twenty-eighth and forty-fourth years, he could hardly have considered himself an old man. The Wanderer has some qualities of character which Wordsworth himself had been striving for and had at least partially achieved. This is really the most that can be said. The difficulties are even greater in the cases of the Pastor and the Poet. The Pastor represents the strictly orthodox viewpoint, which Wordsworth accepted unreservedly neither at the time of writing *The Excursion* nor at any other time in his life. Wordsworth admired the church and was an interested listener to all that could be said for it. This is why the Pastor appears in *The Excursion*. He represents not Wordsworth's own standpoint but a standpoint which Wordsworth admired, respected, and partly shared. The Poet expresses some sentiments which are clearly those of Wordsworth,[4] but he sways naively with the argument more than Wordsworth would have done and is used primarily as a tool to draw out the comments of the other three characters.

Possibly it is significant of Wordsworth's purpose in the character-portrayal of *The Excursion* that none of the characters has a name. This indicates some effort on the part of the poet to omit the irrelevant and to suggest general traits. The most useful generalization that can be made about the characters of *The Excursion* is this: the Solitary represents the metaphysical *terminus a quo* and the Wanderer the *terminus ad quem,* with the Poet falling somewhere between the two and the Pastor presenting a detached special point of view. Wordsworth shows us what he considers the best means of moving from the cynical apathy of the Solitary to the meditative calm of the Wanderer's "pure imaginative soul."[5] Wordsworth himself had made this change, and was still making it. But it is wrong to assume that the entire process is a mere allegory of his own mental history. He presented his problem in a refined and exaggerated form, carefully broadened to include every important aspect of the question in hand, whether or not it was a part of his own particular case history. In philosophical position Wordsworth probably corresponded most closely to the Poet of *The Excursion,* renouncing the extravagances of the Solitary, but making some important concessions to him, and admiring the position of the Wanderer, but unable to achieve it wholly himself.

On the other hand, we must give Wordsworth credit for a great deal of effort to keep his characters specifically in the real world. Not only did

4. See, for example, *The Excursion,* v, 49–59.   5. *Ibid.,* vi, 1065.

he draw them from real people but he also added numerous details and minor characteristics in an attempt to individualize them. Wordsworth has never been given much credit for dramatic power, and certainly he does not deserve it, but for keen insight into human thoughts and feelings, particularly his own, he has seldom been surpassed. The "drama" of *The Excursion* consists entirely of thought and feeling; the measure of its success is the ease with which we come to understand the point of view of each character. The central action of the poem itself is almost entirely metaphysical. All the important external actions are complete when the poem begins and are related in the discourse. Through the story of the Wanderer's past, and through the Solitary's account of his turbulent career, we come to know exactly what each of them stands for and we can interpret the ensuing discourse in the light of what we know about them. Thus the characters do achieve some degree of independence. They are widely diversified in viewpoint, and their past lives and present circumstances are also very different. Their manners of speech alone are not distinguished from one another with sufficient clarity. This must be attributed partly to the nature of the subjects under discussion and partly to Wordsworth's lack of dramatic power.

It has been a common criticism that Wordsworth is "unfair" to the Solitary and that the Wanderer is a "philosophical prig."[6] This criticism is based on the assumption that the two philosophical viewpoints in the poem—those of the Wanderer and the Solitary—are to meet in controversy on equal terms and are to be weighed on equal scales. But such is not the case at all. *The Excursion* does not ask which is better, cynicism and misanthropy or benevolence and meditative calm. Wordsworth assumed that his readers would know which is better. He devoted himself to showing how it is possible for an intelligent and affectionate person to be driven into the worse position, and how it is possible for such a person to be restored to the better position. The Solitary is not an evil man fighting against the good; he is a "sick man" who needs a remedy.[7] The poet specifically describes him as "sick" twice and as "pale" three times. Wordsworth is not unfair to the Solitary as a representative of misanthropy; the Solitary raises many interesting and important objections to the course of the Wanderer's reasoning, and in some instances he forces concessions from the Poet and the Wanderer.[8] He is intelligent and affectionate, and he has a great capacity for appreciation of Nature. The real difficulty in his character arises from the comments that the Poet, as narrator, makes concerning him. For example, the Solitary speaks "with a faint sarcastic smile Which did not please me," "with a careless voice," "somewhat haughtily," "with de-

6. G. M. Harper, *William Wordsworth* (New York, Charles Scribner's Sons, 1916), II, 228.
7. *The Excursion*, II, 612. Compare: "inwardly opprest with malady," II, 305–6.
8. *Ibid.*, v, 242–439; VI, 593–600; VIII, 334–433.

jected look," or "discomposed and vehement." These phrases were intended by Wordsworth merely as descriptions of the sick man's symptoms, but unfortunately they also seem to imply a personal as well as a moral distaste for the Solitary's character. This was not Wordsworth's intention at all, or he would never have devoted the effort he did to establishing the fact that the Solitary is basically a good, intelligent, affectionate man, who is only ill and must be cured. It is a dramatic error on the part of Wordsworth to have given cause for such a misconception. The reader loses some of his sympathy for the Solitary as a result of it.

Somewhat the same error was made in the case of the Wanderer. Wordsworth wanted to present the Wanderer as an almost perfect man, thoroughly wise and completely self-controlled. The difficulty of presenting such a man in dialogue without having him appear priggish, pompous, or dull is self-evident. Wordsworth succeeded very well in painting a convincing background for the Wanderer's character in the story of his life in Book I. The speeches of the Wanderer, while at times they are somewhat too rhetorical and a little difficult to follow, are no more so than those of the other characters, when one considers the burden of thought his speeches have to carry. Wordsworth, in an effort to give the Wanderer normal human reactions and yet to preserve his near perfection of character, made some mistakes. For instance:

> A slight flush
> Of moral anger previously had tinged
> The old Man's cheek.[9]

This sort of superiority—"moral anger"—makes the Wanderer a little distasteful. For lack of a name, Wordsworth is forced to call the Wanderer a "Sage" 8 different times, and he describes him as "venerable" 6 times, and "grey-haired" 9 times. This repetition becomes a little tedious. In Book IV, where the Wanderer speaks for so long a time on such a variety of subjects, the danger is great that he will seem to be preaching, and it is only by a careful effort to understand what he is saying and to see its relationship to what has gone before that the reader can evade a sensation of being lectured. All these difficulties arise from the fact that Wordsworth wanted to make the Wanderer representative of mature wisdom, and to do so he had to make of him a man likely to have acquired wisdom—that is, an old, widely traveled man who is rich in experience. Wordsworth's dramatic powers were again not quite equal to the grandeur of his conceptions; the Wanderer occasionally falls short of the venerability attributed to him by the Poet. He is a little too dogmatic and intolerant to impress us as favorably as Wordsworth wanted him to.

Despite all that can be urged against him, the Wanderer remains the

9. *Ibid.*, v, 621-3.

central character of the poem, with a great deal to recommend him. The choice of a peddler for the leading character of his long poem is a very characteristic decision of Wordsworth. He wanted a wise man who had long been in intimate contact with humble life in all its forms, and he had known peddlers who answered to that description better than any other sort of man. Therefore, since the picture was true in his eyes, he had no other artistic scruples to overcome. The choice offended many, however, and Jeffrey selected it for some of his sharpest barbs.

Did Mr. Wordsworth really imagine, that his favorite doctrines were likely to gain anything in point of effect or authority by being put into the mouth of a person accustomed to higgle about tape, or brass sleeve-buttons? . . . A man who went about selling flannel and pocket-handkerchiefs in this lofty diction, would soon frighten away all his customers.[1]

Hazlitt and Merivale had similar comments to offer. Wordsworth was evidently angered by this criticism, for he came to the defense of his choice of a peddler in 1827 by expanding the second note to *The Excursion,* a quotation from Heron's *Journey in Scotland* describing the "habits of reflection and of sublime contemplation" formed by peddlers in the pursuit of their wandering profession. He also defended his choice in the Fenwick Note.[2]

There can be no doubt that Wordsworth had good authority and real models for the character of a philosophical peddler. Its suitability to his purpose is unquestionable, for he was dealing with country life, and who could be assumed to know more about it than an itinerant peddler?

The Wanderer represents the successful culmination of the unifying impulse of philosophy. He can see the good in seeming evil; he has "Security from shock of mortal accident";[3] he has the "power An agonizing sorrow to transmute";[4] and he has had glimpses of the infinite and eternal.[5] His meditative calm is not passive. He represents an active force of truth, goodness, and love. These are probably the personal ideals of Wordsworth himself—that is, the ideals toward which he aspired. He may have had little expectation of ever perfectly achieving such lofty aims.

3

It is not difficult to realize and remember exactly what "happens" in *The Excursion.* A young poet meets an aged peddler by appointment in front of a ruined cottage on a plain. The peddler tells the poet a story of the former inhabitants of the ruined cottage and then the pair set out to find shelter for the night at an inn. For the next two days they wander

1. *The Edinburgh Review,* xxiv (November, 1814), 30.
2. Fenwick Note to *The Excursion,* Wordsworth, *Prose,* iii, 197.
3. *The Excursion,* iii, 363.   4. *Ibid.,* iv, 168.   5. See *ibid.,* iii, 110–12.

about aimlessly, talking with humble country people and enjoying the beauties of nature. On the third day they climb into the mountains to visit a friend of the peddler, and on the way they see a celebration of the annual Wake. Descending into a secluded valley, they meet a funeral procession, which makes the peddler fear that his friend is dead. Moving on, however, they meet the peddler's friend, who is a misanthropic recluse. He invites them into his apartment for lunch and tells them the sad story of the dead man. After lunch the three men walk to a small recess in the vale where the recluse recounts the long series of personal tragedies which have destroyed his faith in human life. Returning to the abode of the recluse, they pace the lawn while the peddler attempts to show how his friend has brought these tragedies on himself and how his despondency may be remedied. The poet and the peddler spend that night in the home of the recluse. The next morning the three men climb out of the small vale and descend into a large inhabited valley, where they enter the church and inspect it. The mind of the recluse is returned to the discussion of the previous day by the sight of the baptismal font. Moving out into the churchyard, he reopens the discussion, which continues until the arrival of the vicar. The peddler begs the vicar to contribute to the discussion, which he does, first with a few general comments and subsequently with a long series of accounts concerning his parishioners, living and dead. His comments give rise to some further discussion, after which the vicar takes his three friends to his home. There they meet his wife and children and take lunch. After more conversation, they descend to the lake with the vicar's family, and the poet rows them to an island at the far end, where they have a picnic supper. Then they row on to the end of the lake and climb part of the way up a hill overlooking the water, pausing there to look at the sunset, while the parson utters a fervent prayer. The party returns in the dusk to the vicar's home, where the recluse parts from them, promising to rejoin them on the following day.

This is all the external action. It is spread over a period of five summer days and includes only five characters who contribute to the dialogue. Of these the Pastor's wife is the least important. Such a story by itself has very little to recommend it. Obviously the discussions and the illustrative tales must contain the real interest and unity. The doctrinal plot of *The Excursion* is clearly the center of interest. It is, of course, not separable from the outward events of the poem, since it grows directly out of the characters and their stories. The metaphysics have a practical origin and a practical end—their applicability is never forgotten.

The most obvious division of the poem is twofold. First there is a statement of the philosophical position (Books i–v) and then there is a demonstration of its usefulness (Books vi–ix). Perhaps a more valuable dissection of the poem is that which divides it into five main parts: introduction (Books I and II), philosophical problem (Book III), solution of the problem (Books IV and V), illustration of the solution (Books VI and VII), and application of the new position (Books VIII and IX). There is naturally much overlapping or interlinking among these sections, as there should be. Some problems raised early in the poem are not settled until the end, and there are frequent references in later parts of the poem to earlier examples or arguments. To become thoroughly aware of the transitions between ideas and the references from one argument to another, a more thorough familiarity with *The Excursion* is necessary than can possibly be acquired on one reading.

The peregrinations of the characters, with their constant discussions of the scenery, are not mere gratuitous and superfluous decoration. The scenery is used both directly and by analogy in the argument. Its effect on the characters is made the most important collateral evidence of their philosophical standpoints. It turns the mind of the Poet to thoughts of his childhood. It inspires the Pastor to praise of God. In the Solitary there is a conflict between his normal sensibility and his self-imposed determination not to yield to it. The Wanderer's attitude toward nature is the key to the meaning of the whole poem, and so it must be reserved for discussion in a separate section of this chapter.

We turn now to a detailed consideration of the doctrinal plot of *The Excursion*. Perhaps it should first be said that what follows is intended as commentary, not summary, and presupposes a prior reading of Wordsworth's poem. It is not intended to inflame those who have not read the poem with a desire to read it but does pretend to be useful to those who have read the poem and are puzzled by the relation of the parts to the whole.

The first part, or introduction, includes Book I and most of Book II. This section is devoted entirely to the establishment of the scene and the characters but it also gives us a remarkable foretaste of the method to be followed in the later sections, when the story of Margaret and the various landscapes are set as backdrops on which the characters are projected in great detail.

The introductory biographical account of the Wanderer in Book I is in many respects an abbreviated transcript of Wordsworth's own development, particularly in the central importance of nature's ministry. But there is one important difference to be noted: the Wanderer had been free from excessive passion and despondency, so that he achieved earlier the perfect spiritual equilibrium that Wordsworth felt he himself was approaching. The end product of the Wanderer's schooling—in nature, the intellect, and the human passions—was an immunity to worldly disaster. He appreciated fully the great value of life but he could see life end without immoderate grief, since he saw beyond life.

> he kept . . .
> His mind in a just equipoise of love.
> Serene it was, unclouded by the cares
> Of ordinary life; unvexed, unwarped
> By partial bondage . . .
> He had no painful pressure from without
> That made him turn aside from wretchedness
> With coward fears. He could *afford* to suffer
> With those whom he saw suffer.[6]

In the significant preamble to the story of the ruined cottage which follows, there is an interesting affirmation of the sympathy between inanimate objects and human suffering in obedience to the creative power of human passion.[7]

The story of Margaret, with its simple tragic force, is designed to illustrate the Wanderer's attitude toward human suffering, which has been shown in its development in the story of the Wanderer's life. He says of Margaret's fate:

> 'Tis a common tale,
> An ordinary sorrow of man's life,
> A tale of silent suffering, hardly clothed
> In bodily form.[8]

This statement is designed to show that the Wanderer, while he feels a profound sympathy for worldly suffering—there was a tear on his cheek a moment before—sees beyond the earthly agonies, and by means of the power of his active faith in divine wisdom he is able to understand the conversion of seeming evil into good, with the happy result

> That what we feel of sorrow and despair
> From ruin and from change, and all the grief
> That passing shows of Being leave behind,
> Appeared an idle dream.[9]

Therefore the sad tale of Margaret is offered as a source of happiness rather than of despair.[1] In 1845 Wordsworth expanded this concluding passage to make it more specifically Christian in tone, but the meaning remained the same.[2]

The story of Margaret in *The Excursion* serves the purpose of introducing us to the philosophy of the Wanderer. But it must not be for-

6. *Ibid.*, I, 340–81. For further discussion of this quality, see F. R. Leavis, *Revaluation* (London, Chatto & Windus, 1936), pp. 154–202.

7. It is interesting to observe that this antimechanistic concept of a creative power in the mind of man was absent from the poem as originally transcribed by Dorothy in 1798. Wordsworth was still under the influence of Hartley at that time. The passage was added by 1814. *The Excursion*, I, 475–84.

8. *Ibid.*, I, 636–9.   9. *Ibid.*, I, 949–52.

1. The preparation for the story of Margaret and the story itself will be found in Bk. I, 434–956.   2. He added ll. 934–9, 952–5.

gotten that "The Ruined Cottage" was originally an independent poem, praised more extravagantly by Coleridge than anything else Wordsworth wrote.[3] It has considerable merit and is still thought by many to be Wordsworth's finest and most characteristic poem.[4] It provides one of the best measures of Wordsworth's developing powers and changing attitudes during his greatest period, for its subject matter is closely akin to that of "Guilt and Sorrow" (1793–94), but even in its earliest extant form (Dorothy's transcript of 1798) there is evidence of a more calm, sympathetic attitude toward the suffering occasioned by war than the blistering, irate invective of the earlier poem. By studying the additions which appear in 1814 we can see the gradual changes taking place in Wordsworth's ideas, such as the increasing awareness of the mind's activity.[5] The use which Wordsworth made of "Margaret" in *The Excursion* is further evidence of his changing viewpoint, for he evidently no longer felt that the poem was capable of standing alone. The religious additions of 1845 supply the final chapter of this story of Wordsworth's development.

De Quincey, in his essay "On Wordsworth's Poetry,"[6] chose the story of Margaret for his most bitter and cynical remarks. He raised only practical objections, which bear almost no critical weight. For example, he wanted to know why Margaret did not apply to the government to find what regiment Robert was in and where it was located, or why the Wanderer did not try the effect of a guinea in alleviating Margaret's sorrow rather than so many coats of metaphysical varnish. Such comments could have been conceived only in simulated ignorance of Wordsworth's purposes and methods. De Quincey approached the story more like a coroner than a critic.

In Book II, which is also a part of what we have called the introduction, the character of the Solitary is first presented. The story of the Solitary is told first by the Wanderer so that the reader will see the Solitary's position through eyes which recognize the errors and frailties that placed him there and will therefore know that the Solitary is merely a sick man, not a philosopher. The course of the Solitary's inward illness is described as a series of vacillations between different excesses: self-satisfied complacency, sorrow in the face of death, apathy, blind revolutionary ardor,[7] "false philosophy" (rationalism),[8] immorality, and voluptuous misanthropy.[9] Symptomatic of the Solitary's present state is the discovery of his copy of *Candide*, which the Wanderer stigmatizes as "this dull product of a scoffer's pen."[1] This description of *Candide* has perplexed many, but Wordsworth's real objection to Voltaire must

3. See, for example, *Table Talk*, p. 188.
4. See Leavis, *op. cit.*
5. Evidenced in the addition of ll. 475–84.
6. *Tait's Magazine*, September, 1845.
7. *The Excursion*, II, 235–6.
8. *Ibid.*, II, 260.
9. *Ibid.*, II, 311–12.
1. *Ibid.*, II, 484.

have been that Voltaire treats subjects humorously which are really serious and should never be treated with levity. The Wanderer returns to *Candide* in the midst of his argument in Book IV, using it to prove that there is really no refuge for the human mind in levity.

Wordsworth carefully establishes the true sensibilities of the Solitary at the outset, for the Solitary first appears in the act of comforting a bereaved child and shortly gives an inspired account of two nearby mountain peaks which reveals in him a profound feeling for nature and an awareness of the "mute agents stirring there."[2]

The Solitary's story of the poor pensioner serves to introduce him much as the story of Margaret served to introduce the Wanderer. He tells this tale as a justification for his misanthropy. It is an example of outright evil in the form of cruelty and ingratitude, and he takes it as an emblem of all the guilt and error which have driven him into his lonely retreat. He sees nothing beyond the mere outward event and makes no effort to discern the working of a benevolent deity in such tragedies. It merely confirms his utter lack of faith in human virtue and the nobility of the human soul.[3]

The main burden of Book III is the statement of the philosophical problem of the poem in a detailed account of the Solitary's philosophy and an extended narrative of his life, which is designed to show how he developed his philosophy. Wordsworth again prefaces the story of the Solitary with an outburst of inspired rapture from the Wanderer, as if to remind the reader of the sound, mature view of life before exposing the ulcers of the Solitary's *mal du siècle*. The contrast between the two men is presented in considerable detail. The Wanderer's ardent, contemplative love for nature is opposed to the apathy and cynical anti-rationalism of the Solitary, who finds faith, science, and philosophy equally fruitless[4] and who sees in the poets' vision of the Golden Age and in the philosophies of the Epicureans and Stoics the same futile universal impulse toward "confirmed tranquillity, inward and outward,"[5] which has shattered him. In the absence of inward active hope, his childhood joy in nature is gone.[6] The Solitary's autobiography,[7] giving his reasons for his misanthropy, states the real philosophical problem of the poem. He raises further questions later in the discussion but his position is quite clearly established at this point. It may be well to summarize his chief points, since the Wanderer attempts to answer them in the next section.

a) Death blasts domestic happiness.

b) Science and natural philosophy fail to give us insight into the unknown.

2. *Ibid.*, II, 724.
4. *Ibid.*, III, 1–281.
6. *Ibid.*, III, 282–461.
3. *Ibid.*, II, 730–904.
5. *Ibid.*, III, 398–9.
7. *Ibid.*, III, 462–991.

c) The gospel of pure reason fails to bring about the millennium; ignorance prevails over wisdom.

d) Primitive man is not noble but squalid and superstitious.

e) There is no true virtue or love in mankind; evil predominates in all earthly affairs.

f) Apathy in life is the only possible culmination of such sorrow and failure as have attended the Solitary's life. Oblivious death is preferable to life.

The next section is that which we have called the solution of the problem; it includes Books IV and V. In Book IV the Wanderer's argument falls into three sections. First he states his faith (lines 1–196), then he applies it to the problems of the Solitary (lines 197–1106), and finally he shows the Solitary how to restore his faith in God and man (lines 1106–1324). Naturally, the suggestions of remedies for the Solitary are interspersed throughout the discussion, and the Wanderer's arguments are not perfectly orderly, since they are spontaneous and since they are interrupted by the questions and comments of the Poet and the Solitary from time to time. Wordsworth evidently made considerable effort to avoid the appearance of preaching on the part of the Wanderer. A little attention from the reader reveals the fact that the Wanderer really is not preaching. He is more like a garrulous physician diagnosing a patient's illness and giving him a prescription for a remedy. The parallel is most striking in those passages in which the Wanderer recommends plenty of fresh air and regular hours to the Solitary.[8]

The Wanderer's creed is founded on faith in a benevolent superintending providence, first to be perceived and worshiped in nature, which is a temporary spiritual link between man and the Being, a link through which man may also perceive the eternal moral law. Man's chief objective on earth is to strengthen the spiritual bond with the Being, until he no longer needs the help of sense. Through exercise of the godly faculty of imagination, a satisfying view can be fixed on the other world, and then immoderate sorrow in the face of death becomes impossible.[9]

The Wanderer particularly emphasizes the importance of inclusiveness of faith. His constant criticism of the Solitary is that the latter is incapable of going behind outward events to the unities which embrace and transmute those outward events, giving them meanings which they lack for superficial understanding. The Wanderer's own power to transmute an agonizing sorrow arises from his awareness of benevolent purpose in the superintending providence. This creed has much in common with Christianity, but it must not be assumed that it is merely a bald statement of orthodox precepts. It is shot through with Kantian-Coleridgean transcendentalism in the passage on the eternal forms of duty.[1] There is some neoplatonic matter in the passages suggesting pre-exist-

8. *Ibid.*, IV, 481–504.   9. *Ibid.*, IV, 1–196.   1. *Ibid.*, IV, 69 ff., 91–3.

ence,[2] and the concept of childhood mystical experiences as a key to faith is pure Wordsworth. The most strictly orthodox passage was borrowed almost *verbatim* from Christopher Wordsworth's *Ecclesiastical Biography*.[3] There is probably a glimpse into Wordsworth's own state of mind in the passage in which the Wanderer admits the difficulty of sustaining a faith the imagination has achieved and recommends life in accordance with conscience as the most workable rule.[4]

The Wanderer's affirmation of faith provides the assumptive basis for his arguments against the specific attitudes of the Solitary. Because of the need for continuity, dramatic propriety, and poetic expression, Wordsworth was unable to present the Wanderer's arguments in a strictly orderly, systematic fashion; therefore their clarity is somewhat obscured by interruptions, digressions, and poetic analogies. However, a careful study of the argumentative portion of Book IV reveals the following answers to the problems presented by the Solitary in Book III.

a) Death blasts domestic happiness. The Wanderer replies that faith in a superintending providence of infinite benevolence, converting all mortal accidents to good, supplemented by a hope which is founded on a satisfying imaginative concept of the other world, removes almost all necessity for sorrow in the face of death. An overeagerness to realize the vision of the other world and to join the deceased loved ones is an undesirable excess, contrary to the nature which binds us to the earth with innumerable ties.

b) Science and natural philosophy fail to give us insight into the unknown. The Wanderer explains that science and natural philosophy tend to break experience down into minute, unfeeling parts and to concentrate on these small, meaningless segments of experience rather than to search for the links of relationship which make all matter and all thought a unity, differentiated in kind and degree but essentially one. This latter knowledge is what the human soul yearns for, and science will be of value only when its impulse is toward unification, rather than diversification, of knowledge.

c) The doctrine of pure reason fails to bring about the millennium; ignorance prevails over wisdom. The Wanderer points out that the excessive revolutionary faith in human reason erred because it failed to realize the limitations of reason and ignored the eternal truths of the imaginative will. Unassisted reason caused men to develop a presumptuous confidence in the wisdom of their own age, with the result that they overturned some of the most valuable faiths and institutions. This led to schisms and the seizure of control by the evil, who are more unified and earnest than the good. But there is hope that gradually the reasonable

2. *Ibid.*, IV, 50–4, 83–91.   3. See sec. 5 of the preceding chapter of this book.
4. *The Excursion*, IV, 197–238.

way will triumph, and meanwhile no man need become despondent if he has faith.

d) Primitive man is not noble, but squalid and superstitious. The Wanderer replies that even superstition is preferable to apathy. In this instance the Solitary's question really answers itself, for the inference from a shattering of faith in the nobility of natural man is that the faith was erroneous and that the institutions of civilization have ennobled the squalid savage. This inference is confirmed by the panegyric on English institutions in Book vi of *The Excursion*.[5]

e) There is no true virtue or love in mankind; evil predominates in all human affairs. The Wanderer responds that this attitude is self-imposed and is not a result of true experience. He points out that the affection shown by the Solitary for the poor pensioner and for the little child reveals that he himself does not really deny human love. The question is left open for discussion later, in the churchyard scene.

f) Apathy in life and oblivion in death are all that the Solitary wants. The Wanderer demonstrates that apathy has never satisfied man because the spiritual instinct toward love and hope is too strong. Even the primitive modes of belief of the Jews, Persians, Babylonians, Chaldeans, and Greeks all arose from the same basic instincts of admiration, hope, and love. Apathy is contrary to nature—that is, to innate propensities of the human soul—and anyone who studies nature and lives according to nature can easily escape apathy. There is no oblivion in death, because the whole being of man tries to pierce through death, and both faith and reason support the fact of another world.

The Wanderer's nostrum for despondency, the great means of restoration to inner tranquillity, is the energetic cultivation of the Solitary's remnants of human sympathy and appreciation of nature, both of which Wordsworth carefully established earlier in the poem. The Solitary's human sympathies have several times inadvertently exposed themselves, as in the incident of the comforting of the sorrow-stricken child[6] and in his affection for the poor pensioner.[7] His love of nature has overcome his self-imposed apathy several times in the course of the poem, most notably in his account of the twin peaks outside his window[8] and in his narration of the mystical experience he had while descending the mountain after searching for the poor pensioner.[9]

The principal quality of the Wanderer's scheme of redemption is anti-rationalism.[1] As Wordsworth originally expressed it in a passage of the Argument to Book iv which was later omitted, "Happy for us that the imagination and affections in our own despite mitigate the evils of that

5. *Ibid.*, vi, 1–74.
6. *Ibid.*, ii, 502–11.
7. *Ibid.*, ii, 730–895, especially 757–63, 801–4. See also *ibid.*, 447–8.
8. *Ibid.*, ii, 694–725.
9. *Ibid.*, ii, 827–77. See also *ibid.*, iii, 307–24.
1. *Ibid.*, iv, 1127–32.

state of intellectual Slavery which the calculating understanding is so apt to produce."[2] Nature by herself provides impulse and utterance. Through open communion with nature, the Solitary is to discover the "pure principle of love"[3] in nature, which he will link with kindred love among his fellow creatures, thus ultimately discovering the moral and spiritual oneness of things and learning lessons of duty and love from all experience. Then science and reason find their true position, as supports and guides for the imaginative (*"excursive"*) powers of the mind. The whole process, if properly begun, is almost automatically self-effecting.[4]

It is interesting to notice how far removed the Wanderer's remedy is from the Christian scheme of penitence and redemption. A Christian faith, or something very like a Christian faith, is the end of the system; but the means are purely Wordsworthian. It seems almost a matter of indifference whether or not the faith at the end of the process is achieved. The emphasis is all on the intermediate steps—appreciation of the mute agents which stir in nature and love for one's fellow-beings—and they seem to be important ends in themselves, as well as means to the ultimate faith in God. The "passages through which the ear converses with the heart"[5] are the real key to the whole process, for there sensation and intuition are fused. The Poet intimates that the Wanderer himself has been through a similar process in the development of his powers, for he started with experience and then went through persuasion, belief, and faith, which finally became passionate intuition.[6] There is a great deal of emphasis on duty in this system of regeneration, with the implication that a firm sense of duty is the mainstay of virtue, while in the long run virtue is the key to happiness.

In Book v the problem of the predominance of evil in human affairs is reopened by the Solitary's attack on baptism as an empty pretense[7] and the Poet's reply that such rites show man's great aspiration to rise from his fallen state. Henry Crabb Robinson, after a meeting with Shelley at Godwin's, recorded that this passage on baptism is hard to defend, from which we may conclude that Shelley attacked it.[8] Wordsworth offended some by the apparent hyperorthodoxy of his representation of baptism as actually washing away the stains of original sin.[9] His allusion here to man's fallen condition, together with the Wanderer's account of the early legends of Christianity, is the only specific affirmation of a fall in *The Excursion*. Therefore the poem can hardly be said to fulfill that requirement of Coleridge.[1] The Poet is probably voicing

2. See Argument to Bk. iv, edition of 1814, after the words, "Personal appeal."
3. *The Excursion,* iv, 1113.   4. *Ibid.,* iv, 1207–74.
5. *Ibid.,* iv, 1154.   6. *Ibid.,* iv, 1291–5.
7. *Ibid.,* v, 1–292.
8. *Henry Crabb Robinson on Books and Their Writers,* p. 212.
9. *Ibid.,* p. 158.   1. *Letters of Samuel Taylor Coleridge,* ii, 643–50.

something like Wordsworth's own attitude when he admits that in the "smooth and solemnized complacencies"[2] of the church, "Profession mocks performance,"[3] an imposture which he attributes not to inherent falsehood in the institution but rather to individual human delinquency. There is also a strong Wordsworthian flavor to the Solitary's next new argument, that there is a progressive decline in the value of life from youth to age.[4]

The Pastor's contribution to the discussion of the predominance of good or evil, of progress or decline, in human affairs[5] is to emphasize the limitations of human reason in judging of such matters and to suggest the relativity of human happiness to the individual viewpoint.[6] It is agreed that an inward principle is necessary to give effect to the arguments of "naked reason"[7] and that the inward principle is best acquired by exercise from visible nature; this antirationalism is carried a step further when the Poet suggests that virtue is inversely proportional to reason[8] and the Solitary cynically announces that happiness is the property of ignorance.

The Pastor, having been asked to supply specific examples from life in place of abstract arguments,[9] offers the story of the quarryman as proof that happiness and virtue do exist even in conditions of arduous poverty, but the Solitary counters with a new reference to the poor pensioner, an example of ingratitude and undeserved suffering.[1] In a passage which is closely related to the "Essay upon Epitaphs," the graveyard is then indicated as evidence of the universality of human love and sympathy, feelings which spring not from reason but from the very soul. The foundation of the great English institutions is attributed to the same impulses.[2a]

This brief suggestion of the benevolent origin of public institutions is to be associated with the antiprimitivistic passage at the end of Book III. Wordsworth's thesis is that natural man is not necessarily good, intelligent, or noble, but that he has innate propensities of soul which are good. Institutions actually do not stifle man's natural nobility but are designed to curb his ignoble side and to bring forth his propensities for good. Therefore institutions, at least in their origin, are an expression of man's love and respect for his fellow-creatures. This idea inspires the lofty panegyric on the English Church and State which opens Book VI, spoken by the Poet. The sentiments are probably Wordsworth's own and they are not to be interpreted as plain Toryism and orthodoxy, as we shall see below. His admiration for the leaders and martyrs of the church was probably stimulated by his brother's *Ecclesiastical Biography*.[3a]

2. *The Excursion*, v, 376.   3. *Ibid.*, v, 378.   4. *Ibid.*, v, 292–439.
5. *Ibid.*, v, 440–84.   6. *Ibid.*, v, 484–557.   7. *Ibid.*, v, 562.
8. *Ibid.*, v, 595.   9. *Ibid.*, v, 558–657.   1. *Ibid.*, v, 658–892.
2a. *Ibid.*, v, 892–1016.   3a. *Ibid.*, VI, 1–74

This completes the third main section of the poem, which has been called the solution of the philosophical problem. The question of good and evil in human life, which was left partially unanswered in Book IV, has now been answered by the Pastor, who has been called in as a specialist for consultation. The argument is therefore essentially complete; but the Solitary has raised two new questions. Can the Wanderer's theories meet the test of reality? How can the falling-off in the value of life after youth be explained according to the theories of the Wanderer? The Pastor now proposes to show the human affections in operation and to show moral successes and failures by relating some stories of his parishioners. Subsequently the Wanderer will apply his theories to practical problems of the moment and will answer the objection that life gradually decreases in value.

First comes the fourth section (Books VI and VII), the illustration of the new attitude toward humanity which arises from the philosophy of the Wanderer. This illustration takes the form of a long series of tales, some tragic and some not. Wordsworth does not punctuate his stories with specific, outspoken morals, as did Crabbe, for instance:

> Ah! fly temptation, youth, refrain! refrain!
> Each yielding maid and each presuming swain![4]

Wordsworth's failure to draw a lesson from each tale has occasioned some scholarly discussion. One opinion holds that in telling his stories, both in *The Excursion* and in his shorter poems, Wordsworth omitted specific morals because he was a member of the eighteenth-century school of sentimental morality, which held that there is a "moral sense" in man which is superior to reason and experience, and since this moral sense can be identified with public good, sympathy is an expression of the moral sense. By this token the stories in *The Excursion* are told to awaken sympathy in the Solitary and, through sympathy, to stimulate his moral sense.[5] Another theory is offered by those who hold that Wordsworth was an enthusiastic adherent of the associationist psychology of Hartley. Hartley held that there was almost no transfer directly from outward events to the moral sense but that the experience must go through a long process of assimilation and transmutation by the faculties of sensation, imagination, ambition, self-interest, sympathy, and theopathy before it could fortify the moral sense. From this it is inferred that Wordsworth's failure to make his moral intention specific was based on the Hartleian principle that the moral sense is a part of a mechanical structure, which can be reached only by way of the supporting parts of the same structure, and efforts to reach it directly

4. *The Parish Register*, II, 187–8.
5. O. J. Campbell, *Sentimental Morality in Wordsworth,* University of Wisconsin Studies in Language and Literature, Ser. II, No. 11 (Madison, 1920), pp. 21–57.

are in vain. In short, Wordsworth simply told his stories without didactic adornment, in order that they might fall upon the fallow field of the human mind in the form of mere sensational experience and then might be transmuted into moral truths by the mechanical operation of the human mind.[6]

There is absolutely nothing, to my knowledge, which indicates that Wordsworth had the Hartleian mechanism in mind when he told his stories. The doctrine of sentimental morality seems to have a closer relationship to Wordsworth's method, but this doctrine does not include those stories which evidently are not intended to arouse sympathy. In short, both these efforts to provide a philosophical motivation for Wordsworth's method of telling stories are superfluous. In the works of such poets as Shenstone and Cowper, Wordsworth had ample precedent for his manner of permitting stories of real life to speak for themselves. To impose a metaphysical motivation on such frank simplicity seems quite unnecessary. Wordsworth explained his motivation in these simple words: "It is not enough for me as a Poet, to delineate merely such feelings as all men *do* sympathise with; but it is also highly desirable to add to these others, such as all men *may* sympathise with, and such as there is reason to believe they would be better and more moral beings if they did sympathise with."[7] He saw the relationship between sympathy and morality, but his primary concern was to broaden the sympathies. Finally, it must be pointed out that Wordsworth gave a great deal more attention to explaining the moral purposes of the stories in *The Excursion* than has been generally recognized. Most of the tales in this poem have some remarks either in the course of the narration, in the subsequent conversation, or in the Argument at the beginning of the particular book, which indicate clearly the purpose they are intended to serve.[8] Some of the tales require no explanation of their morals. For instance, when the story concerns a man of great virtue, as do several in *The Excursion,* there can be no need to point out that praise of a virtuous man is in itself a moral. In addition, there are three separate passages which apply to all the stories related by the Pastor and make perfectly clear the function which they are intended to serve. In the first of these it is indicated that the stories are to solve the doubts raised by the Solitary concerning the predominance of good or evil in human life, the abilities of religion to fortify people against calamity, and the reality of human affection, in order that the Poet, the Solitary, and the Wanderer may learn to love human life.[9] In the second such passage it is stated that the stories are intended to excite feelings of love, esteem, and admiration,

6. A. Beatty, *William Wordsworth,* University of Wisconsin Studies in Language and Literature, No. 24 (Madison, 1927), 271–5.

7. Wordsworth to Wilson, June, 1802, *EL,* p. 298.

8. For example, the purposes of the story of Margaret are clearly indicated in Bk. 1, 626–36, 933.   9. *The Excursion,* v, 630–57.

and to declare the native grandeur of the human soul.[1] And finally, after all the stories have been told, it is repeated that their purpose has been to teach patience in affliction, faith, hope, love, and reverence for the dust of man.[2] It seems clear that through these means the Solitary's sense of "belonging" to life and his zest for life are to be restored. Stories as well fortified as these can hardly be said to fall on the fallow field of the associative process. They are simply examples from real life which throw some light on the discussion between the Solitary and his three companions and which constitute one major step in the Solitary's regenerative process.

The first story,[3] which tells how a rejected lover was restored from despondency to health, affection, and inward calm by giving himself "To Nature's care,"[4] is clearly an illustration of the efficacy of the means of restoration recommended to the Solitary by the Wanderer in Book IV.[5] The story of the persevering miner is given its application by the Wanderer, who says that those who have a hope in God as this miner had a hope in his work should show a similar perseverance in the face of adversity, which is, of course, something which the Solitary has not done.[6] The Pastor's account of the young prodigal[7] is designed to illustrate qualities diametrically opposite to those of the persevering miner. At this point the Solitary seeks self-justification by asking for stories about men who took refuge in renouncing the world, but the Pastor gives him instead the story of the Jacobite and Hanoverian who found hope and peace in their solitude through a development of affection.[8] The Solitary is now forced to state his question more explicitly. He asks why no stories are being told about men who struggle against a ruthless destiny or an overpowering fatality in vain. The relation of his question to his own past life is obvious. The Pastor replies that in the Christian system there is no such thing as a ruthless destiny or an overpowering fatality. Adversity is an exercise, a test for faith. His system does not deny sympathy for those who commit crimes, those who are the victims of disasters, or those who are degraded by brutish vice, but he would prefer not to discuss them, since they are better left in the peace Heaven has granted them. Mortal ignorance and frailty claim some forbearance. The Solitary admits this but insists that they remember that to see the whole truth they must keep the sordid side of life in mind. The Pastor agrees to limit the stories to subjects of love, esteem, and admiration.[9] But in order to show that much can be learned from perverse selfishness as well,[1a] he tells the story of the jealous, miserly scholar-mother who finally achieved peace by realizing

1. *Ibid.*, VI, 646–74.   2. *Ibid.*, VII, 1054–7.   3. *Ibid.*, VI, 88–211.
4. *Ibid.*, VI, 183.   5. *Ibid.*, IV, 1106–1274.   6. *Ibid.* VI, 212–75.
7. *Ibid.*, VI, 275–375.   8. *Ibid.*, VI, 376–521.
9. This is Wordsworth's characteristic deliberate limitation of his subject. See G. W. Meyer, *Wordsworth's Formative Years* (Ann Arbor, University of Michigan Press, 1943), pp. 247–9.   1a. *The Excursion*, VI, 522–674.

the transience of all to which she had devoted her unhealthy passions.[2]

The next two stories illustrate the effects of remorse and repentance. In the beautiful and deeply moving tragedy of Ellen[3] are seen the purifying and ennobling powers of suffering, while the story of Wilfred Armathwaite[4] shows the lifelong agony of a noble man's self-reproach after sin. Book VI closes with a happy account of the enduring domestic affections of a widower and his six daughters,[5] probably designed to show the Solitary the great amount of joy that can survive acute personal grief.

At the beginning of Book VII, the courtier-parson's strength of mind in resigning himself to a humbler way of life and his perfect spiritual equanimity in the midst of keen domestic anguish[6] are probably an intentional contrast with the Solitary's despondency. The priest called "Wonderful," who is next described, is particularly noteworthy for his lifelong adherence to one humble but very useful position, and for his great personal virtues.[7]

There follows a pair of stories dealing with physical afflictions. First is the story of a deaf man who lived a rich and full life in spite of his loss.[8] This story is an example of courage and domestic affection. Next, in the tale of a blind man, Wordsworth emphasizes the compensations which are given for such physical deficiencies, so that they seem to be even a blessing.[9]

The passing of a lumberman drawing away a mighty oak[1] shifts the subject to the transience of all life on earth; three stories illustrate this theme. The first recounts the courage of a family which loses its only daughter,[2a] the second tells of the untimely death of a beloved young soldier,[3a] and the third recalls an Elizabethan knight, now all but forgotten.[4a] The theme is further developed in the Wanderer's comments on the transience of all merely human arrangements, such as fortunes, class privileges, and even happiness.[5a] This leads to another criticism of the excessive self-confidence of the revolutionary spirit. Wordsworth believes that there is a linear progression toward better things in worldly affairs, but he cautions once more against the presumptuousness of any effort to bring about the millennium overnight. At the close of the fourth section, which we have called the illustration of the philosophical solution, there is a general comment on social ferment and revolution.[6a]

The purpose of the foregoing summary has been to indicate the applicability of the Pastor's stories to the previous discussion. It will be remembered that the Solitary insisted on the predominance of evil in human affairs and that he denied the reality and permanence of human affection. He also called into question the ability of religion or philosophy

2. *Ibid.*, VI, 675–777. 3. *Ibid.*, VI, 787–1052. 4. *Ibid.*, VI, 1079–1114.
5. *Ibid.*, VI, 1115–91. 6. *Ibid.*, VII, 31–310. 7. *Ibid.*, VII, 310–95.
8. *Ibid.*, VII, 395–481. 9. *Ibid.*, VII, 482–536. 1. *Ibid.*, VII, 537–631.
2a. *Ibid.*, VII, 632–94. 3a. *Ibid.*, VII, 695–890. 4a. *Ibid.*, VII, 921–75.
5a. *Ibid.*, VII, 1000–7. 6a. *Ibid.*, VII, 976–1057.

thoroughly and permanently to sustain anyone under mortal affliction. Of the 17 stories related by the Pastor, 10 are devoted to an affirmation of human affection and to a demonstration of the efficacy of religion in giving fortitude to the afflicted. Two stories illustrate repentance after error, and one shows the blessings that accrue to even the humblest faith. Finally there are two pairs of stories, one contrasting perseverance with prodigality and the other showing death as a leveller which strikes youthful promise as well as old age which has outlived its time. These are the more specific applications of the stories. Wordsworth is more insistent on their general application and their cumulative force.

Turning to the final section, which may be considered the application of the Wanderer's philosophy to contemporary problems, we assume a broader social outlook. In an admirably clear-sighted passage the Wanderer describes the vast change being wrought in the social fabric by the industrial revolution and the wide spread of commerce in Wordsworth's day. He exults in man's great material progress and his conquests over the titanic forces of nature, but he is gravely aware of the abuses which come with these advances, particularly long working hours, poor working conditions, child labor, and the materialistic philosophy. He feels that the greatest hope for the future lies in a realization by man that all rests upon the moral law.[7]

Wordsworth was much alarmed during his later years by what he considered the decay of the priceless old domestic morals and affections in urban industrial areas, and he here attributes it, with considerable acrimony, to the institution of child labor, which enslaves modern youth to weakness and stupidity. By far the saddest result in Wordsworth's eyes is total insensitivity to the teaching and healing powers of nature. Characteristically facing bravely up to the most serious objections that can be raised to his theories, Wordsworth has the Solitary ask whether there have not always been ignorant, oppressed children and whether stultifying penury and unremitting toil are not also common among the rustics, who are in daily contact with nature.[8] The scene in the Pastor's home which closes Book VIII seems to be calculated to impress on the Solitary the ideal rural domestic situation and to prepare the way for the Wanderer's climactic speech at the beginning of Book IX.[9]

This speech, affirming the existence of a universal, beneficent, *"active principle,"*[1] describing the spiritual riches of the mature mind,[2] and condemning as contrary to nature any treatment of man as a means rather than as an end in himself,[3] is perhaps the most important single pronouncement in the entire poem. In the first place, it is designed to refute the Solitary's contention that there is a falling-off in the value of life after youth.[4] It will be recalled that the Wanderer himself made an

7. *Ibid.*, VIII, 1–230.   8. *Ibid.*, VIII, 231–433.   9. *Ibid.*, VIII, 434–601.
1. *Ibid.*, IX, 3.   2. *Ibid.*, IX, 81–92.   3. *Ibid.*, IX, 93–137.
4. *Ibid.*, V, 390–439.

opening for this criticism earlier in the discussion when he admitted that his youthful raptures and mystical experiences were gone and that he now looked back upon them as convincing glimpses into eternity.[5] At that time he implied that all that was left for old age was the memory of the visionary powers of youth and a sort of Christian stoicism. This is comparable to the theme of the "Ode: Intimations of Immortality from Recollections of Early Childhood," where the same sort of hopeful resignation is the result of advancing age. But in Book IX of *The Excursion* there is a great effort to make an advance over that position by an insistence on the positive accession of new spiritual riches which awaits the active mind in old age. We will defer our examination of the precise manner in which this is brought about to the next section of this chapter.

The other great purpose of this crucial speech by the Wanderer is to clarify the position of external nature in the cosmological processes he has been describing. We have been told repeatedly in the earlier parts of the poem that nature provides "impulse and utterance," that there are "mute agents stirring" in nature, that there is an energy or a spiritual presence in nature. These forces are described in so many different terms that there is considerable confusion in the mind of the reader concerning their exact character. Their importance to the plot of *The Excursion* cannot be overemphasized, for they are made the basis of the regenerative process which is to correct the despondency of the Solitary. Furthermore, as we have just seen, their absence from the experience of children who are enslaved to industry explains the resultant ignorance and immorality. In this passage at the beginning of Book IX, it was evidently Wordsworth's intention to increase our understanding of the active force, as he conceived it. This passage tells us a great deal about it.

a) It exists in all things and circulates from one to another.

b) Although it is removed from sense and observation, it becomes more sensible in exact proportion to the increase in human knowledge; it is spiritual—of the soul.

c) Its most apparent home is in the human mind.

d) It communicates good to objects beyond itself.

e) It is not to be identified with the Deity, since it is "assigned."

It is probably by this process of "circulation" that the principle was to be communicated from nature to the mind of the Solitary and to start the regenerative process. The principle is not only good but is a "pure principle of love," as we were told in Book IV.[6] This is probably one reason for the fact that the human mind is its "most apparent home." The relation of the sense of duty to this spiritual force in nature is one of the most difficult and interesting problems of *The Excursion*. It is clear from Book IV that the laws of duty are eternal and transcendental,

5. *Ibid.*, IV, 103–39.   6. *Ibid.*, IV, 1213.

they also exist in the human mind itself, they may be learned from all the forms of nature, and obedience to them is virtue, which is the key to happiness.[7] When Wordsworth tells us that the active principle of the universe has power to spread *good* beyond itself,[8] it must be the laws of duty to which he refers. This clarifies the discovery by the shepherd boy in Book IV of a moral law within himself and also the Wanderer's statement in Book IV that a study of the forms of nature in the relation which they bear to the human mind enables a man to learn his duties from all forms.[9] Wordsworth affirms, later in Book IX, that the laws of duty are just as liable as the forms of nature to be rendered inaccessible by premature slavery to labor and ignorance.

From this definitive speech the argument returns to the objection raised by the Solitary that poverty and ignorance are as prevalent in rural areas as in industrial centers. The answer now offered, in the light of the new definitions, is that the primal duties—the moral truths—are by nature equally available to all, but human injustice brings about social inequalities which obstruct them. In a passage which became the target of Arnold's [1] special abuse, universal compulsory state education is suggested as a first step toward a remedy. From this beginning the development toward a humanistic imperial world utopia rests entirely with the "British Lawgivers."[2]

The sharp contrast between this glittering idealistic vision and the sad facts of modern life reawakens the Solitary's brooding sense of human ingratitude, helplessness, and hopelessness. He expresses it in a melancholy outburst which is obviously connected with the story of the poor pensioner in Book II,[3] the recurrence to that story in Book V,[4] and the Wanderer's comments on the use of man as a means,[5] "A senseless member of a vast machine."[6] This recurrent countertheme here suggests a doubt that man's apparent progress is really progress after all. The Pastor's concluding prayer partially resolves the doubt by pointing out that the valley before them was once the scene of idolatrous sacrifices. The inference is that progress must be viewed as a much slower, more gradual process than it has seemed in the past.

The conclusion of the Pastor's prayer, which ends the doctrinal plot, is appropriately an effort to sanctify the forms of nature and the active principle which pervades them.[7a]

This brings us to the end of the last section, which we have called the application. It may be well to review the objects to which the Wanderer's philosophy has been applied in this section.

a) Human life. The decay of the bodily senses with the resultant loss

7. *Ibid.*, IV, 69–76, 225, 800–10, 1240.   8. *Ibid.*, IX, 10–11.

9. *Ibid.*, IV, 800–10, 1240.   1. "Wordsworth," *Essays in Criticism,* Ser. II, p. 152.

2. *The Excursion,* IX, 138–415.   3. *Ibid.*, II, 732–895.

4. *Ibid.*, V, 880–90.   5. *Ibid.*, IX, 113–22.

6. *Ibid.*, IX, 159.   7a. *Ibid.*, IX, 416–754.

of youthful transport is not a deprivation, for by the removal of the physical media between the mind and the active principle of love and good in the universe, old age achieves a higher and more enduring insight into eternal things than the fitful transports of youth can give.

b) The industrial revolution. The abuse of the new discoveries and the overcentralization of power are spreading ignorance, delinquency, and poverty; for long hours and child labor obstruct the necessary forms of nature and break up the domestic foundations of love and morality.

c) Education. Moral truth is equally available to all, but inequality of educational opportunity perpetuates grave social injustice.

d) Government. It is the duty of the legislators to curb the abuses of the manufacturing system and to provide perfect equality of educational opportunity.

e) The future. There is a slow progress perceptible in human affairs toward better things. This progress is much slower than self-flattering minds realize, but it may be made much more rapid if the English legislators will only fulfill their destiny.

These applications are partly designed to answer the specific problems of the Solitary, by showing that life is not a gradual decline and that there is a perceptible progress in human affairs, which holds forth great hope for the future. There is also some effort to catch the Solitary's interest in contemporary problems by pointing out remediable abuses and by showing an example of the domestic bliss (in the Pastor's home) which is the foundation of morality and intelligence and which is being threatened by the spread of ignorance and delinquency. The ideas grow very naturally out of the preceding discussions, and considerable pains were taken by Wordsworth to show their bearing on the central problem of the poem. Wordsworth was not merely taking advantage of an opportunity to express his political prejudices.

The Solitary is not rehabilitated at the end of *The Excursion*. Wordsworth said that it was his intention to resume the wanderings of these characters in a subsequent work and to show how the Solitary was finally won back to faith and hope by witnessing a religious ceremony in his native region, which recalled his childhood to him.[8] This explanation is interesting in the light of the Advertisement to *The Excursion,* where we are told that only in the second of the three parts of *The Recluse* are the intervention of speaking characters and a dramatic form to be employed, while in the first and third parts the meditations are to be in the author's own person. But if *The Excursion* is the second part, there would have to be some dramatic material in the third part to complete the story of the Solitary's regeneration as proposed at the end of *The Excursion* and in the Fenwick Note. The explanation of this problem is simply that Wordsworth had not planned the other two

8. Fenwick Note to *The Excursion,* Wordsworth, *Prose,* iii, 210.

parts of *The Recluse*. According to the original plan, *The Recluse* was
to have been entirely in the form of abstract meditations. When Coleridge's anticipated contributions failed to appear, Wordsworth made
his first retreat, which was an admission of dramatic material into the
second part. Perhaps the suggestion that the dramatic material was to
be continued in the third part represents another retreat by Wordsworth from the formidable task of a sustained metaphysical effort. That
no dramatic material was considered in the original plan we may conclude from Coleridge's attack on that very aspect of *The Excursion* in
his *Table Talk:* "Can dialogues in verse be defended? I cannot but
think that a great philosophical poet ought always to teach the reader
himself as from himself. . . . I have no admiration for the practice of
ventriloquizing through another man's mouth.[9]

Our effort in this long summary of the doctrinal plot of *The Excursion*
has been twofold. In the first place, a prose paraphrase of the didactic-
philosophical element in the poem should be helpful, for many important
passages have long been neglected or misinterpreted, and the progression
and interrelations of the presiding ideas have never been appreciated.
In the second place, it has been our concern to show the exhaustive
efforts devoted by Wordsworth to the unification of the many vastly
different parts of *The Excursion*. The most obvious examples of this
interlinking process are : the evidences of sensibility in the Solitary which
are given in Books II and III to be used in Book IV; the recurrence to the
story of Margaret later in the poem by the Poet, and the recurrence to
the story of the poor pensioner by the Solitary; the raising of a question in one part of the poem to be answered much later, as the Solitary's
claim of a falling-off in the value of life in Book V is answered by the
Wanderer in Book IX; and the repeated hinting at metaphysical themes
which are not resolved until the end, as the active principle in nature
and the exploitation of human beings as means to selfish ends are both
repeatedly suggested throughout the poem but finally stated explicitly
only in Book IX. The characters themselves, as they represent philosophical viewpoints, lend a further unity to the poem.

4

In the preceding section of this chapter we have endeavored to show
the development of ideas in *The Excursion* in their context, so that all
possible light might be thrown upon Wordsworth's exact meanings. In
order to come to a fuller understanding of some of the foremost doctrines which appear in the poem, we will now attempt to isolate them
and to fit them into their historical background.

Heretofore the most complete study of *The Excursion* has been that

9. *Table Talk*, p. 188.

of Professor Arthur Beatty, in his interesting and provocative book, *William Wordsworth: His Doctrine and Art in Their Historical Relations*.[1] In a sense this is unfortunate, since Professor Beatty's efforts were devoted almost exclusively to showing the relationship of Wordsworth's poetry to the sensational-associational tradition of English philosophy. Subsequent criticism has shown that Professor Beatty's effort to find a thoroughgoing Hartleian in Wordsworth was mistaken.[2] The sensational bias of that study prevented it from grasping Wordsworth's modifications and reservations in his acceptance of sensationism and his occasional forthright intuitionism.

As we have seen in the first section of this chapter, Coleridge's influence was diametrically opposed to sensationism. Coleridge wanted Wordsworth to demolish the "sandy sophisms" of Locke and the mechanists and to substitute a thoroughgoing intuitional philosophy. Wordsworth himself abandoned complete sensationism, if he ever really adopted it, fairly early, although some of the peculiar tenets of that philosophy, and much of its vocabulary, continued to influence him for a great many years. Coleridge was more fickle in his philosophical affiliations than was Wordsworth. He could "overthrow" by one intellectual effort a system to which he had been thoroughly devoted for some time, and soon be equally devoted to another system. Wordsworth, who was not so avid a metaphysician, was probably sounder and more cautious. At some time early in their acquaintance these two men devoted themselves to a synthesis of thought and feeling, of intuition and sensation. Coleridge tended rather soon to move into a Christian transcendentalism which denied first validity to sensory data but developed the senses from the mind, which had an intuitive grasp on a far higher reality than the senses could ever approach, and which gave the sensory data their meaning. Wordsworth was moving in the same direction, but perhaps not so specifically. Coleridge regarded Wordsworth as engaged in the same effort as himself, but the failure of *The Excursion* to demolish the mechanists emphatically was a source of keen disappointment to Coleridge, for it revealed the chasm which separated them. Wordsworth could not bring himself to abandon that cardinal principle of empiricism which says that sensory experience of nature is the ultimate source of all our finest thoughts, for this concept sanctioned the most important and influential of his own past experiences. Clinging to this precept involved him in contradictions and difficulties from which he was at some pains to extricate himself. It was particularly difficult for him to recon-

1. University of Wisconsin Studies in Language and Literature, No. 24 (Madison, 1927), pp. 241–84.
2. See G. M. Harper, *Literary Review* (July 21, 1923), p. 842; M. M. Rader, *Presiding Ideas in Wordsworth's Poetry;* and A. E. Powell (Mrs. E. R. Dodds), *The Romantic Theory of Poetry in the Light of Croce's Aesthetic* (London, E. Arnold, 1926), chap. v.

cile this empirical tenet with his growing impulse toward transcendental-ism.

Apart from this one fundamental doctrine, which incidentally Words-worth modified to suit his purposes, all that was left of the sensational-associational philosophy when Wordsworth wrote *The Excursion* was an occasional use of the language of associationism. Even in Words-worth's own day it was recognized that the primary impulse of his poetry was away from mechanistic philosophy. In 1818 John Wilson stated specifically in an article in *Blackwood's*[3] that Wordsworth's phi-losophy was "at variance with the philosophy at present most fashion-able in this country," which has "been directed chiefly towards the laws of intellect and association."

We have already seen that the associationistic explanation of Words-worth's stories has little to recommend it.[4] Professor Beatty makes some effort to show that the doctrine of the three ages of man is one asso-ciationistic tenet which plays an important part in *The Excursion,* but his examples[5] fail to bear out this contention, and it is far from clear that that doctrine is really associationistic. It certainly fails to figure in Hartley's work. In *The Excursion* the ages of man are usually four or more, and a great deal more spiritual insight is conceded to the child than any mechanical system of the mind's growth could allow. Words-worth seems also to have been untouched by Priestley's doctrine of the materiality of the soul. The doctrine of necessity, which is taught by both Hartley and Godwin, has left several traces in *The Excursion,* even though we know Wordsworth had abandoned it by 1801.[6] The idea of necessity continued to appeal to Wordsworth, but he could not admit it without qualifications.

> while inspired
> By choice, and conscious that the Will is free,
> [We] Shall move unswerving, even as if impelled
> By strict necessity, along the path
> Of order and of good.[7]

Wordsworth came to prefer using the term "necessity" to describe the constraint which governs the life of the very poor as a result of social injustice.

> Whence came he?—clothed
> In tattered garb, from hovels where abides
> Necessity, the stationary host
> Of vagrant poverty.[8]

3. *Blackwood's Edinburgh Magazine,* IV (December, 1818), 257–8.
4. See the previous section of this chapter.
5. *The Excursion,* I, 77–433; IV, 66–196; IX, 29–86.
6. See Coleridge, *Letters,* I, 348–9.
7. *The Excursion,* IV, 1266–70. For an affirmation of free will, see *ibid.,* IX, 223.
8. *Ibid.,* VI, 323–6. See also *ibid.,* VII, 147; VIII, 287; V, 594.

The mechanical theory of the human mind from Locke to Hartley denied the human mind any power to originate or create new ideas. As Locke expressed it, ". . . it is not in the power of the most exalted wit or enlarged understanding, by any quickness or variety of thought, to *invent* or *frame* one new simple idea in the mind . . . ."[9] Because of this derivative nature of all thought, Hartley believed it possible, by a study of the laws of association, to resolve all thought back into simple sensation.

One may hope, therefore, that, by pursuing and perfecting the doctrine of association, we may sometime or other, be enabled to analyse all that vast variety of complex ideas, which pass under the name of ideas of reflection, and intellectual ideas, into their simple compounding parts, *i.e.* into the simple ideas of sensation, of which they consist.[1]

Wordsworth was specifically attacking this idea in *The Excursion*, for he was affirming the mind's *excursive* power. He disparages the effort to dissect the human mind, to break it down by a constant process of division.[2] Repeatedly he mentions the creative powers of the human mind, the human soul, and the human passions.[3] The mind contributes to sensation just as much as sensation contributes to the mind.[4] In his creative synthesis, Wordsworth did not indulge in Coleridge's multiple classification of the powers of the mind. He called the creative power "imagination," with reason, understanding, fancy, and all the others serving on a lower level. Hartley assigned a much lower function to the imagination. By imagination Wordsworth did not mean simply the power of the mind to summon up images not known to experience. Imagination for him was a sort of passionate intuition. It was the faculty by means of which we apprehend eternal and infinite truths, which exist partly within the mind itself, partly in the active principle which pervades nature, and partly in some transcendental realm. The following passages may serve to clarify the functions assigned to this highest of all human faculties by Wordsworth.

> . . . many a tale . . .
> Nourished Imagination in her growth,
> And gave the mind that apprehensive power
> By which she is made quick to recognise
> The moral properties and scope of things.[5]

> Imagination . . . is left free
> And puissant to range the solemn walks
> Of time and nature . . . .[6]

9. *An Essay Concerning Human Understanding*, Bk. II, chap. ii, sec. 2.
1. David Hartley, *Observations on Man, His Frame, His Duty and His Expectations* (London, J. Johnson, 1791), I, 75–6.   2. *The Excursion*, IV, 957–78.
3. *Ibid.*, I, 480–1; III, 940; IV, 833; V, 571 ff.   4. *Ibid.*, III, 940.
5. *Ibid.*, I, 165–9.   6. *Ibid.*, IV, 819–25.

> Access for you
> Is yet preserved, to principles of truth,
> Which the imaginative will upholds
> In seats of wisdom, not to be approached
> By the inferior Faculty that moulds,
> With her minute and speculative pains,
> Opinion, ever changing![7]

> . . . these imaginative heights, that yield
> Far-stretching views into eternity.[8]

> . . . the hopes divine
> Of pure imagination . . . .[9]

> . . . Thanks to his pure imaginative soul
> Capacious and serene . . . .[1]

> . . . to the imagination may be given
> A type and shadow of an awful truth . . . .[2]

Both Locke and Hartley denied the existence of innate ideas or instincts. The only origin of knowledge is sensory experience in their systems. Wordsworth, on the contrary, specifically affirms the existence of innate ideas of the supernatural and of moral truth.

> . . . his innate capacities of soul . . . .[3]

> By thy grace
> The particle divine remained unquenched;
> And, mid the wild weeds of a rugged soil,
> Thy bounty caused to flourish deathless flowers,
> From paradise transplanted . . . .[4]

> . . . thou, who didst wrap the cloud
> Of infancy around us.[5]

> . . . The native grandeur of the human soul . . . .[6]

> . . . the endowment of immortal power . . . .[7a]

> . . . the soul
> Inherits an allegiance . . . .[8a]

Another interesting example is that of the shepherd-boy who "perceives, within himself, a measure and a rule."[9a] The diametrical opposition of Wordsworth and Hartley on this point is so evident that in one place it seems almost as if Wordsworth were attempting a specific contradiction of Hartley.

7. *Ibid.,* iv, 1126–32.   8. *Ibid.,* iv, 1188–9.   9. *Ibid.,* v, 909–10.
1. *Ibid.,* vi, 1065–6.   2. *Ibid.,* vii, 526–7.   3. *Ibid.,* iii, 934.
4. *Ibid.,* iv, 51–4.   5. *Ibid.,* iv, 84–5.   6. *Ibid.,* vi, 666.
7a. *Ibid.,* iv, 205.   8a. *Ibid.,* iv, 1023–4.   9a. *Ibid.,* iv, 807–8.

Hartley	*The Excursion*, v, 562–3
The moral sense is . . . generated necessarily and mechanically.[1]	Moral truth Is no mechanic structure, built by rule . . . .

Wordsworth's concept of the moral intuition as innate and immutable, divine but obstructable, is distinctly transcendental. The moral laws exist not only in the soul and in the mysterious spiritual underpresence in nature but also in some heavenly realm distinct from time and space.

> Duty exists . . . where time and space are not.[2]
>
> The primal duties shine aloft—like stars . . . .[3]
>
> A light of duty shines on every day
> For all . . . .[4]

Wordsworth specifically refutes Godwin's doctrine that such truths can be approached only by an arduous course of reasoning;[5] he believes them to be equally available to all. The innate measure or rule by which we learn our moral duty cannot be acquired exclusively from sensation or reason; Wordsworth is unequivocal in his insistence that there is needed an

> inward principle that gives effect
> To outward argument.[6]

This inward principle is the conscience

> —conscience reverenced and obeyed,
> As God's most intimate presence in the soul,
> And his most perfect image in the world.[7]

This passage, which in its entirety develops the concept of the ideality of space and time in the face of the eternal laws which are supplied by an abstract intelligence, has a distinctly Kantian flavor. The same is true of the passage in Book IX in which Wordsworth says that men should never be treated as means, but only as ends in themselves;[8] this seems like a concise statement of the Kantian concept of a Kingdom of Ends. But it is not necessary to doubt Wordsworth's claim of ignorance concerning Kant, for Coleridge knew Kant, and both of these Kantian concepts appear in *The Friend*, which was originally written in the presence of Wordsworth.[9]

As for the constantly recurring idea in *The Excursion* that nature— human or external—is the ultimate source of all our highest thoughts and

1. *Op. cit.*, I, 504.   2. *The Excursion*, IV, 73–6.   3. *Ibid.*, IX, 238.
4. *Ibid.*, v, 383–4.   5. *Ibid.*, IX, 229–40.   6. *Ibid.*, v, 572–3.
7. *Ibid.*, IV, 225–7.   8. *Ibid.*, IX, 113–22.
9. For the ideality of space and time, see *The Friend* (1818 ed.), sec. I, Essay III; for the concept of ends and means, see *ibid.*, sec. I, Essay IV. This was pointed out by R. Wellek, *Kant in England*, pp. 159–62.

feelings, it may well seem difficult to reconcile this with such tran-
scendental-intuitive doctrines as we have just been considering and to
distinguish it from mechanical theories of the growth of the human mind.

> . . . by nature tuned . . .
> To sympathy with man . . . .[1]

> The glorious habit by which sense is made
> Subservient still to moral purposes . . . .[2]

> Whate'er we see,
> Or feel, shall tend to quicken and refine;
> Shall fix in calmer seats of moral strength,
> Earthly desires . . . .[3]

Such passages are easily mistakable for sensationism, as are also the
facts that the regenerative method prescribed by the Wanderer begins
with nature, the abuses of industry are condemned because they obstruct the forms of nature, and the Solitary was to have been returned
to his native hills to begin his rehabilitation. Although the ideas may
have originated in empiricism, such passages as they appear in *The
Excursion* have almost no relation to strict sensationism or associationism. They do not refer to simple sensory perception of external physical
properties. In the first place, Wordsworth's nature is shot through with
divine, spiritual, active principles and with esthetic values; and, in the
second place, the mind itself is endowed with creative and intuitional
powers which enable it to grasp these recondite properties. The union of
mind and the mysterious substratum of external objects is consummated
on a much higher level than Locke's impressions on a *tabula rasa*. It
is a reciprocal intuition, the mind half-creating and half-receiving, and
the imagination is at once the source and the receptacle.

But the fact remains that Wordsworth could not bring himself to dis-
credit the senses so thoroughly as Coleridge desired. After all his insistence on intuition, there remained a considerable emphasis on sensation
in *The Excursion,* and the resultant paradox between the active, creative mind and the passive, receptive mind is difficult to resolve.

One important clue to Wordsworth's synthesis of these seemingly
antagonistic theories has never been pointed out. The problem of the
duality of mind and matter was particularly pressing in Wordsworth's
age. Locke had opened the controversy by starting a stream of thought
which culminated in the belief that all is matter, while Berkeley had
taken a diametrically opposite viewpoint in claiming that all is mind. As-
suming that both Coleridge and Wordsworth started from the same objectivist, Lockian position, it is easy to see their gradual swing to the
subjectivist viewpoint. Coleridge proclaimed his transition not only in

1. *The Excursion,* I, 362–4.   2. *Ibid.,* IV, 1247–9.   3. *Ibid.,* IV, 1270–4.

letters but in the naming of his sons, Hartley (b. 1796) and Berkeley (1798). Wordsworth never became so nearly thoroughgoing a subjectivist as Coleridge. Coleridge wanted Wordsworth in *The Recluse* to "inform" the senses from the mind rather than to compound a mind from the senses. But Wordsworth, while he had come to place more emphasis on what the mind contributes, kept a high estimate of the role of the senses—too high to suit Coleridge. The relation of the senses to the mind, or rather to the soul, remained a very real problem to both men, but particularly to Wordsworth. In *The Prelude* Wordsworth speaks of "The incumbent mystery of sense and soul."[4]

By the time he came to complete *The Excursion,* Wordsworth had achieved a synthesis between the senses and the soul. This he did by partially fusing the two. He gave the soul sensory faculties, not by a mere literary analogy but by a distinct belief that the soul has powers which correspond to, and are linked with, the bodily senses.

> . . . Powers
> Of soul and sense mysteriously allied . . . .[5]

The most explicit statement of the doctrine of the senses of the soul comes in Book v of *The Excursion.*

> . . . the pure soul, the soul sublime and pure;
> With her two faculties of eye and ear,
> The one by which a creature, whom his sins
> Have rendered prone, can upward look to heaven;
> The other that empowers him to perceive
> The voice of Deity, on height and plain . . . .[6]

This, then, and not automatic processes of simple perception, aggregation, and association, is

> The glorious habit by which sense is made
> Subservient still to moral purposes,
> Auxiliar to divine.[7]

The analogy between sense perception and spiritual intuition is common in English poetry, particularly in the romantic movement. But a close scrutiny of Wordsworth's poetry reveals that this idea occurs more frequently and with greater insistence than mere metaphor would warrant. It can be found in an early poem such as "Tintern Abbey";[8] *The Prelude* contains many examples, some of them occurring at crucial points in the poem;[9] and the following lines, from "Yes it was the mountain Echo," are a striking instance.

---

4. *The Prelude,* xiv, 285.   5. *The Excursion,* iii, 842–3.
6. *Ibid.,* v, 986–91.   7. *Ibid.,* iv, 1247–9.   8. Lines 45–9.
9. *The Prelude,* ii, 348–52, 405, 415–18; iii, 155 ff.; v, 453; vi, 471, 600–2; vii, 735; x, 444; xii, 128 ff.; xiii, 21, 52, 304, 369 ff.; xiv, 88.

Have not *we* too?—yes, we have
Answers, and we know not whence;
Echoes from beyond the grave,
Recognised intelligence!

Such rebounds our inward ear
Catches sometimes from afar—
Listen, ponder, hold them dear;
For of God,—of God they are.

Wordsworth uses many curious expressions in an effort to state or suggest this distinction between outward and inward senses: "bodily eye" (7 times), "bodily sense" (3 times), "fleshly ear," and "human eye" for the former; and for the latter, "inner eye," "under-sense," "peculiar eye," "inward ear," "inward eye," and "inward sense." The distinction is also made in many longer, more circuitous expressions, using particularly words like "audible" and "visible."

In *The Excursion* the inward senses are frequently mentioned and play a major role in the system of regeneration recommended to the Solitary.

. . . visionary powers of eye and soul . . . .[1]

. . . living things, and things inanimate,
Do speak, at Heaven's command, to eye and ear,
And speak to social reason's inner sense,
With inarticulate language.[2]

. . . the soul perceives . . . .[3]

. . . his inward sense perceived
The prolongation of some still response,
Sent by the ancient Soul of this wide land . . . .[4]

. . . the freedom of the universe;
Unfolded still the more, more visible,
The more we know . . . .[5]

. . . Music of finer tone; a harmony,
So do I call it, though it be the hand
Of silence, though there be no voice . . . .[6]

Intuition is represented as an act of perception throughout *The Excursion*. In childhood the senses of the soul are closely allied with the bodily senses, so that the child is in direct sensory contact with the manifestations of divinity.

1. *The Excursion*, IV, 111.   2. *Ibid.*, IV, 1204–7.   3. *Ibid.*, V, 305.
4. *Ibid.*, VII, 894–6.   5. *Ibid.*, IX, 16–18.   6. *Ibid.*, II, 710–12.

> While yet a child, and long before his time,
> Had he perceived the presence and the power
> Of greatness . . . .[7]

> . . . from the power of a peculiar eye . . .
> He traced an ebbing and a flowing mind . . . .[8]

> . . . in the mountains did he *feel* his faith.[9]

> . . . nor did he believe,—he *saw*.[1]

In time of mystical experience, the bodily senses are overwhelmed by the vast perceptions of the soul.

>   . . . great objects . . . lay
> Upon his mind like substances, whose presence
> Perplexed the bodily sense.[2]

>   Sound needed none,
> Nor any voice of joy; his spirit drank
> The spectacle: sensation, soul, and form,
> All melted into him; . . . they were his life.[3]

The outer and inner senses seem to be connected through the higher emotions, or "feelings." Anything which denies or restricts these higher "feelings" severs or weakens the connection. Thus the linkage between the bodily senses and the senses of the soul may be broken by enslavement to industry and ignorance, by excessive worldly concern, by blind devotion to analytical reason, or by apathy, with the result that the inward senses are obstructed, and consequently the outward senses, though continuing to function mechanically, lose their true value as an avenue for intercourse between the divine force in nature and the soul of man. Such is the Solitary's "illness" in *The Excursion*. And yet his inner senses have not completely atrophied, but occasionally receive insights in spite of him, as in the moment of his visionary experience while descending the mountain after searching for the poor pensioner.

> That which I *saw* was the revealed abode
> Of spirits in beatitude.[4]

But he denies the validity of such experience. It is, however, precisely through this remnant of inner sensibility that the Wanderer proposes to cure the Solitary, by restoring the function of the blind eye and re-opening the closed passages "Through which the ear converses with the heart," so that the Solitary may once more receive the impulse, the utterance, and the inspiration provided by nature.[5] The Wanderer states in another connection the weakness of the outer senses alone.

7. *Ibid.*, I, 134–5.   8. *Ibid.*, I, 157–61.   9. *Ibid.*, I, 226.
1. *Ibid.*, I, 232.   2. *Ibid.*, I, 137–9.   3. *Ibid.*, I, 205–10.
4. *Ibid.*, II, 873–4.   5. *Ibid.*, IV, 1147–75.

> . . . these visual orbs,
> Though inconceivably endowed, [are] too dim
> For any passion of the soul that leads
> To ecstasy; and all the crooked paths
> Of time and change disdaining, takes its course
> Along the line of limitless desires.[6]

Only when the outer perceptions are linked to inner perceptions through perfect feeling is man capable of achieving the balance and contemplative tranquillity of true maturity. Overindulgence in feeling is likewise an excess, for it rebels against the outer senses, which bind us to the earth. In speaking of the sorrow of those who mourn the dead and long to follow them into the unknown, the Wanderer says:

> Deem not . . . that, having ceased to see
> With bodily eyes, they are borne down by love
> Of what is lost, and perish through regret.
> Oh! no, the innocent Sufferer often sees
> Too clearly; feels too vividly; and longs
> To realize the vision, . . . —there—there lies
> The excess, by which the balance is destroyed.[7]

The blind man and the deaf man in Book VII of *The Excursion* offer an interesting opportunity for Wordsworth to clarify his meaning in this matter. Here is his concluding comment on those two stories.

> . . . proof abounds
> Upon the earth that faculties which seem
> Extinguished, do not, *therefore,* cease to be.
> And to the mind among her powers of sense
> This transfer is permitted, . . .
> That to the imagination may be given
> A type and shadow of an awful truth.[8]

This idea of compensation for the loss of physical sight by a sharpening of the inner sight is strongly reminiscent of Milton:

> So much the rather thou celestial Light
> Shine inward, and the mind through all her powers
> Irradiate, there plant eyes, all mist from thence
> Purge and disperse, that I may see and tell
> Of things invisible to mortal sight.[9]

But for Wordsworth the eyes of the soul were not merely a metaphor for spiritual insight. They were definitely related to the physical eyes and served an independent function after the physical eyes grew weak. In the instance of the deaf man, the senses of the soul are shown to survive

6. *Ibid.,* IV, 180–5.   7. *Ibid.,* IV, 169–78.   8. *Ibid.,* VII, 518–22, 526–7.
9. *Paradise Lost,* III, 51–5.

death with the soul. This is the only interpretation which clarifies the following passage to my satisfaction.

> —And yon tall pine-tree, whose composing sound
> Was wasted on the good man's living ear,
> Hath now its own peculiar sanctity;
> And, at the touch of every wandering breeze,
> Murmurs, not idly, o'er his peaceful grave.[1]

The implication here seems to be that the physical sound of the tree murmuring was lost on the physical ear of the deaf man, so that the two active principles involved were unable to "circulate"; but after his death, when he was relieved of the encumbrance of faulty physical ears, the ears of his spirit could hear the rustle and "the mute agents stirring there."[2]

Wordsworth's application of this doctrine of inward senses to the problem of old age is also interesting. The youthful perceptions, which bear with them the certainty of the infinite, eternal, and divine, may be founded on some sort of Platonic recollection of a previous state of existence for the soul. This doctrine appears clearly in the "Ode: Intimations of Immortality from Recollections of Early Childhood," despite Wordsworth's equivocation elsewhere on that subject. The fact that Wordsworth held some such belief is confirmed by his note to some lines in *The Excursion* which suggest pre-existence of the soul: "This subject is treated at length in the Ode—'Intimations of Immortality.' "[3] In any event, the strength and number of these youthful raptures diminish as a man grows older, not only because of the diseases noted in the case of the Solitary but also because of a weakening in the powers of the bodily senses, and possibly because of a dimming of the recollections from the previous state. When Wordsworth wrote the "Ode," he was lamenting the loss of his visionary powers. As we have seen, his stoicism in that instance was echoed in Book IV of *The Excursion*.[4] But in Book IX of *The Excursion* he announces the discovery of new and greater visionary powers.[5] When the bodily senses lose their power to grant insight into the unknown, the mind must become disencumbered of them in order to give the senses of the soul free rein to pierce into the realms of power. Thus in old age man perceives directly with the senses of the soul, as he perceived directly with the bodily senses in childhood.

> . . . the gross and visible frame of things
> Relinquishes its hold upon the sense . . . .
> This he is freed from, and from thousand notes

---

1. *The Excursion*, VII., 477–81.   2. *Ibid.*, II, 724.
3. Wordsworth's note to *The Excursion*, IV, 205–6.
4. *The Excursion*, IV, 109–29.   5. *Ibid.*, IX, 63–87.

(Not less unceasing, not less vain than these,)
By which the finer passages of sense
Are occupied; and the Soul, that would incline
To listen, is prevented or deterred.

                    .   .   .

And may it not be hoped . . . .
            . . . that the severing should confer
Fresh power to commune with the invisible world,
And hear the mighty stream of tendency . . . .[6]

This is Wordsworth's advance over the position of the "Ode." Passionate intuition has returned to him, this time through the senses of the soul, which bring the unknown to his mind much more clearly, for they are free of the accidents and impediments which clogged the bodily senses. The world is no longer too much with us, for we now can hear the mighty stream of tendency, that is, the infinite meanings which circulate through nature. It is important to notice that nature is never absent from this concept of Wordsworth's, even after death. The doctrine of the senses of the soul helps us to understand the manner in which Wordsworth believed the mind absorbs the active principle in nature. It is neither subjectivist nor objectivist, for the inner senses, alive with feeling, half create by intuition and half receive by perception. This creative sensibility[7] links the senses with the imagination, by which man apprehends the awful truths. The perfect product of these processes is the meditative calm of the pure imaginative soul.

Lest it should be thought that this evidence from *The Excursion* itself is inconclusive without some historical evidence for such a belief on the part of Wordsworth, it may be well to indicate a few passages in the sources and analogues of *The Excursion* which suggest the senses of the soul. We have already seen the similar passage from Milton. In *The Seasons* Thomson speaks of "the mind's creative eye."[8] In *The Task* Cowper says,

There is in souls a sympathy with sounds,

                    .   .   .

Some chord in unison with what we hear
Is touched within us . . . .[9]

In Berkeley's *Alciphron*, the following phrase appears: ". . . the mind of man sees without eyes, and apprehends without hands."[1] Priestley, in the third introductory essay to his edition of Hartley, which Words-

6. *Ibid.*

7. As I understand it, the doctrine of the senses of the soul is an adjunct of, rather than a substitute for, the doctrine of creative sensibility. See F. Christensen, "Creative Sensibility in Wordsworth," *Journal of English and Germanic Philology*, XLV (1946), 361–8.

8. "Autumn," 1016.   9. *The Task*, VI, 1–5.   1. Dialogue IV, sec. 24.

worth probably used, wrote as follows: ". . . let it be considered how exceedingly different, to the *eye of the mind,* as we may say, are our ideas of sensible things from any thing that could have been conjectured concerning their effect upon us . . . ."[2] Certainly the most important treatment of the subject from the standpoint of possible influence on Wordsworth is that of Coleridge. There can be little doubt that the problem was discussed by the two men. In Coleridge's *Omniana* (1812) there is a paragraph entitled "Inward Blindness," which contains the following sentences: "Talk to a blind man—he knows he wants the sense of sight, and willingly makes the proper allowances. But there are certain internal senses, which a man may want, and yet be wholly ignorant that he wants them."[3] Also among the *Omniana* there is an essay entitled "The Soul and Its Organs of Sense."[4] This is a rambling discussion of the mysterious relationship between the mind and the senses, in which it was Coleridge's purpose to prove "that the mind makes the sense, far more than the senses make the mind," which, it will be remembered, is what Coleridge wanted Wordsworth to prove in *The Recluse.* After a careful division of the powers of the mind into physical senses, imitative power, imagination, fancy, understanding, speculative reason, will, and choice, he considers the effect of the loss of any of these powers on the others. He concludes the essay with a series of examples from real life which show that the mind can compensate for the loss of any of the bodily senses and continue to function with perfect normality. Among his examples, John Gough of Kendal, who was the model for Wordsworth's blind man in *The Excursion,* is most prominent. Coleridge says of him: "Why, his face sees all over! It is all one eye! I almost envied him . . . ." It certainly seems significant of some relationship that both men, writing at about the same time, should use the same concrete example to prove roughly the same metaphysical theory. The doctrine of the senses of the soul also appears occasionally in Coleridge's poetry.[5]

Wordsworth went further than any of these men in the development of the idea of the senses of the soul, because it was a very useful concept to him. It enabled him to strike a middle course between subjectivism and objectivism. However, it is not to be thought that Wordsworth formulated and adopted the doctrine by an orderly process of conscious logic. His expression of the idea is often tentative, equivocal, and apparently paradoxical. There is always considerable ambiguity in Wordsworth's descriptions of his own inner experience and personal beliefs.

2. *Hartley's Theory of the Human Mind,* J. Priestley, ed. (London, Johnson, 1790), p. xxxviii.

3. *Table Talk,* p. 341.   4. *Ibid.,* pp. 360–4.

5. See, for example, "Frost at Midnight," 59 ff.; and "Hymn: before Sunrise in the Vale of Chamouni," 13 ff. In a passage in *The Friend* ("First Landing-Place," Essay 5. 1818 ed.) Coleridge explains that his phrase "the mind's eye" refers to reason.

This probably arises in part from his effort to invest common words with new meanings in order that he might express uncommon shades of thought and feeling with their full sense of freshness and originality. The mystical nature of many of his experiences puts too great a strain on language, involving him in occasional obscurities and contradictions, which are usually accepted by the reader because they bear the stamp of genuine and important experience. Another cause for Wordsworth's ambiguities in the language of metaphysics is the semiformed condition of many of his beliefs. It is a grave error to think of Wordsworth as a profound and systematic metaphysician. He was never such. But he was a courageous, independent, and cautious thinker. He accepted nothing that was either useless or unattractive to him. His constant effort was to synthesize thought and feeling, belief and experience. His philosophy could be naive, derivative, and incomplete but it had to be consistent, useful, and sound. That is why he abandoned strict empiricism, because it did not include all his feelings; and that is why he could not reach the extreme intuitionist viewpoint of Coleridge, because it denied first validity to the evidence of the senses. His development of the idea of the senses of the soul served in part to reconcile these warring elements in his mind. It is a strange and naive solution but it is characteristic of Wordsworth.

Wordsworth's treatment of reason in *The Excursion* is very interesting. He did not attempt to maintain a clear-cut distinction between higher and lower reason, or between reason and understanding. He seems to have acknowledged that it is all one process, to be differentiated only by the functions it fulfills. His distinction is between right reason and wrong reason, or between the use and abuse of reason. Under wrong reason or the abuse of reason he included pure science and the revolutionary rationalism which was given its most extreme statement by Godwin.

Wordsworth's antagonism to science is somewhat more bitter than his purpose warrants. His purpose is to show that science pursued for its own sake is of little value. The important truths elude such painstaking, uninspired research. The important function of science is to search out the fundamental unity of all creation rather than to break creation down into ever smaller units which have less and less relation to the object of all men's search, which is the fundamental unity. Science, as the glorification of fact, ignores the feelings, without which fact is meaningless and far from truth.

> . . . rather would I instantly decline
> To the traditionary sympathies
> Of a most rustic ignorance,
>   . . . than see and hear
> The repetitions wearisome of sense,

Where soul is dead, and feeling hath no place;
Where knowledge, ill begun in cold remark
On outward things, with formal inference ends;

      . . .

Lost in a gloom of uninspired research;
Meanwhile, the heart . . . can nowhere find, the light of truth.[6]

Wordsworth's most forthright attack on the general scientific tendencies
of his age comes in a passage, already quoted in part, in which he ac-
cuses science of working against truth, of warring against the soul, and
of treading upon forbidden ground.[7] Of scientists he says,

                . . . shall they in fact
Prove a degraded Race? and what avails
Renown, if their presumption make them such?
Oh! there is laughter at their work in heaven![8]

The animosity he felt for uninspired research reached its fullest expression in the cynical descriptions by the Solitary of the herbalist and the
geologist.[9] They are represented as utterly insensitive to the beauty and
unity of nature, in their eager devotion to minute fact and classification.
But science is not condemned outright. Wordsworth saw its usefulness
but he also saw that, in its ignorance of the values of experience and its
exclusive concentration on the facts of experience, it was missing the
truth. I cannot resist quoting at length Eliza Hamilton's record of Wordsworth's response to an accusation by her brother that Wordsworth had
slighted science in *The Excursion,* for it clarifies Wordsworth's attitude toward science in *The Excursion* better than any other possible
comments.

He then defended himself, with a beautiful mixture of warmth and tem-
perateness, from the accusation of any want of reverence for Science, in the
proper sense of the word—Science, that raised the mind to contemplation of
God in works, and which was pursued with that end as its primary and great
object; but as for all other science, all science which put this end out of view,
all science which was a bare collection of facts for their own sake, or to be
applied merely to the material uses of life, he thought it *degraded* instead of
raising the species. All science which waged war with and wished to ex-
tinguish Imagination in the mind of man, and to leave it nothing of any kind
but the naked knowledge of facts, was, he thought, much worse than useless;
and what is disseminated in the present day under the title of "useful knowledge," being disconnected, as he thought it, with God and everything but
itself, was of a dangerous and debasing tendency. For his part, rather than
have his mind engrossed with *this* kind of science, to the utter exclusion of
Imagination, and of every consideration but what refers to our bodily com-

---

6. *The Excursion,* IV, 613–30.   7. *Ibid.,* IV, 941–94.
8. *Ibid.,* IV, 953–6.   9. *Ibid.,* III, 159–93.

forts, power and greatness, he would much prefer being a superstitious old woman.[1]

The salvation of science will have to be in an acknowledgment of the feelings, the emotions, the qualities, or the values of experience, and in a redirection of its purposes to include these things; by this means it will tend to move upward instead of downward, to unify rather than divide, and to support and guide man's search for truth rather than to break down cold fact into infinite littleness.

> Science then
> Shall be a precious visitant; and then,
> And only then, be worthy of her name:
> For then her heart shall kindle; her dull eye,
> Dull and inanimate, no more shall hang
> Chained to its object in brute slavery;
> But taught with patient interest to watch
> The processes of things, and serve the cause
> Of order and distinctness, not for this
> Shall it forget that its most noble use,
> Its most illustrious province, must be found
> In furnishing clear guidance, a support
> Not treacherous, to the mind's *excursive* power.[2]

Wordsworth's evident assumption that the eyes of all scientists are chained to their object in brute slavery, as well as his ill-disguised impatience with science as a whole, somewhat weakens his case.

Wordsworth is on sounder ground when he turns to the popular philosophy of pure reason. This overconfidence in the powers of pure reason he felt to be an abuse of reason, or reason misdirected. Like science, reason needs a unifying principle beyond itself. Alone it is impotent to approach truth. Wordsworth called it "false philosophy."[3] Reason alone can produce only opinion; truth is the special sphere of imagination.

> Access for you
> Is yet preserved to principles of truth,
> Which the imaginative will upholds
> In seats of wisdom, not to be approached
> By the inferior Faculty that moulds,
> With her minute and speculative pains,
> Opinion, ever changing.[4]

There are several attacks on rationalistic philosophy in *The Excursion*,[5] the chief objection to it seeming to be that it is capable of error if unguided by something outside itself, such as the imaginative will. An

---

1. This conversation took place in 1829. *The Life of Sir William Rowan Hamilton,* I, 312–14.   2. *Ibid.,* IV, 1251–63.   3. *Ibid.,* II, 260.
4. *Ibid.,* IV, 1126–32.   5. *Ibid.,* IV, 941–94, 1152; VIII, 223–7.

excellent example of this misdirection is to be found in the rationalistic enthusiasm of the French Revolution, where "false conclusions of the reasoning power"[6] led men into

> A proud and most presumptuous confidence
> In the transcendent wisdom of the age,
> And her discernment.[7]

The entire story of the Solitary is an illustration of the abuse of reason. After the deaths of his family, the Solitary takes refuge in abstract reasoning,[8] which fails to bring him any comfort, and later he plunges himself into the extravagant rationalism of the French Revolution, which again leads him astray. The final result of this observation of the errors to which the unassisted reason is prone is a forthright discrediting of pure reason. The Wanderer says that even the wildest superstition is preferable to pure reason,[9] and the Poet says that the humble and ignorant rustics, who are forced by their circumstances to "follow reason's least ambitious course," probably err the least.[1] Unaided reason is opposed to faith, and a good faith must be able to withstand

> The worst that human reasoning can achieve,
> To unsettle or perplex it . . . .[2]

But it must not be concluded that Wordsworth is an unqualified anti-rationalist. He did not entirely abominate the exercise of human reason. On the contrary, he recognized reason as an invaluable faculty, to be used invariably within its proper sphere. What Wordsworth was trying to do was to delimit the area in which pure reason is operative. There are some subjects with which it is unqualified to grapple—the subjects of the spirit. In this realm of the transcendental truths, the reason can support and assist the findings of the imagination, but alone it is powerless.

> . . . the mind's repose
> On evidence is not to be ensured
> By act of naked reason.[3]

> . . . who can best subject
> The will to reason's law, can strictliest live
> And act in that obedience, he shall gain
> The clearest apprehension of those truths,
> Which unassisted reason's utmost power
> Is too infirm to reach.[4]

> Reason, best reason, is to imperfect man
> An effort only, and a noble aim;

6. *Ibid.,* IV, 1126. 7. *Ibid.,* II, 235–7. 8. *Ibid.,* III, 695–705.
9. *Ibid.,* IV, 613–26. 1. *Ibid.,* V, 594–622. 2. *Ibid.,* IV, 197–8.
3. *Ibid.,* V, 560–3. 4. *Ibid.,* V, 517–22.

> A crown, an attribute of sovereign power,
> Still to be courted, never to be won.[5]

Although reason is an imperfect faculty, its great purpose is to act as a support to faith, and in this role it is most useful, if only as a secondary evidence for the truths of the heart.[6] In all other affairs reason is simply sound judgment and should be exercised always to the best of one's ability.[7]

It is an almost hopeless task to distinguish all the different concepts of nature which meet in *The Excursion*. Mr. Beach's excellent book, *The Concept of Nature in Nineteenth-Century English Poetry*,[8] gives a good idea of the tremendously complicated meanings of the word "nature" in Wordsworth's day. The sacredness of nature was almost a first datum of consciousness by the end of the eighteenth century. The extreme form of this belief was of course pantheism, which held that nature *is* God. At the opposite extreme was the viewpoint of Leibnitz that the universe is in the same relationship to God as a watch is to the watchmaker. Wordsworth, in an important letter to Catherine Clarkson defending *The Excursion* against the criticisms of one of her friends, specifically repudiates both these extreme viewpoints, although admitting that there is something "ordinarily (but absurdly) called *Spinosistic*" about the famous passage on the sea shell.[9]

> She condemns me for not distinguishing between Nature as the work of God, and God himself. But where does she find this doctrine inculcated? Whence does she gather that the author of *The Excursion* looks upon Nature and God as the same? He does not indeed consider the Supreme Being as bearing the same relation to the Universe, as a watch-maker bears to a watch. In fact, there is nothing . . . that appears to me so injurious as perpetually talking about *making* by God.[1]

Wordsworth does not, in some instances, distinguish clearly between God and the works of God in dealing with Nature in *The Excursion* but it is fairly clear throughout that he wishes to maintain some such distinction between the Deity and the manifestations of Deity in nature. He is certain that there is a unity of some sort which joins all objects of nature, animate and inanimate. There was a multitude of theories as to the exact nature of this divine underpresence in nature ready to Wordsworth's hand. For example, there was Cudworth's concept of "plastic nature" as an unbroken chain of material phenomena united in the intelligent substance, as a drudge or servant of God. Cudworth's book, *The True Intellectual System of the Universe,* was read by Cole-

5. *Ibid.*, v, 501–4.   6. *Ibid.*, I, 412–13; IV, 158–61; v, 1008–10; IX, 101–13.
7. See, for example, *ibid.*, IV, 260–72.
8. (New York, Macmillan, 1936), chaps. i–vi.
9. *The Excursion*, IV, 1132–47.   1. December, 1814, *MY*, p. 618.

ridge in 1795–96[2] and was in Wordsworth's library.[3] Berkeley's *anima mundi* in *Siris* may have more in common with the "all-pervading Spirit"[4] of *The Excursion* because it has the neoplatonic cast of many of Wordsworth's descriptions. The *"active principle"* also seems close to Shaftesbury's descriptions in *Characteristics,* where he repeatedly calls it an "active principle."[5] This book was also in Wordsworth's library.[6] Newton's immaterial effluvium as God's means of causing motion in matter is very similar.[7] It has recently been pointed out that Wordsworth used both Stoic ideas and Stoic language in the passage on the *"active principle"* at the beginning of Book IX and that *The Excursion* "is everywhere bulwarked with the ethics of Stoicism."[8] But all these different concepts of nature are fused into one in *The Excursion.* Some idea of the heterogeneity of the doctrine in *The Excursion* may be gained by listing the different names given by Wordsworth to the divine underpresence in nature in that poem.

Book	Line	Name
I	135–6	the presence and the power of greatness
I	161	an ebbing and a flowing mind
II	724	mute agents stirring
III	424	earth's native energies
IV	412	plaintive spirit of the solitude
IV	520	a presence or a motion
IV	600	the breeze of nature stirring [in his soul]
IV	927	A spiritual presence
IV	969	all-pervading spirit
IV	1,145	ebb and flow, and ever-during power
IV	1,213	pure principle of love
V	991	The voice of Deity on height and plain
VI	90	the spirit of the place
VI	392	the Genius of our hills
VI	524	nature's language
VII	896	the ancient Soul of this wide land
VII	897	Spirit of its mountains and its seas
IX	3	An *active* principle
IX	47–8	the stir of hopeful nature

2. Kaufman, "The Reading of Southey and Coleridge," *Modern Philology,* XXI (1923–24), 319–20.

3. "Rydal Mount Library," Lot 220.   4. *The Excursion,* IV, 969.

5. *Characteristics,* Treatise V, Pt. III, sec. I.   6. "Rydal Mount Library," Lot 430.

7. On this resemblance, see an excellent article by S. G. Dunn, "A Note on Wordsworth's Metaphysical System," *Essays and Studies by Members of the English Association,* XVIII (1932), 74–109.

8. Jane Worthington, *Wordsworth's Reading of Roman Prose* (New Haven, Yale University Press, 1946), pp. 52–3, 67.

IX	87	the mighty stream of tendency
IX	617	effluence of thyself [i.e., God]
IX	619–20	local transitory type Of thy paternal splendors
IX	626	The faint reflections only of thy face

These are some of the names Wordsworth gives to the divine principle in nature. The ambiguity of its relationship to the Deity appears rather clearly in these names. There is an intermingling of intuitive animism, neoplatonism, and physico-theology. This heterogeneity does not necessarily reflect any doubt or indecision on Wordsworth's part. The plain truth probably is that he knew all the various theories concerning the sanctity of nature and could bring himself to deny acquiescence only to the two extremes of pantheism and deism. Each of the others had something to recommend it to him, and no two of them conflicted because they were never allowed to come into collision. Wordsworth probably felt that it was impossible to arrive at any specific conclusions, and, since all these explanations satisfied him and pleased him and since they presented no further obstacles themselves, he accepted them all. They sanctioned his most memorable and important experiences since early childhood. The one basic requirement, for an active, beneficent divinity in nature, was satisfied, and he was free to make what use he could of the various means. The principle he accepted can be described only negatively: it was not pantheistic, since it was "assigned"; it was not mechanistic, since it was "active"; and it was not materialistic, since it was insensible.[9]

For the purpose of *The Excursion* there are three attributes of nature which are particularly important. The first of these is the active force of love in nature.[1] By apprehending and partaking of this benignity of the spirit of nature, man is made aware of human affection and divine love. The first experience of love in nature comes to the child as a revelation. This appears clearly in the account of the Wanderer's boyhood.

> . . . he had felt the power
> Of nature, and already was prepared,
> By his intense conceptions, to receive
> Deeply the lesson of deep love which he,
> Whom Nature, by whatever means, has taught
> To feel intensely, cannot but receive.

Then comes the mystical experience.

> Far and wide the clouds were touched,
> And in their silent faces could be read

9. All these attributes will be found in the opening passage of Bk. IX.
1. For other examples than those given here of the doctrine of the benignity of nature, see *The Excursion*, III, 809; IV, 427–8; V, 975; VIII, 58–9; IX, 10–11, 99–100.

Unutterable love.
. . . it was blessedness and love !²

The whole purpose of communion with nature in the remedy prescribed for the Solitary by the Wanderer is to reveal the pervading benignity.

. . . the man—
Who, in this spirit, communes with the Forms
Of nature, . . . —needs must feel
The joy of that pure principle of love . . . .³

From this the Solitary is to be led to love for his fellow-men. In fact, one whole facet of the central theme of *The Excursion* may be summed up in these climactic words of the Pastor : "Life, I repeat, is energy of love."⁴

A second important attribute of nature in *The Excursion* is its unity. All the various forms are linked together in outward manifestations as well as in inward principle. This is the concept of the scale or chain of being, which Pope describes in *An Essay on Man*. According to Wordsworth, God is the "Source of all that in the scale of being fill their place."⁵ The importance of this concept to *The Excursion* lies in its relation to science. The Wanderer, in telling the Solitary how he should approach the study of nature, places his greatest emphasis on investigation of the interrelationships of the various forms of nature. This study will teach love, as opposed to cold science, which divides nature endlessly into fact. The Solitary should explore

All natures,—to the end that he may find
The law that governs each ; and where begins
The union, the partition where, that makes
Kind and degree, among all visible Beings ;

. . .

Through all the mighty commonwealth of things ;
Up from the creeping plant to sovereign Man.
Such converse, if directed by a meek,
Sincere, and humble spirit, teaches love . . . .⁶

Subsequently, in a very interesting passage, the Wanderer traces this community of love among all natural beings.⁷ He includes moles, emmets, flies, rooks, and ducks in his description. All are pervaded by benignity, and this is their unity. Even mountain crags share the benefits of the commonwealth. The active principle is universal, or, as Wordsworth expresses it,

Spirit that knows no insulated spot,
No chasm, no solitude ; from link to link
It circulates, the Soul of all the worlds.⁸

2. *Ibid.*, I, 185–218.   3. *Ibid.*, IV, 1207–13.   4. *Ibid.*, V, 1012.
5. *Ibid.*, IV, 81.   6. *Ibid.*, IV, 332–50.   7. *Ibid.*, IV, 427–65.
8. *Ibid.*, IX, 13–15.

The importance of this concept of a chain of being to the remedy prescribed in *The Excursion* is self-evident. To Wordsworth it had still further importance because it permitted him to grasp the whole of nature as involved in the tonality of the particular instance.[9] Since such experiences had been of first importance in his own development, he felt that they could be the same to others.

The third important attribute of nature in *The Excursion* is quite apart from the metaphysical concepts of nature which we have been considering above. This is the concept of nature as a norm for conduct. Wordsworth seems to have felt that a comparison of human problems to nature somehow could reveal a solution. Nature in its processes is the quintessence of normality and propriety and can teach men lessons for their outward conduct as well as for their inward state of soul. The first example of this concept in *The Excursion* comes in the middle of the story of Margaret, when the Wanderer breaks off and contrasts the sadness which that tale arouses with the joyousness of nature, at high noon on a summer day.

> Why should we thus, with an untoward mind,
> And in the weakness of humanity,
> From natural wisdom turn our hearts away;
> To natural comfort shut our eyes and ears;
> And, feeding on disquiet, thus disturb
> The calm of nature with our restless thoughts?[1]

In pointing out to the Solitary the excesses of which he has been guilty, the Wanderer points to the revolutionary desire to effect the millennium overnight as a presumptuous faith. The important social changes are wrought gradually, and such violent upheavals often do more to hinder than to help the causes which they pretend to support. Again nature is made the criterion: "By nature's gradual processes be taught."[2] The same remedy is prescribed by the Wanderer for the Solitary's irregular habits of living.

> . . . withdraw yourself from ways
> That run not parallel to nature's course.
> Rise with the lark![3]

The Pastor uses the same measure in the case of Ellen. When Ellen's employers discovered that she was spending a great deal of time weeping over her child's grave, they forbade her to go out at all. Of this the Pastor says,

> . . . Nature might not thus be crossed,
> Thus wronged in woman's breast . . . .[4]

---

9. Whitehead, *op. cit.*   1. *The Excursion*, I, 599–604.
2. *Ibid.*, IV, 288.   3. *Ibid.*, IV, 489–91.   4. *Ibid.*, VI, 998–9.

These are the three most important special uses which are made of nature in *The Excursion*. There are many other uses, less important but still a part of the whole texture of the poem. For instance, the ministry of pleasure in nature appears most memorably in several passages, such as the following.

> . . . sweep distemper from the busy day,
> And make the chalice of the big round year
> Run o'er with gladness; whence the Being moves
> In beauty through the world; and all who see
> Bless him, rejoicing in his neighborhood.[5]

Nature is also frequently personified as a sort of guardian of the life-processes in man.[6] The "powers of nature" are variously used as the principle of life in man, the active principle, and an influence exerted by nature on man.[7]

The Christianity of *The Excursion* presents many interesting problems. It is surprising that *The Excursion* is regarded as the first great example of Wordsworth's ultimate "apostasy," his "retreat" into orthodoxy, for the Christianity of *The Excursion* is incomplete and occasionally heterodox, and recent scholarship has tended to break down the customary sharp distinction between the "early Wordsworth" and the "later Wordsworth," finding much more unity and consistency in Wordsworth's ideas over the years than has previously been acknowledged.

Wordsworth's temporary pantheism was really a deviation from his fundamental beliefs, a deviation which, while it provided him with certain useful ideas, never completely satisfied him; and his later orthodoxy was not a retreat from naturalism but actually a return to an earlier position.[8] This return was not a sudden shameful abandonment of independent thought but a gradual, difficult, and creditable intellectual accomplishment. The revisions of *The Prelude* reveal no "retreat," no systematic effort by the older poet to conceal his youthful convictions.[9]

There is evidence that Wordsworth's religious thought continued along independent lines long after 1814, when he wrote, "I am a professed admirer of the Church of England."[1] For example, on January 3, 1815, Crabb Robinson recorded that Wordsworth had said to him, "I have no need of a Redeemer."[2] In 1836 Robinson wrote a brief sum-

---

5. *Ibid.*, IX, 133-7.   6. *Ibid.*, III, 809; VI, 301-3; VII, 873.
7. *Ibid.*, VII, 465; I, 135-6; IV, 1190-2, respectively.
8. Elizabeth Geen, "The Concept of Grace in Wordsworth's Poetry," *PMLA,* LVIII (September, 1943), 689–715.
9. Mary E. Burton, *The One Wordsworth* (Chapel Hill, University of North Carolina Press, 1942).   1. *MY*, p. 622.
2. This may be a recollection by Robinson of a conversation which took place on May 24, 1812, when Robinson made the following record of Wordsworth's statement: "I can feel more sympathy with an orthodox believer who needs a Redeemer and who, sensible of his own demerits flees for refuge to Him (though perhaps I do not want

mary of what he had gathered of the beliefs of Wordsworth from conversations with the poet. There are several criticisms of orthodoxy, and the summary concludes with a statement by Robinson that he had told Wordsworth that he *tried* to believe and that Wordsworth had replied, "That is pretty much my case."[3] In 1842 Aubrey de Vere recorded the following conversation.

[Miss Fenwick] spoke of her great desire to see Mr. Wordsworth become a Catholic-minded man, and pass his evening of life under the shadow of some cathedral[.] Heard Mr. Wordsworth say—'I cannot raise myself to this state of feeling. I feel and lament my own unworthiness, but the feeling of penitence is lost in sympathy with the virtues of others, or contemplation of our Saviour's character, so that I seem to remember my own shortcomings no more.'[4]

In 1843 "Wordsworth declared in strong terms his disbelief of eternal punishment . . . ."[5] Wordsworth became a professed high churchman and frequently expressed admiration for the aims and accomplishments of the Oxford Movement.[6] His identification with that movement, however, was apparently without much foundation, for he admitted a limited knowledge of the Tracts,[7] his approval was restricted to the broad beneficial effects,[8] and he remained critical of the methods of the movement.[9] After his death his friends expressed regret at the selection of his extremely high-church nephew as his biographer because they felt the poet would be shown in a false light.[1] Thus it seems that in religion, as in other fields of thought, Wordsworth moved slowly, with courageous independence and generally with fidelity to long-term fundamental principles.

   With the Christianity of *The Excursion,* as with so many others of the doctrines of that poem, there is difficulty in determining exactly when Wordsworth is speaking and when the characters are speaking. Charles Lamb felt this problem and boldly asked Wordsworth in a letter, ". . . Are you a Xian? or is it the Pedlar and the Priest that are?"[2] The letter in which Wordsworth replied to this question has not been preserved, but his answer has. Lamb recorded that Wordsworth replied,

---

one for myself) than with the cold and rational notions of the Unitarian." *Henry Crabb Robinson on Books and Their Writers,* pp. 87, 158.
   3. *Ibid.,* pp. 481–2.   4. Wilfred Ward, *Aubrey de Vere,* p. 69.
   5. *Henry Crabb Robinson on Books and Their Writers,* p. 628.
   6. Ellis Yarnall, *Wordsworth and the Coleridges* (New York, Macmillan, 1899), p. 42.
   7. *The Correspondence of Henry Crabb Robinson with the Wordsworth Circle,* p. 396; Ward, *op. cit.,* p. 65.
   8. *The Correspondence of Henry Crabb Robinson with the Wordsworth Circle,* p. 472.
   9. See Wordsworth's sonnet on "Young England."
   1. *The Correspondence of Henry Crabb Robinson with the Wordsworth Circle,* pp. 729, 731, 754.   2. Lamb, *Works,* VI, 443–6.

"When I am a good man *then* I am a Christian."[3] This certainly seems equivocal, which is exactly what Robinson called it.[4] Montgomery, in his review of *The Excursion,* decided that the Pastor's religious speeches were not an integral part of the main doctrine of the poem:

The pastor of 'the church among the mountains' indeed, touches delightfully on the Christian's hopes on each side of the grave; but this is only in character, and *his* sentiments are *not* vitally connected with the system of *natural religion,* if we may call it so, which is developed in this poem.[5]

Montgomery's only severe criticism of the poem is that its scheme of redemption is not Christian but rather a combination of nature-worship and self-reliance. It is true that, in the very midst of his most passionate arguments for aspirations heavenward, Wordsworth specifically emphasizes the importance of earthly awareness.[6]

In 1828 Wilson published in *Blackwood's* an essay entitled "Sacred Poetry," a large part of which was devoted to an attack on the Christianity of *The Excursion: ". . .* is it Christianity? No—it is not. There are glimpses given of some of the Christian doctrines; just as if the various philosophical disquisitions . . . would be imperfect, without some allusion to the Christian creed."[7] This article suggested that the panegyric on the church at the beginning of Book vi is mere lip service.

How happened it that he who pronounced this eloquent panegyric—that they who so devoutly inclined their ear to catch it—should have been all contented with "That basis laid, these principles of faith announced," and yet throughout the whole course of their discussions, before and after, have forgotten apparently, that there was either Christianity or a Christian Church in the world?[8]

The Excursion was a much less Christian poem in its original (1814) form than in the form in which it is usually read today. A great many of the passages of specific Christianity which appear in the final version of the poem were not added until 1845.[9] It may very well be that Wordsworth was moved by the criticisms of Montgomery to make the poem more Christian, for it is known that he held Montgomery in high regard and the review in the *Eclectic* is the only one he is known to have read with great care.[1] Others of the most Christian parts of *The Excursion* were drawn from Christopher Wordsworth's *Ecclesiastical Bi-*

3. *Letters, Conversations, and Recollections of S. T. Coleridge,* T. Allsop, ed. (London, E. Moxon, 1836), I, 205.
4. *Henry Crabb Robinson on Books and Their Writers,* p. 469.
5. *The Eclectic Review,* New Series, Vol. III (January, 1815), 20.
6. *The Excursion,* IV, 418–26.
7. *Blackwood's Edinburgh Magazine,* XXIV (December, 1828), 925–6.
8. *Ibid.,* p. 926.   9. See pp. 25 ff. of this book.
1. See *MY,* pp. 638, 652, 655–6.

ography, and still others can perhaps be explained by Coleridge's pressure on Wordsworth to affirm a thoroughly Christian creed in *The Recluse.*

When all these things are taken into consideration, there is really a very small residue of orthodox Christianity in *The Excursion.* Before we consider the positive side of the Christianity of *The Excursion,* however, we must notice two negative aspects. In Book IV, the Old Testament story of the creation, the fall, and the miracles is classed with the exploded primitive myths of the Persians, the Chaldeans, and the Greeks.[2] And in Book V Wordsworth makes the surprisingly critical comment:

> Who can reflect, unmoved, upon the round
> Of smooth and solemnized complacencies,
> By which, on Christian lands, from age to age
> Profession mocks performance?[3]

Turning to the positive side of Christianity in *The Excursion,* we find that it is both incomplete and somewhat unorthodox.

The Deity of *The Excursion* is not very clearly distinguished from His works, as we have seen. He is called "God" 27 times; "Providence" 8 times; the "Being" 6 times; "Father" only 4 times; "Master," "Ruler," and "Lord" once each; and "Creator" and "Giver" not at all. He is also called such vague names as "an abstract intelligence," an "all-pervading Spirit," and a "Great Artificer." These expressions merge with the great variety of names, already indicated, that Wordsworth applied to the divine underpresence in nature. The relation of God to nature is ambiguously presented, and, while there is some effort to distinguish between God as a person and His extension in nature, the latter is obviously still an important and attractive aspect to Wordsworth. The attributes of God as they appear in *The Excursion* do not throw much additional light on His nature. He is benevolent, mysterious, infinite, eternal, and merciful. There is little else to be said of Him.

A thorough survey of the diction of *The Excursion* reveals that the language of Christian dogma is as scarce in this poem as elsewhere in Wordsworth, and several theological terms which appear in *The Prelude* and the shorter poems are not used at all, or are used less frequently, in *The Excursion.* Very few such words occur significantly more often in *The Excursion* than in Wordsworth's other works. Christ is mentioned only three times in the entire poem, twice as "Christ" and once as "Jesus." The word "Redeemer" appears only twice, and in one of these instances it is used cynically. The word "Saviour" does not appear at all, nor is there any mention of the incarnation, the atonement, the resurrection, the communion, the blood, or the wounds. The cross is mentioned five times; but there is no allusion to eternal punishment, and the word

2. *The Excursion,* IV, 631-70.   3. *Ibid.,* V, 375-8.

"hell" appears only in one figurative use. Sin is mentioned only three times, penitence twice, and the fall, which Coleridge wanted Wordsworth to affirm in some sense, appears only twice, once in the Wanderer's account of ancient beliefs and once when the poet speaks of man as "now fallen." There can be little doubt that Wordsworth was familiar with the language of theology.[4] His avoidance of it in *The Excursion* may be attributable to the fact that it was not particularly germane to his purpose and to the fact that he felt his handling of such material was frigid. Even the Pastor, who was evidently designed as a spokesman for orthodoxy, equivocates blandly, says very little in specific support of his faith, and shows a strange neoplatonic natural piety at times.

There are some important themes in the poem which do seem to be specifically Christian. For instance, the theme of hope runs through the entire poem and adds to the impression of orthodoxy. Hope is acknowledged to be a necessary attribute of faith. It is also a necessity of life: "We live by Admiration, Hope, and Love."[5] The Solitary lacks hope and one of the central purposes of the poem is to restore it to him. Nevertheless, when we isolate and analyze this hope in *The Excursion,* it proves to be of a strangely calculating, utilitarian species. It seems to consist in fixing a satisfying view upon the afterlife.[6] It is a function of the imagination, our faculty for piercing the unknown, and it seems to be merely the putting of an attractive semblance on one's imaginative conception of the afterworld. If we have hope (i.e., if we can imagine that the afterlife is better than the worldly life), then we can live in peace and we have the power "to transmute" "an agonizing sorrow."[7]

Duty is another important theme in *The Excursion.* It appears primarily as an abstract concept—a sort of categorical imperative. There are four passages which set forth this concept.

> Duty exists;—immutably survive,
> For our support, the measures and the forms,
> Which an abstract intelligence supplies;
> Whose kingdom is, where time and space are not.[8]

> So shall they learn . . .
> Their duties from all forms . . . .[9]

> A light of duty shines on every day
> For all; and yet how few are warmed or cheered![1]

> The primal duties shine aloft—like stars.[2]

4. See Geen, *op. cit.*
5. *The Excursion,* IV, 763. The substitution of "Admiration" for "Faith" here and elsewhere in the poem is perhaps indicative of his tendency to make mental reservations.
6. *Ibid.,* IV, 158.   7. *Ibid.,* IV, 168.   8. *Ibid.,* IV, 73-6.
9. *Ibid.,* IV, 1239-40.   1. *Ibid.,* V, 283-4.   2. *Ibid.,* IX, 238.

There is also a passage which indicates that these primal duties exist in one's own mind, as an innate moral sense,[3] a conscience apparently of divine origin. They also seem to exist in the forms of nature and in the eternal and infinite realm, so that it can be said that they are coexistent with the Deity, established by the Deity, and binding to the Deity Himself.[4] There is little to indicate that Wordsworth had Christian duty in mind. There is no trace of the Ten Commandments or of the Beatitudes. Wordsworth's treatment of duty seems to have more in common with classical Stoicism.[5] The longing for complete submission to duty, as a sort of refuge from the fluctuating passions and desires of life, which appears in the "Ode to Duty" (1805), is transmuted in *The Excursion* into a more positive, active creed; but here it is no more detailed or specific, and it takes on a transcendental flavor which it lacked in the earlier poem. As Wordsworth conceived it, duty evidently meant primarily the property of fortitude by which we are enabled to carry on in social life after severe affliction. Nevertheless, it also included the fulfillment of all the necessary round of minor obligations which each person contracts in social life. It seems to bear some relationship to Christian duty, but it is not very carefully defined. Wordsworth's concept of duty, like his concept of hope, seems to be somewhat utilitarian. There is just enough sense of duty in *The Excursion* to support the characters under affliction and to keep them active in life when life has lost much of its interest and pleasure.

The most unequivocal articulations of faith in *The Excursion* are those which deal with the Deity Himself and those which mention immortality. The statement by the Wanderer of his creed at the beginning of Book IV is the clearest expression in the entire poem. It affirms faith, hope, love, and a firm belief in immortality. These are all beliefs that Wordsworth himself held. But they must not be inspected too closely. His impressions of Deity are heterodox and his belief in immortality carries with it no clear conception of heaven. There is in *The Excursion* also some effort to express a belief in the transience of all worldly affairs, even including nature.[6] This belief was probably a reaction to the deaths in Wordsworth's family; the concern he shows for worldly affairs in the last two books of *The Excursion*, together with his abiding faith in nature throughout the poem, indicates that he had considerable difficulty in preserving a mental state of otherworldliness.

Analysis of *The Excursion* reveals that Wordsworth avoided the vocabulary of Christianity, that his presentation of the Christian faith was incomplete, and that he entertained convictions concerning the divinity of nature and man's self-reliance which are almost contrary to Christianity. Nevertheless, the poem does teach Christian faith and vir-

---

3. *Ibid.*, IV, 800–10.   4. *Ibid.*, IV, 96–9.   5. Worthington, *op. cit.*, pp. 61–2.
6. *The Excursion*, IV, 100–2, 140; VII, 976–1007.

tue, and in many respects it is more specifically religious than Wordsworth's previous works. Yet, most important of all for a clear understanding of *The Excursion,* we must recognize that the Christian faith is not the specific solution for the problems of *The Excursion.* It is a minor force in the doctrinal plot.

It has been commonly held that the politics of *The Excursion* are reactionary and that Wordsworth was a thoroughgoing Tory long before he began writing this poem. It is true that on February 6, 1812, Wordsworth wrote to Lord Lonsdale, asking him to procure a government position for him,[7] but this is no assurance of his political convictions. His early radicalism was certainly much tempered by the events in France following his departure from that country, and some of the "Poems Dedicated to National Independence and Liberty" show that he was a critical English patriot—but still an English patriot—as early as 1803. During this same year he joined the Grasmere Volunteers. But that he had not abandoned his democratic principles appears clearly in Haydon's statement that in 1809 Sir George Beaumont said to him and Wilkie: "Wordsworth may perhaps walk in; if he do, I caution you both against his terrific democratic notions."[8] Wordsworth really remained faithful to the democratic ideal throughout his life; his later conservatism was purely a matter of application and surface opinion.[9]

In *The Excursion* Wordsworth criticizes the French Revolution as an excess, an illusory and presumptuous faith in man and in the wisdom of the age, a faith misplaced because men of evil intent are firmer in purpose and more energetic in action than men of good intent.[1] He also criticizes the excessive faith in pure reason which was at the fountainhead of the revolution and indicates his belief that upheavals do more to hinder social progress than to aid it. A gradual process of legislation promises more than violence.[2] All men are fundamentally equal;[3] the political restraints and privileges which destroy this equality are lamentable.[4] The government should control industry and child labor to abolish the abuses which are increasing and perpetuating inequalities. Above all, the government should establish universal compulsory state education to remove the inequalities of moral and intellectual opportunity which have reduced so great a portion of the population to slavish ignorance and poverty. Humble life is frankly championed throughout *The Excursion.*[5]

These are not the political principles of a hardened Tory. They are

7. *MY*, pp. 485–6.
8. *The Autobiography and Memoirs of Benjamin Robert Haydon,* T. Taylor, ed. (London, P. Davies, 1926), I, 97.
9. See Vida Scudder, *The Life of the Spirit in the Modern English Poets* (Boston, Houghton, Mifflin, 1895), pp. 58–92.   1. *The Excursion,* IV, 260–331.
2. *Ibid.,* IV, 283.   3. *Ibid.,* VI, 950.   4. *Ibid.,* IX, 245–54.
5. *Ibid.,* I, 340–7.

progressive ideals with a practical basis and a practical end. His attack on the new mechanical civilization is based on broad moral and humanitarian principles. He condemns it because it encourages greed for wealth and because it reduces the laboring classes to a new slavery. With a keen critical eye he figures up the total gains and losses of the factory system, exposing its abuses as they have never been exposed before, noticing the smoke, the dirt, the slums, the fouling of streams, the turning of night into day, the exploitation of childhood, the lessening of man's sense of dignity and freedom, the tendency to make man a mere tool, the impairment of the moral sense, and the decadence of the old domestic morals.[6] Wordsworth anticipated Carlyle by 19 years in all this, and it is important to notice that he did not recommend a return to the past as a cure for these evils. He wanted the government to control and direct the new forces. He anticipated compulsory elementary education in England by 66 years.[7] The nearest approach to Toryism in *The Excursion* is in the first 16 lines of Book VI, and this tribute to his native land really cannot be taken as a token of his whole political viewpoint. It is still possible to say that in *The Excursion* we have that higher ethical socialism which anticipates the work of social revolution and that "The poet of 'The Excursion' and the poet of 'Prometheus' bear the standard of the future side by side."[8]

Perhaps it is now possible to answer the question, what is the message of *The Excursion?* We are justified in seeking a message because Wordsworth always insisted that his first purpose was to teach. In *The Excursion,* furthermore, his first purpose was to teach philosophy. But it must not be thought that *The Excursion* contains a complete and detailed philosophical system: "It is not the Author's intention formally to announce a system: . . . the Reader will have no difficulty in extracting the system for himself."[9] *The Excursion* is a dramatic presentation of philosophical ideas. The plot and characters are of first importance; the ideas which are developed apply primarily to the particular problems raised in the dramatic development and should not be considered without reference to the plot. The central doctrines have now been considered both in and out of their context.

There is no single message in *The Excursion.* There are many problems raised and many solutions provided. Following are perhaps the most important lessons taught by the poem.

a) We live by faith in a benevolent providence, hope for a desirable after life, and love for our fellow-creatures. Faith must be inclusive

6. See C. H. Patton, *The Rediscovery of Wordsworth* (Boston, Stratford, 1935), pp. 125–37.

7. Wordsworth later changed his mind about state education, but still on the basis of the same general principles. *LY*, pp. 326–35.

8. Scudder, *op. cit.*, pp. 91–2.   9. Preface to the edition of 1814.

enough to embrace all accidents of mortal existence. The duties which are the standard for a virtuous life exist in nature, man, and infinity.

b) A man who has lost these fundamental principles of life may be restored to them in the following way. By communion with nature he will become aware of the divine love which is active in nature. This will cause him to recognize a similar love within himself and to seek it in his fellow-men, where he will find it. He will then come to see his duty in everything which he experiences.

c) Human reason is not commensurate with the whole of experience and is an illusory god. The imagination is the highest human faculty, for by means of it alone can we see into the unknown. Reason serves best as a guide and support to pure imagination.

These are vastly oversimplified statements and they fail to embrace a great many minor lessons which are in the poem; but they are the central truths which Wordsworth wished to convey in *The Excursion*.

V

The Style of The Excursion

I

WHEN Matthew Arnold said that Wordsworth has no style,[1] he meant that the peculiar quality of Wordsworth's best poetry is the simplicity, exactitude, and directness of inevitability, and hence the absence of ornament and elaborate contrivance. The poet himself, in the famous Preface, with its Appendix and Supplementary Essay, made it clear that the conventionalized artifices of poetry, particularly as practiced in the eighteenth century, were repugnant to him and were to have no part in his idiom. Naturalness and intelligibility he always avowed to be his main stylistic objectives. Thus simplicity and plainness approaching austerity have generally been regarded as the characteristic virtues of Wordsworth's style at its best, and a multitude of examples among his shorter poems is familiar to all.

Much of *The Excursion,* however, is written in a style which cannot be described as brief, simple, direct, and devoid of ornament. As Arnold expressed it, "In the *Excursion* we have his style, as an artistic product of his own creation; and although Jeffrey completely failed to recognise Wordsworth's real greatness, he was yet not wrong in saying of the *Excursion,* as a work of poetic style: 'This will never do.' "[2] The style of *The Excursion* is clearly not the style of "My heart leaps up" and "The Solitary Reaper." It abounds with conscious artifice and elaborate pictorial and emotional effects. Spontaneity is largely replaced by careful, painstaking artistry. If the estimate of Wordsworth's greatness is to rest, as Arnold would have it, on the great short poems, then this new departure in poetic style of the later Wordsworth must inevitably be considered a falling-off, as indeed it has been generally considered since Wordsworth's own day.

The most common objection to Wordsworth's later style, and particularly to the style of *The Excursion,* has been that rhetoric replaces poetry, the result of which is diffuseness and sonorous prolixity.[3] In fact, mere length has been called the most serious shortcoming of *The Excursion.*

1. "Wordsworth," *Essays in Criticism,* Ser. II, p. 155.
2. *Ibid.,* p. 156.
3. F. H. Doyle, "Wordsworth," *Lectures on Poetry,* Ser. II (London, Smith, Elder, 1877), pp. 1–77.

The most fatal fault of the Excursion is, that it is too long. I do not mean long in respect to quantity, (for I have heard a longer sermon of fifteen minutes than one of fifty,) but long in respect to the quantity of idea spread over a surface of words. Every thing is long in it, the similes, the stories, the speeches, the words, the sentences (which are indeed of a breathless length),—and yet, awful to relate, it is only a third part "of a long and laborious work!"[4]

The reason usually given for this artificiality and length is the decline of poetic power with advancing age. It must at least be admitted as a possibility, however, that this "rhetoric" is attributable to a cause other than the sudden lapse of inspiration, and that this length grows out of circumstances other than the mere pompous prolixity of a senescent poet.

The recent publication of the first really thoroughgoing study of the revisions of *The Prelude*[5] has done much to dispel the persistent popular belief that there were two Wordsworths, a rakish, radical, inspired young poet and a pontifical, reactionary, garrulous old poseur, the division between which is clearly established at some point in the year 1808.[6] That study shows that the later Wordsworth was in most technical respects a more competent craftsman than he had been in 1805; that he was capable of ingenious condensation, more forceful expression, greater clarity and grammatical propriety, more vivid imagery, and more polished expression; and that he was more careful to avoid the semblance of prose. This development of artistic richness is apparently an outgrowth of a mature study of poetic technique, increasing familiarity with great models, and long experience and experimentation.

The "rhetoric" of *The Excursion* is perhaps due largely to the awakening of this greater artistic awareness, which, while it was perhaps inchoate and therefore excessive in 1813, must give us pause in the customary assumption that wherever the style of *The Excursion* differs from the style of the acknowledged great poems it is a bad style.

The length of the poem, of its similes, stories, speeches, words, and sentences, and the consequent difficulty of reading it are certainly to be accounted for partly by the subject matter of the poem, which is abstruse and difficult itself. The burden of the poetry, some of the most elaborate philosophizing ever committed to verse, is clearly among the chief determining factors of the style. This is especially apparent when the narrative books, particularly Books VI and VII, are contrasted with the more speculative books, particularly Books IV and V. The former have

---

4. "An Essay on the Theory and Writings of Wordsworth: Part III," *Blackwood's Edinburgh Magazine*, XXVI (November, 1829), 781.

5. Burton, *The One Wordsworth.*

6. A recent reiteration, for popular consumption, is that of Max Eastman, "The Strange Case of Will and William Wordsworth," *Reader's Digest*, XLVIII (April, 1946), 131–4.

been considered characteristic of Wordsworth at his very best[7] and are written in a simpler language, with generally shorter and clearer sentences, than the speculative books. This in itself is evidence that the complexity and difficulty of many speculative passages in the poem result from the demands of a complex and difficult subject matter, for Wordsworth demonstrated in the same poem the continuing high level of his narrative and descriptive powers. Also to be considered is the fact that much of the poem is in dialogue form, and the nature of this dialogue is determined to some extent by the characters of the speakers —a philosopher, a pastor, and a religious poet on one hand and a former preacher and philosopher on the other. It is only proper that conversation among such men should have something of pulpit eloquence and philosophical abstraction about it. Indeed, when the demands of the subject matter and the characters and situation are fully considered, it is surprising that the poem is so nearly fit for popular consumption as it is. Perhaps only a Wordsworth could see in such essentially philosophical problems so much that is concrete and human, fit for simple narrative treatment.

In defending the style of *The Excursion*, Wordsworth himself appealed to the nature of the subject matter and the varied demands of the different parts of the poem.[8]

2

The diction of *The Excursion* constitutes one of the most marked deviations of Wordsworth from his earlier practice and theory. It has long been recognized that in *The Excursion* the effort to approximate the real language of country people and to observe the prose order and choice of words has been largely abandoned. One critic has even stated that much of the diction of *The Excursion* is more than in most poets elaborate and stately.[9]

There is really a surprising resemblance between many phrases in *The Excursion* and the "poetic diction" of eighteenth-century poets that Wordsworth denounced in the famous Preface and Essay Supplementary to the Preface of *Lyrical Ballads*. The following list of some of the more striking examples will illustrate this correspondence. Wherever necessary for clarity, the example is followed by a parenthetical translation into "the real language of men."

7. See, for example, S. Banerjee, *Critical Theories and Poetic Practice in the "Lyrical Ballads"* (London, Williams & Norgate, 1931), pp. 178–84.
8. Wordsworth to Catherine Clarkson, December, 1814, *MY*, pp. 617–21.
9. Doyle, *op. cit.*, p. 68.

Book	Line	Phrase
II	100	the fleet coursers they bestride
II	719	[the sun's] substantial orb
III	3	[falcons'] clamorous agitation
III	42	copious rains have magnified the stream
III	50	a semicirque of turf-clad ground
III	541	shining giver of the day diffuse (sun)
IV	180	visual orbs (eyes)
IV	450	the feathered kinds (birds)
IV	460	etherial vault (sky)
IV	858	blazing chariot of the sun
IV	1,179	Athwart the concave of the dark blue dome (across the night sky) [1]
V	138	sacred pile (church)
VII	834	The forkèd weapon of the skies (lightning)
VIII	461	A reverend pile (parsonage)
IX	491–4	A hawk . . . cleaves . . . With correspondent wings the abyss of air.

These flowery circumlocutions would hardly be recognized as Wordsworthian, yet they are in the best tradition of poetic embellishment and probably indicate a greater familiarity with both eighteenth-century poetry and books of style and rhetoric.

A similar extension of style is apparent in Wordsworth's choice of modifiers in *The Excursion*.

Book	Line	Phrase
III	17	spot so parsimoniously endowed
III	523	unendangered myrtle
III	974	conglobulated bubbles
IV	245	reiterated steps
IV	456	sedentary fowl
IV	793	contiguous torrent
IV	884	goat's depending beard
IV	1160	circumambient walls
V	84	copious stream
VII	193	unsedentary master
VII	620	fleece-encumbered flock
VII	745	indefatigable fox
VIII	66	Examples efficacious
VIII	450	commodious walk
VIII	557	capacious surface [of a smooth blue stone!]
IX	6	unenduring clouds

1. Wordsworth speaks of "the concave" of the sky 3 times in *The Excursion*.

There are many other expressions in *The Excursion* which have this tone of verbose formality and which are not simple and plain. For example:

Book	Line	Expression
Passim		from out
I	49	nothing willingly
V	269	amusive
VI	18	what time [when]
VII	6	" " "
IX	781	peradventure

Occasionally words appear in *The Excursion* which seem distinctly prosaic. It is perhaps hazardous to call any particular word a prose word, because it is easy to imagine a Donne or a Dickinson making very successful poetic use of almost any word that may be suggested. However, Wordsworth did not have their transforming skill, and therefore it is safe to say that the following words, among others, are distinctly prosaic in his hands. He used them only in *The Excursion*.

appendage	hatchment
cognizable	incalculably
connatural	preponderates
contiguous	presumptuousness
deciphered	self-disparagement
discomfitures	unambitiously
disencumbering	unobnoxious
disesteem	unstigmatized
disproportioned	

There are occasional archaisms in *The Excursion,* but they occur with no greater frequency than elsewhere in Wordsworth's poetry and therefore represent no significant factor in the development of his style from plainness to ornateness.

It is noticeable even in the lists already presented in this chapter that words of Latin derivation predominate over those of Old English derivation. This represents a real trend in Wordsworth's diction by the time of *The Excursion*. A study of 781 words which occur with significantly greater frequency in *The Excursion* than elsewhere in Wordsworth reveals that among such words those of Latin origin predominate over those of Old English origin in a ratio of approximately 5 to 2, and a list of 717 words which occur only in *The Excursion* shows almost invariably Latin derivations. Conversely, in a list of 392 words which occur significantly less frequently in *The Excursion* than elsewhere in Wordsworth, Old English derivations are in the majority. The same proportions hold true for the lengths of these words and show a marked tendency on the part of Wordsworth to adopt and make use of more and more trisyllables and polysyllables and at the same time to depend less on monosyllables. Thus the vocabulary of *The Excursion* is made up of decidedly longer and more Latin words than is the vocabulary of his previous works, which accounts for the impression of sonorousness and verbosity made by the poem.

Another pronounced tendency of the diction of Wordsworth in *The Excursion* is the increasing use of negative adjectives. Probably in an effort to lend depth or variety to his vocabulary, Wordsworth frequently used the negative form of an adjective of opposite meaning from the positive adjective which might be expected. In fact, there are over a hundred negative adjectives in *The Excursion* which occur nowhere else in Wordsworth, many of them exceedingly awkward. For example:

unambitious	unobnoxious
unavengeable	unredressed
uncountenanced	unsearchable
undistempered	unseconded
unelbowed	unsubstantialized
unescutcheoned	unvoyageable
unimprisoned	unwealthy

A similar increase in the use of hyphenated forms, also occasionally producing awkwardness, seems to result from a desire for greater accuracy and detail of description. Over 125 hyphenated forms were used by Wordsworth in *The Excursion* which occur nowhere else in his works.

It is interesting to notice in passing that in most of the tendencies discussed so far in this chapter the diction of *The Excursion* corresponds much more closely with that of *An Evening Walk, Descriptive Sketches,* and *The Borderers* than with that of the intervening works, which might indicate that in *The Excursion* Wordsworth was in some respects returning to the more detached, topographical, traditional diction of these early works.

Some of the shifts in diction apparent in *The Excursion* may reflect the changing interests of an older man. For example, words often associated with the security of later life, such as "peace," "rest," "tranquillity," "stillness," "calm," "comfort," and "leisure," are increasingly used in *The Excursion,* as are words referring to death and the transience of life, and words showing an awareness of pain and misery. Words reflecting domestic concern are also more frequent: "house," "habitation," "household," "parent," "husband," "partner," "matron," "maternal," "children," and "little-one." However, many of these increases are called for by the subject matter of the poem and their value as evidence of a changing Wordsworth must not be insisted upon.

The Excursion has been called "a tissue of elevated but abstract verbiage,"[2] and one of the commonest criticisms of the poem has been that the diction is too abstract and lacking in the concrete sensuousness

2. Arnold, *op. cit.*, p. 150.

that usually characterizes poetry. Wordsworth, it is felt, has abandoned minute observation of nature and turned to metaphysical and political speculation. However, a careful survey of the diction of the poem reveals that Wordsworth was really continuing to extend his vocabulary among the minutiae of nature even while he was adopting more long and Latin words. For example, the following words he used only in *The Excursion*.

bind-weed	heath-plant	sweet-briar
carnations	heath-cock	trouts
chicken	knoll	vulture
currants	magpies	water-fowl
foot-path	mocking-bird	water-lily
fossils	snipe	whortle-berries
grasshoppers	stone-crop	willow-flowers

It is noteworthy that this list includes 9 plants and 7 birds, which testifies to Wordsworth's continuing study of and ever growing familiarity with nature. The following words occur with significantly greater frequency in *The Excursion* than elsewhere in Wordsworth.

air	leaf	shrub
beams	mountain	sods
cloud	oak	soil
dew	path	sun
dust	pool	tufts
echo	rill	turf
fowl	seas	vale
hound	seed	waves
insect	shade	wren
land	shadows	

These words also seem evidence of greater attention and enduring devotion to the small details of nature. To be compared with these are the nature words which the poet used less frequently in *The Excursion* than elsewhere.

birds	lake	rose
cataracts	moonlight	sands
fountain	morning	tempest
gleam	ocean	water
horse	pines	
island	river	

This list is so brief that one hesitates to draw inferences from it, but it is perhaps significant that a comparatively general word like "birds" occurs less frequently, while the names of several specific birds are used for the first time, and that the poetically more conventional natural details —"cataracts," "tempest," "fountain," "moonlight," "rose"—are relinquished, while the words used more in *The Excursion* are generally more concrete and detailed, apparently the result of closer observation and study.

Apart from nature words, *The Excursion* includes a great many concrete details, many of them as homely as anything in "Goody Blake." Used only in *The Excursion:*

awning	cube	hemp
axle-tree	cupboard	hoe
bracelet	curd	knife
chimney-top	football	maps
chip	hay-field	quoit
copper	hay-makers	sofa

Used significantly more often in *The Excursion* than elsewhere:

bread	fire	roof
carpet	floor	shelf
cheek	limbs	sound
circle	lip	spade
coffin	liquid	veil
ear	loom	voice
eye	pillar	warmth
fabric	plough	wheel
finger	porch	

Thus it can be seen that the diction of *The Excursion* is not exclusively "abstract verbiage." Domestic details and details descriptive of physical man seem to be on the increase.

As a final bit of evidence that Wordsworth was not utterly given to high-flown abstraction in *The Excursion,* a sampling of the adjectives and verbs should be made. Used only in *The Excursion:*

bare-headed	skyey
body-bending	thyme-besprinkled
brazen	ticked
cackling	turf-built
nibbled	whining
pelting	wormy
roof-high	

Used significantly more often in *The Excursion* than elsewhere:

cool	moist	tall
crooked	pale	tattered
crystal	rough	tremble
dark	rugged	vapoury
fanning	shaggy	wintry
flat	slender	wooden
hear	soft	

It is perhaps also worthy of notice that the words "red," "green," "blue," "grey," "gold," and "silver" occur more frequently in *The Excursion* than elsewhere, while only "black" and "yellow" are used less.

The diction of *The Excursion* shows Wordsworth extending his poetic vocabulary to include more long and Latin words, partly to meet the demands of a more difficult subject matter and partly in an effort to achieve a more stately, sonorous, and varied style. The most surprising result of this tendency is the frequent resemblance of the diction of *The Excursion* to the "poetic diction" of eighteenth-century poets against which he always inveighed so strenuously. The diction of *The Excursion* also offers some evidence of an effort by the poet to develop greater accuracy in description and to include more variety of concrete and sensuous detail. There are still many simple and homely words in his poetic vocabulary.

3

The first sentence of *The Excursion* is 17 lines long and of a rather rambling construction. This serves as a foretaste of much that is to come, for there are many long, loose, rambling sentences[3] in the poem, occasionally extending over 30 lines[4] and requiring close attention for comprehension. Some of them have as many as 15 connectives,[5] and some sentence structures are exceedingly broken and difficult to follow.[6] The most common means of thus stringing out the sentence structures are the offering of numerous alternatives with "whether" or "either" and "or"; the making of exceptions with "except," "save," and "else"; the piling up of long series of elements, sometimes complex themselves; and the interposing of long parenthetical elements with dashes or parentheses. Such sentences are not always merely confusing and breathtaking, however, but occasionally have a dignity and eloquence approaching the grand style.

> Ah! what avails imagination high
> Or question deep? what profits all that earth,
> Or heaven's blue vault, is suffered to put forth
> Of impulse or allurement, for the Soul
> To quit the beaten track of life, and soar
> Far as she finds a yielding element
> In past or future; far as she can go
> Through time or space—if neither in the one,
> Nor in the other region, nor in aught
> That Fancy, dreaming o'er the map of things,
> Hath placed beyond these penetrable bounds,

3. For example, *The Excursion*, II, 65–80; IV, 79–99, 103–22; V, 331–48, 903–21, 934–52.
4. *Ibid.*, IV, 663–93.   5. *Ibid.*, IV, 611–30.
6. *Ibid.*, I, 453–9; III, 626–36, 173–89; VI, 599–604; VIII, 501–6.

Words of assurance can be heard; if nowhere
A habitation, for consummate good,
Or for progressive virtue, by the search
Can be attained,—a better sanctuary
From doubt and sorrow, than the senseless grave?[7]

The natural prose or conversational order of words was no longer
a fetish with Wordsworth by the time of *The Excursion,* for there is
hardly a line in the poem which does not show at least one inversion of
normal word order, and often the inverted order is used where the
normal order would be a metrical equivalent, so that the inversion is not
required by the meter. Occasionally these inversions seem really awkward,[8] and when they occur in conversation they give the speeches a
distinctly nonconversational tone.[9]

The most common inversions of normal word order in *The Excursion*
are those which transpose adverbial elements, occasionally extensive and
numerous, to a position between subject and verb.[1] In fact, this construction is so common in *The Excursion* that merely to read a list of
examples gives much of the tone of the poem. Another common inversion
is that which transposes adverbial elements to a position between auxili-
ary and past participle.[2] And finally one more characteristic alteration of
normal word order is the use of relative clauses introduced by "who,"
the antecedent of which is in an awkward or subordinate position,[3] or
omitted and understood ("There are who . . . ."[4]).

There are several other formal, nonconversational syntactical habits
apparent in *The Excursion.* Reflexive pronouns are often used alone as
subjects ("Myself have seen . . . ."[5]) and "nor" is overworked to introduce negative clauses or predicates after positive elements ("Benevolence is mild, nor borrows help . . . ."[6]). "Not . . . but" and "not
only . . . but also" constructions are numerous, as are the expressions
"cannot but" and "could not but." Sentences are repeatedly started
with brief absolute phrases, like "This done, . . ." and "That basis
laid, . . ."[7a] There are numerous qualifying parenthetical clauses, such
as "so deem I"[8a] and "as might seem."[9a] The double negative, always a
favorite device with Wordsworth, is much too common in *The Excursion,*
occurring about 115 times and often obscuring the meaning. Wordsworth's other great besetting sin, the use of parentheses, is also prevalent.
There are about 79 interruptions in parentheses in *The Excursion,* some
over 5 lines in length, and there are also numerous parenthetical elements
enclosed by dashes, some rather long and confusing.[1a]

7. *Ibid.,* III, 209–24.
8. *Ibid.,* II, 393–8; v, 250–1.
9. *Ibid.,* II, 140 ff., 457–8.
1. For example, *ibid.,* I, 793; III, 77; IV, 142–3.
2. *Ibid.,* I, 830.
3. *Ibid.,* III, 77; VI, 491.
4. *Ibid.,* VI, 491.
5. *Ibid.,* VII, 963; see also v, 426–7; VII, 271.
6. *Ibid.,* VII, 1030.
7a. *Ibid.,* VI, 88; IX, 755, 768.
8a. *Ibid.,* III, 173.
9a. *Ibid.,* v, 964.
1a. *Ibid.,* III, 574–82.

The punctuation of *The Excursion* is not noteworthy, apart from a surprising quantity of exclamation marks, which probably testify to the poet's earnestness, and the excessive use of dashes already mentioned.

The syntax of *The Excursion* does not show the simplicity and plainness usually associated with Wordsworth. There is evident an advance toward greater length and complexity in the sentences, and although a high level of intelligibility is still maintained, clarity is occasionally lost in intricacy. Some of this development must be recognized as an effort by the poet to achieve a greater majesty of cadence, a more Miltonic tonal sweep. The requirements of a complex subject and the qualities of the characters speaking must also be taken into account in any consideration of syntactical peculiarities.

The final estimate of the syntax of *The Excursion* must be that Wordsworth's experimentation with longer and more involved sentence structures and with more "poetic" rhetorical devices resulted in occasional passages of magnificent eloquence and a constant high level of dignity and nobility, while at the same time artifice occasionally smothered art, and when the fire of inspiration burns lowest, the result is a rather intricate, prosaic obscurity.

The versification of the poem requires little comment, since it is of the uniform excellence of most of Wordsworth's blank verse. The changing habits of diction and syntax proved no great impediment to the poet's metrical skill, and only in the occasional prosaic passages does the line lose its magic. Skillfully distributed extra unaccented syllables, feminine endings, and other variations in the normal metrical pattern relieve the monotony of regularity; Wordsworth himself regarded variety of rhythm and music as one of the chief virtues of the poem.[2] The verbal contractions resulting from metrical necessity which are to be found in nearly all of Wordsworth's works are slightly less frequent in *The Excursion*. Transposed accents, on the other hand, are slightly more common,[3] usually requiring accent of a final *-ed*.[4] The long, parenthetically interrupted sentences in some of the less inspired passages of the poem are permitted to approach too close to prose cadence by excessive running-on and breaking-up of lines. Although the verse occasionally falters and seldom takes wings quite as it does in *The Prelude*, the general level of metrical craftsmanship is still very high, and there are passages of real sublimity in *The Excursion*.

4

The Excursion marks the emergence of a less brilliant, more accurate and elevated imagery in Wordsworth's poetry. The foregoing

2. Wordsworth to Catherine Clarkson, December, 1814, *MY*, p. 617.
3. E.g., *pérspective*, *The Excursion*, VIII, 537; *aspécts*, IV, 327.
4. *Ibid.*, IV, 639; V, 152, 211; VI, 52, 919; VII, 834; VIII, 489; IX, 444.

analysis of the diction of *The Excursion* has shown the inclusion of a mass of concrete detail, an increase in the use of color, and an extended vocabulary of other descriptive words. In *The Excursion* the clock ticks,[5] the poet waves the insects away from his face,[6] and a single insect imperceptibly sucks its nourishment from a leaf.[7] Such details are important in that they show Wordsworth's powers of observation unimpaired and his faith in the poetic efficacy of minutiæ unshaken. The descriptions in the poem, although occasionally too matter-of-fact in detail, are often magnificent and moving, and sometimes aglow with mystical insight.

But perhaps the most important fact about the imagery of *The Excursion* is that its function is frequently decorative and ornamental, and that its relation to the idea or event in hand is seldom close or functional. This becomes particularly evident in an analysis of the similes, which are the most conspicuous figures in the poem.

The similes in *The Excursion* are long, very often extending over 3 lines and occasionally continuing for over 20 lines. They are frequently almost independent, detachable set pieces and are thus eminently quotable. Here, more unquestionably than with the diction and syntax, length and intricacy are functions of conscious artifice on the part of the poet, results of his striving toward a more dignified and stately style. It is true that some of these long similes have a machine-made quality and seem superfluous embellishments, but generally they are admirably conceived and successfully developed, so that they constitute one of the chief attractions of the poem. There is a sort of classical, Miltonic quality about the best of them which is probably precisely what Wordsworth was striving for. Nevertheless, in most of them the Wordsworthian element continues plain, for the comparisons are usually drawn from minute observation of nature and rural life, and the poet never hesitates to parallel lofty abstractions and humble concrete details when some point of similarity suggests the comparison to him. For example, the course of human life is twice compared to a mountain stream,[8] the wandering herbalist is compared to a fine-nosed hound,[9] and devotion to external forms is paralleled with an insect's attachment to a leaf.[1] Man's celestial spirit is compared to the moon seen through trees,[2] an optimist to a nesting bird,[3] love to a lake,[4] a small grave to a lamb,[5a] Ellen's child-love to a traveller's first view of the morning light,[6a] age to a mountain prospect,[7a] social upheaval to cracking ice fields,[8a] rowing to hawk-flight,[9a] the universe to a sounding sea shell,[1a] and the soul's reception of old songs to the

5. *Ibid.*, II, 645–6. 6. *Ibid.*, I, 24. 7. *Ibid.*, III, 579–81.
8. *Ibid.*, III, 967–91; VI, 736–40. 9. *Ibid.*, III, 169–71.
1. *Ibid.*, III, 579–81. 2. *Ibid.*, IV, 1062–70. 3. *Ibid.*, V, 840–3.
4. *Ibid.*, V, 916–21. 5a. *Ibid.*, VI, 787–90. 6a. *Ibid.*, VI, 911–16.
7a. *Ibid.*, IX, 56–91. 8a. *Ibid.*, IX, 340–3. 9a. *Ibid.*, IX, 491–4.
1a. *Ibid.*, IV, 1132–47.

parched ground's reception of irrigation.[2] Occasionally the comparison is more intricate and two related objects in nature are compared to two related objects in life, as the Wanderer and the Pastor are compared to an oak and a sycamore,[3] death with and without hope to a graveyard seen from the sunny and snowy sides,[4] a man and his wife to the setting sun and its attendant cloud,[5] two boys to a brook and a lake,[6] and the seas Britain's ships sail to the air through which bees fly.[7] Some of the comparisons have a more literary, fanciful tone, as when a small lawn is compared to a mariner's deck,[8] the Solitary's discourse to Lethe,[9] the Wanderer's discourse to that of an Indian chief,[1] the strength of middle age to that of a pillar which is stronger for what it supports,[2a] despondents to exiles and sentinels,[3a] and the Pastor's wife to a ship homeward bound.[4a]

All these similes are at least three lines long, and most of them are longer. Although the aptness of the comparisons is not always immediately evident, the descriptions and the play of fancy involved are often truly brilliant, and the resulting succession of memorable tableaux throughout the poem makes one of its chief beauties. There is something Homeric, or perhaps more precisely Miltonic, about these semidetached, elaborate similes, but the Wordsworthian element is still usually apparent in the details.

Wordsworth's early aversion to personification was gradually abandoned in his later poetry. Mary E. Burton found over 25 personifications added in the revision of *The Prelude*.[5a] This tendency was already incipient in *The Excursion,* for there are numerous personifications throughout the poem, including Contemplation, Nature, Chance, Fancy, Truth, Folly, Experience, Time, Solitude, and Silence. Obviously personification was no longer "utterly rejected, as an ordinary device to elevate the style, and raise it above prose."[6a]

Allusions are likewise more common in *The Excursion* than in Wordsworth's earlier works. There are numerous references to authors, mythology, history, and literature.

It is surprising to find in the imagery of *The Excursion* so many points of resemblance to classical and Miltonic poetry. The imagery, while still firmly founded on minute observation of nature, is generally more polished, elegant, and elaborate than Wordsworth's previous practice and shows a conscious endeavor by the poet to add some of the dignity and detachment of the traditional embellishments to his verse.

2. *Ibid.*, I, 70–3.
5. *Ibid.*, VII, 230–7.
8. *Ibid.*, IV, 246–50.
2a. *Ibid.*, V, 964–6.
5a. *Op. cit.*, pp. 206–7.

3. *Ibid.*, V, 455–61.
6. *Ibid.*, VIII, 576–85.
9. *Ibid.*, IV, 1122–6.
3a. *Ibid.*, VI, 534–8.

4. *Ibid.*, V, 531–57.
7. *Ibid.*, IX, 369–78.
1. *Ibid.*, IV, 1277–82.
4a. *Ibid.*, VIII, 506–18.
6a. Preface to *Lyrical Ballads* (1800).

5

The large form of *The Excursion* must be considered as an element of style. The stylistic disparity between the narrative, the speculative, and the exhortatory parts of the poem has been said to damage the unity of effect of the whole. However, if the varied styles are well adapted to the varied subjects and purposes, the unity of style must depend largely upon the unity of structure and idea. Now, *The Excursion* does have a structural unity, indicated in some detail in Chapter IV, Section 3, of this study. To be sure, the structure is somewhat creaky and archaic, reminiscent of the long eighteenth-century didactic and topographical poems, but nevertheless a clearly conceived and carefully fitted unity of purpose and idea governs the poem. This unity must be permitted at least partially to embrace the disparity of style, for if speculation and narration can be successfully yoked together, certainly they should still be written in their respective styles and not forced to conform to some compromise style which would be unsuitable for both. Unity is not necessarily uniformity.

It is possible that Wordsworth was attempting to achieve some degree of epic unity in *The Excursion*, perhaps in imitation of Homer's and Milton's practice. Thus the action of the poem is confined to five days and all the important preliminary action of the Wanderer's and Solitary's backgrounds is revealed in flashbacks, while the action of the poem proper is restricted to the one main object of reclaiming the apathetic Solitary, the ultimate outcome of even this action remaining untold and merely foreshadowed at the end. This epic tendency would seem to be indirectly supported by the presence of Homeric similes and of other classical or neoclassical stylistic traits, but there is no further evidence to support it and it must remain speculation.

Turning to smaller structural matters, *The Excursion* was early taxed for unevenness, for the ruining of carefully contrived good effects by the inclusion of grotesque, ridiculous lines.[7] There is unquestionably some of this anticlimax in the style of *The Excursion,* almost invariably resulting from the use, at an inappropriate point, of some particularly prosaic or homely word or detail, or from the treatment of homely detail in an absurdly lofty and dignified manner.

> . . . The winds of March, smiting insidiously,
> Raised in the tender passage of the throat
> Viewless obstruction . . . .[8]

Wordsworth did occasionally lack the insight which would have permitted him properly to evaluate the individual effectiveness of such

7. "An Essay on the Theory and Writings of Wordsworth: Part III," *Blackwood's Edinburgh Magazine,* XXVI (November, 1829), 786.
8. *The Excursion,* VII, 683–5.

touches, but his habitual idiom required their use, and in their proper position they are effective. When Wordsworth nods in *The Excursion,* the resultant incongruity is accentuated by the general loftiness of tone. The occasional approach to prose in such lapses is undeniable; and Wordsworth removed at least one passage stigmatized in a review as prosaic, harsh, dragging, and mathematical.[9]

Wordsworth was apparently also sensitive to the charge of prolixity and, when needless repetition was pointed out in a review,[1] he removed it in revision, which of course is also in conformity with the general tendency toward condensation in revision.

6

There are many fine passages in *The Excursion,* although none of them individually seems to approach in quality the best passages in *The Prelude.* The poem contains such a variety of material, however, that it affords examples of all Wordsworth's best styles, and there is hardly a passage in the poem that has not been singled out by some critic for praise, even though the same passage may have been vilified by other critics. Thus in its variety the poem offers every reader some sort of satisfaction; there is at least something in the poem to please every palate.

One of the most characteristic features of *The Excursion* is the frequent punctuation of the flow of thought and action by more or less independent passages of eloquent invocation, panegyric, or complaint. Such are the prayers of the Pastor, the eulogy of church and state at the beginning of Book VI, the admonition to the British Lawgivers in Book IX,[2] the passage praising natural but mute poets in Book I,[3] and the Solitary's complaint against the rewards of imagination in Book III.[4] There are several other such passages in the poem, many of them having the stately eloquence of oratory and others resembling brief classical odes.

There are expressions of enthusiastic transport and mystical insight in *The Excursion,* as in the great crucial poems of Wordsworth's earlier years. Though their fire is somewhat less intense than that of similar earlier lines, they show clear recollection and perhaps occasional reverberation of the famous "spots of time." The description of the Wanderer's youthful transports in Book I[5] seems clearly autobiographical. The Solitary's speech on the twin peaks and their natural music[6] and his account of the ending storm and his mystical vision[7] seem to have the excited

9. Wordsworth removed from Bk. VI, between lines 148 and 149, a passage containing the phrase "the sedentary art of penmanship," which was attacked in "An Essay on the Theory and Writings of Wordsworth: Part III," p. 780.

1. *Ibid.,* p. 787. The sense of Bk. I, 118–19, was originally repeated after line 196, and Wordsworth removed this repetition after it was criticized.

2. Lines 398 ff.   3. Lines 77 ff.   4. Lines 209–24.
5. Lines 198–221.   6. *The Excursion,* II, 696–725.   7. *Ibid.,* II, 827–81.

immediacy of more recent experience. Autobiography is again apparent
in the child's imaginative flight, initiated by listening to minstrels, described at the beginning of Book VII, and a similar enthusiasm burns in
the Solitary's account of his love in Book III.[8]

The unfaltering power of Wordsworth's descriptive talent and his
continuing joy in nature are apparent in countless passages throughout
the poem, both in elaborate paintings like that of the white ram reflected
in a calm lake in Book IX[9] and in small deft strokes like this:

> When stormy winds
> Were working the broad bosom of the lake
> Into a thousand thousand sparking waves,
> Rocking the trees, or driving cloud on cloud
> Along the sharp edge of yon lofty crags . . . .[1]

Finally, there are many individual passages and lines which are noteworthy for particular reasons. Some give an expression with the stamp
of finality to characteristic attitudes of the poet.

> . . . that mighty orb of song,
> The divine Milton.[2]

> The keen, the wholesome, air of poverty . . . .[3]

> . . . sometimes his religion seemed to me
> Self-taught, as of a dreamer in the woods.[4]

> The smoke ascends
> To heaven as lightly from the cottage hearth
> As from the haughtiest palace.[5]

Others are memorable for a trick of expression that makes them seem
particularly original and quotable. The famous account of the Greek
shepherd's religion[6] and the passage on the sea shell[7] in Book IV are
longer examples, while the following are some of the briefer.

> . . . the good die first,
> And they whose hearts are dry as summer dust
> Burn to the socket.[8a]

> . . . the crust wherein his soul
> Sleeps, like a caterpillar sheathed in ice.[9a]

> They sweep distemper from the busy day,
> And make the chalice of the big round year
> Run o'er with gladness . . . .[1a]

8. Lines 480–549.
2. *Ibid.*, I, 249–50.
5. *Ibid.*, IX, 245–7.
8a. *Ibid.*, I, 500–2.

9. Lines 439–51.
3. *Ibid.*, I, 306.
6. *Ibid.*, IV, 851–87.
9a. *Ibid.*, VIII, 418–19.

1. *The Excursion*, VII, 409–13.
4. *Ibid.*, I, 409–10.
7. *Ibid.*, IV, 1132–50.
1a. *Ibid.*, IX, 133–5.

These are some of the individual stylistic gems of *The Excursion.* They show some advance by the poet into new fields of poetic expression, particularly that of the nonessential adornment which, while it may be a lovely thing independently, is not a necessary functional part of the poem in which it stands and can be removed without serious damage either to itself or to the poem.

When, in a consideration of the style of *The Excursion,* all allowances have been made for the demands of the difficult subject matter, for the requirements of the dialogue form and the sort of character depicted, and for the apparent experimentation by the poet with a loftier, more dignified tone, it must be admitted that there is a residue of dull prosaism and inflated rhetoric and verbosity which no degree of tolerance can ennoble with the name of poetry. It can only be urged that the stylistic richness and beauty of most of the poem should excuse these lapses.

Perhaps the most surprising fact that emerges from a study of the style of *The Excursion* is the astonishing resemblance the poem bears to much that has always been called classical. It may seem a gross solecism to suggest that in *The Excursion* a classical Wordsworth emerges, for the name of Wordsworth has traditionally symbolized the antithesis of classicism, but when the evidence is reviewed this conclusion seems almost inevitable. The points of resemblance between *The Excursion* and Milton and between *The Excursion* and eighteenth-century poetry are numerous, and the evidence that Wordsworth was seeking to elevate and dignify his style in *The Excursion* by the use of traditional artifices is overwhelming. Certainly the simplicity, concreteness, and homeliness of the early Wordsworth are not altogether superseded by this impulse, but it does represent a new and important departure in the later Wordsworth, of which perhaps the happiest results are "The River Duddon" and certain of the "Evening Voluntaries." It may serve as a useful starting-point in the modern revaluation of the later Wordsworth.

VI

Conclusion

THE purpose of this study has been to reach a fuller, fairer understanding of *The Excursion* than has hitherto been possible because of the incomplete state of our knowledge of the facts about the poem. Modern scholarship has neglected *The Excursion* principally because popular taste has neglected it. Enthusiasm for long speculative poems has reached its lowest ebb, and when a long work has been widely condemned as dull and wordy sermonizing, there can be little hope for a revival of interest in it. Nevertheless there was an era in which *The Excursion* overcame critical stigma and gained a wide circle of discriminating admirers. As we have seen, it has suffered an unparalleled eclipse in the last seventy years—an eclipse from which it may never emerge. However, the last quarter-century has seen a steady growth of interest in Wordsworth both as a man and as a thinker. The woeful lack of information about *The Excursion* is a serious gap in the history of Wordsworth's thought.

It is to be hoped that the present study has made at least some progress in the direction of filling that gap. We have attempted to show that *The Excursion* cannot be dismissed as the dull and pompous preaching of an aged poet in his decline. We have seen that *The Excursion* should be almost exempt from the common accusation of excessive orthodoxy and Toryism. We have also seen that Wordsworth himself was intellectually and emotionally involved in almost every line of it, much as he was in *The Prelude*. *The Excursion* represents the inner psychological and philosophical struggles of Wordsworth himself, as well as of a great mass of his contemporaries. It bears clear evidence of several important strides forward in the poet's mental development. It came from the pen of a more profound, more serene, and wiser Wordsworth than did most of the previous works. Nevertheless it still represents "the one Wordsworth," for most of his early convictions are still to be found in this later poem. Nature is still represented as a better teacher than books,[1] and the highest religious act is still communion with nature.[2] Dislike for rank, privilege, wealth,[3] and the individual hardships caused by international misrule[4] continue, as do the admiration for Swiss popular equality,[5] faith in the superiority of rural life,[6] belief in human progress,[7] and clear

1. *The Excursion*, I, 163. 2. *Ibid.*, I, 215–16, 226. 3. *Ibid.*, VII, 988; IX, 206, 253.
4. *Ibid.*, I, 379–81. 5. *Ibid.*, V, 92 ff. 6. *Ibid.*, I, 344–7; IV, 365–8.
7. *Ibid.*, VII, 1005.

recollection of the enthusiasm which marked the early stages of the French Revolution.[8] *The Excursion* also bears the stamp of real conviction, of exciting discovery, and of inward growth. These characteristics appear only with sympathetic and painstaking study, but we cannot deny a poem the attention its author deserves, and we must not mistake difficulty for dullness. Wordsworth was not unaware that *The Excursion* is serious as a whole and abstruse in part, and he knew that for these reasons it could never achieve a lasting popularity. Nevertheless, he did not doubt that it would always find a select audience of understanding and appreciative readers. Perhaps it was his belief that he had earned our attention and that attention to *The Excursion* would be rewarded. The student or teacher of Wordsworth cannot fully understand or appreciate the poet until he has made the necessary effort to grasp the full meaning and beauties of *The Excursion*. There are delicate shades of meaning which will always elude the rapid reader.

Apart from Book iv and Book v the poem is not difficult to follow or to remember. In this respect it is easier than *The Prelude*. There is a great deal of action and variety, and a background of incomparable scenery. But a failure to grasp the full significance of those two central books deprives the whole poem of its unity of impulse and idea, leaving it a mere polyglot collection of varied fragments. *The Excursion* was not published as a miscellany of Wordsworthian blank verse collected from manuscripts on hand. It grew out of a few central ideas, closely interrelated, which had occupied Wordsworth's thoughts and efforts for many years. Every line has some bearing on these central themes.

Everything considered, *The Excursion* cannot be called a thoroughly satisfactory poem. The characters lack conviction and fail to hold our sympathies. They are also open to Coleridge's criticism of Wordsworth for "ventriloquizing." The transitions between ideas in the speculative parts of the poem are not always marked with sufficient clarity, and the bearing of the nonspeculative parts on the central problem is not stated specifically enough in the poem, although it becomes clear with study. The style, while it provides an excellent vehicle on the whole, occasionally lapses into verbosity and rhetoric. It may still be thought with some justification that it was a grave error on the part of Wordsworth ever to have undertaken a poem of the scope of *The Excursion*. But he did undertake it and, ill suited though it may have been to his powers, he was still Wordsworth, which in itself is enough to indicate that *The Excursion* must contain much wisdom, much beauty, and very little that does not in some way bear the stamp of a great mind.

Perhaps, in closing, it would be appropriate to quote Edward Quillinan's final estimate of *The Excursion:* "It *will* do, in spite of my Lord Jeffrey, and its occasional defects . . . ."[9]

8. *Ibid.,* ii, 210 ff.; iii, 706 ff.
9. *Henry Crabb Robinson on Books and Their Writers,* p. 548.

APPENDIX I

The Reviews of The Excursion

1. *The Examiner,* (August 21, 28, and October 2, 1814). Hazlitt. Possibly instigated by Hunt, this essay was predominantly favorable in its original form, but it contained a brilliant and cynical attack on country manners and raised objections to the narrative element. Subsequent political and other differences with Wordsworth caused Hazlitt to alter the essay, making it much less favorable as it was published in *The Round Table.*

2. *The Edinburgh Review,* XLVII (November, 1814), 1–30. Jeffrey. "This will never do." The apex of the slashing review, this essay condemned *The Excursion* and its author most emphatically. It went a long way toward crushing the poem. Dishonest and vehement, it nevertheless touches on a few real flaws and many beauties.

3. *The Quarterly Review,* XII (October, 1814, published January 6, 1815), 100–11. Lamb. In its original form, which was lost, this essay was most favorable, but it was altered for the worse by Gifford. However, even in its final form there is not one strong adverse criticism. If at all, it damns only with faint praise.

4. *The Eclectic Review,* New Series, Vol. III (January, 1815), 13–39. Montgomery. Rather favorable on the whole, this review points out the incompleteness of the Christianity in *The Excursion.* This is the only review Wordsworth is known to have read with great care.

5. *The Monthly Review,* Second Series, LVII (January, 1815), 123–36. Merivale. Imitation of Jeffrey is patent in this very hostile review. Merivale praises Wordsworth's versification and native genius but decides that all must fall with the "system."

6. *The British Critic,* New Series, Vol. III (May, 1815), 449–67. Anonymous. Mainly laudatory but rather narrow and unappreciative. Esteems Wordsworth's nature poetry more than his grappling with human values. Deplores his preoccupation with his "system."

7. *The British Review and London Critical Journal,* VI (August, 1815), 50–64. William Roberts. A thoroughly favorable review, distinctly anti-Jeffreian. A religious bias.

8. *The Philanthropist,* No. 20, Vol. V (October ?, 1815), 342–63. Anonymous. A strong defense of the poem against Jeffrey. Written by a Quaker, it stresses the moral teaching of *The Excursion.* Sermonizing.

9. *The Analectic Magazine,* New Series, VI (October, 1815), 273–94. The same review as that in *The British Critic.*

10. *The Monthly Magazine: or, British Register,* XXXVIII (1815), 638–49. Lengthy quotations, prefaced by a laudatory note.

11. *The London Chronicle,* CXVI, Nos. 8690, 8718 (August 27–29, November 1–2, 1814), 230, 451. Two brief notices containing a bald combina-

tion of condemnation and commendation, followed by substantial quotations. The only notice received by *The Excursion* in a newspaper.

12. *The Literary Gazette,* III (1820), 837. A favorable review of the octavo edition of 1820.

13. *Blackwood's Edinburgh Magazine,* No. 21, Vol. IV (December, 1818), 257–63. "Essays on the Lake School of Poetry; No. II: On the Habits of Thought, Inculcated by *Wordsworth.*" John Wilson. This essay deals primarily with *The Excursion* and it is important because it recognizes the fact that Wordsworth's doctrines are "at variance with the philosophy at present most fashionable in this country," which is "directed chiefly towards the laws of intellect and association."

14. *Blackwood's Edinburgh Magazine,* No. 146, Vol. XXIV (December, 1828), 917–38. "Sacred Poetry." John Wilson. This essay contains a blistering indictment of *The Excursion* for the "utter absence of Revealed Religion," alleging that the panegyric on the Church of England at the beginning of Book VI is mere lip service.

15. *The Literary World,* V (New York, 1849), 463–4. A review of the C. S. Francis (etc.) edition (see Appendix II, No. 8), containing an interesting comparison of the Solitary to Job.

16. *The Athenaeum,* No. 1637 (March 12, 1859), 361. A review of the 1859 edition of selections, dealing exclusively with the Fraser etchings.

APPENDIX II

The Editions of The Excursion

Separate Editions of *The Excursion*

1. First edition. There were at least four distinct issues,[1] for the Yale and Amherst copies all differ in a few details from that described by T. J. Wise (*A Bibliography of Wordsworth* [London, 1916], pp. 80–3) and from one another. 500 copies were printed, in quarto with large print on heavy paper, price two guineas. The edition is not rare, at least 21 copies being located in major libraries. It can still be purchased for the original price. Following is a summary of the contents.

Page	
iii	"The Excursion,/ Being a Portion of/ The Recluse,/ A Poem./ By/ William Wordsworth/ London:/ Printed for Longman, Hurst, Rees, Orme, and Brown,/ Paternoster-Row./ 1814."
iv	"T. Davison, Lombard-street,/ Whitefriars, London."
v	Dedicatory sonnet to William, Earl of Lonsdale, with the date: "Rydal Mount, Westmoreland, July 29, 1814."
vii–x	Preface.
x–xiv	Fragment of *The Recluse,* printed as a prospectus.
xv–xx	Summary of contents.
1	"The/Excursion."
3–423	Text.
425–47	Notes, including the "Essay upon Epitaphs" on pages 431–446. After the last note on page 447: "The End."
448	"T. Davison, Lombard-street,/ Whitefriars, London."

2. Second edition. London, Longman, Hurst, Rees, Orme, & Brown, 1820. 8vo.

3. In 1827 *The Excursion* was incorporated in a collected edition with the rest of the works of Wordsworth, Volume v being devoted to *The Excursion*. That volume was also supplied with a different title page in order that it might be sold as a separate edition. London, Longman, Reese, Orme, Brown, & Green, 1827.

4. London, Longman & Co., July, 1832. 8vo, fcp., 7s.

5. A new edition. London, E. Moxon, 1836.

6. A new edition. London, E. Moxon, 1841 [ie., 1843].

7. A new edition. London, E. Moxon, 1847.

8. New York, C. S. Francis; Boston, J. H. Francis, 1849.

9. New York, C. S. Francis; Boston, J. H. Francis, 1850.

10. New York, C. S. Francis; Boston, J. H. Francis, 1852–55.

---

1. C. H. Patton, *The Amherst Wordsworth Collection* (Amherst, Trustees of Amherst College, 1936), p. 7.

11. A new edition. London, E. Moxon, 1853. 12mo, 6*s.*

12. A new edition. London, E. Moxon, 1857. 12mo, 3*s.* 6*d.*

13. London, Society for the Promotion of Christian Knowledge, 1859. 8vo.

14. With topographical notes by Lindsley Aspland. Windermere, J. Garnett; London, Whittaker, 1860. 8vo, 1*s.* Part of "Garnett's Series."

15. A new edition. London, E. Moxon, 1864.

16. A new edition. London, E. Moxon, 1869. 12mo.

17. A new edition. New York, J. Miller, 1870.

18. With a biographical sketch. New York, Clark & Maynard, 1881 (English Classics Series).

19. With explanatory notes. New York, Effingham, Maynard, 1889.

20. G. C. Moore Smith, ed. London, J. M. Dent, 1904 (The Temple Classics).

21. Preceded by Book 1 of *The Recluse,* E. E. Reynolds, ed. London, Macmillan, 1935. With introduction and notes.

22. Muses Library, L. Magnus, ed. New York, Dutton, n.d.

23. With topographical notes. London, Simpkin, Marshall; Windermere, J. Garnett, n.d. (Garnett's Series).

Editions of Selections from *The Excursion*

1. *The Deserted Cottage (The Excursion,* Bks. I, II), *A Poem.* Illustrated with 21 designs by Birket Foster, J. Wolf, and J. Gilbert. London, Routledge, 1858–59. Post 8vo, 7*s.* 6*d.*

2. *Passages from Wordsworth's Excursion.* Illustrated with etchings on steel, by Agnes Fraser. London, Colnaghi, 1859. 4to, £1 1*d.*

3. *The Wanderer.* Edited with introduction by D. C. London, 1863. 8vo (*The Excursion,* Bk. I).

4. *The Wanderer (The Excursion,* Bk. I). Edited with notes to aid in grammatical analysis and in paraphrasing by H. O. Robinson. London, Hamilton, 1863.

5. *The Excursion, Book* I. With Introduction. London, E. Moxon, 1863. 12mo, 9*d.*

6. Second edition of No. 4, above, 1864.

7. *The Deserted Cottage.* Illustrated. London, Routledge, 1864. Small 4to, 5*s.*

8. *The Excursion, Book* I. With full notes and a treatise upon the analysis of sentences. C. H. Bromby, ed. London, Longmans, 1864. 12mo, 1*s.* 6*d.*

9. *Wordsworth's Excursion, Book* IX, *Discourse of The Wanderer, and an Evening Visit to the Lake.* London & Edinburgh, W. Chambers & R. Chambers, 1870 (Chambers' English Classics for Use in Schools).

10. *The Excursion: Book* I (Book III). With introduction and notes. Glasgow, W. Collins, Sons, 1874. 8vo (Collins' School Classics).

11. *The Wanderer (The Excursion,* Bk. I). With life, introduction, and notes by H. H. Turner. London, Rivington's, 1874. 77 pp. (English School-Classics).

12. *The Excursion, Book* I. Edited with life and notes by the Rev. C. Ivens.

Manchester, J. Heywood, 1879. 12ᵐᵒ, *2d*. (J. Heywood's Annotated Series of School Classics).

13. A new edition of No. 11, above, 1880.

14. A new edition of No. 11, above, 1886.

15. *Wordsworth's Excursion, Book* 1. Edited with introduction and notes by M. T. Quinn. London, Bell & Sons, 1897. xlii, 82 pp. Cr. 8ᵛᵒ, 1*s*. 3*d*. (Bell's English Classics).

16. A new edition of No. 11, above, n.d.

17. *The Excursion, Book* 1. New York, Oxford University Press, n.d. (Oxford Plain Texts).

18. *The Excursion, Book* 1, *and Ode on Immortality*. New York, Maynard, Merrill, n.d. (Maynard's English Classics).

APPENDIX III

The New Oxford Edition

THE long-awaited appearance of the new Oxford edition of *The Excursion* [1] makes available for the first time complete information on the surviving manuscripts of the poem. In general, this material confirms the description of the history of the poem in Chapter II above. However, there is some interesting additional information, and there is one important difference.

It is now evident that early drafts of a few passages in *The Excursion* can be dated with some probability as early as 1795. These are particularly lines corresponding to *The Excursion,* I, 502–70, 582–91.[2] Thus it seems that the central problem of the Margaret story and the setting of the ruined cottage had perhaps taken shape in the poet's mind somewhat earlier than was previously apparent. However, there is no new evidence to fix the date of lines 871–916 of Book I, which Wordsworth said were the first to be composed, any earlier than 1798.

It is also interesting to learn that many short but interesting passages in Book IV, in addition to lines 1,207–74, appear in early drafts dating from 1798–99.[3] This is further evidence of the fundamental unity of Wordsworth's thought, his later fidelity to earlier convictions and insights. The same is true of the passage from Book VIII (282–333) on the disastrous effects of child labor, the similar lines in Book IX (128–52), and particularly the opening lines of Book IX (1–26), all of which are to be found in a manuscript dating from 1798–99.[4] Two of the stories ultimately used in Book VI can be dated 1800.[5] Early drafts of a few other passages in different parts of the poem were written in the years 1804–6.[6] The first three books were essentially complete in 1806.[7] In general, therefore, it can be said that the manuscripts confirm my statement that at least one third of the poem had been written by 1808, and the possibility still exists that as much as one half may have been written by that time.

The greatest discrepancy between the history of the poem given in Chapter II above and that given in the New Oxford edition is that while I have treated "The Pedlar" as a temporarily independent poem composed of the overflow of the Wanderer's character from "The Ruined Cottage," the editors of that edition regard "The Pedlar" as merely an alternative name for "The Ruined

---

1. *The Poetical Works of William Wordsworth,* v, E. De Selincourt and H. Darbishire, eds. (Oxford, Clarendon Press, 1949), (hereafter referred to as Wordsworth, *Poetical Works*).
2. *Ibid.,* v, 365, 369, 377.
3. *Ibid.,* v, 423.
4. *Ibid.,* v, 471.
5. *The Excursion,* VI, 1080–191. Wordsworth, *Poetical Works,* v, 461.
6. *The Excursion,* V, 1–200; IX, 437–48.
7. Wordsworth, *Poetical Works,* v, 410.

Cottage." It may be well to summarize the evidence on which I based my conviction that "The Pedlar" was an independent poem.

a) In her journal Dorothy speaks of "The Pedlar" on October 6, 1800, and December 21 and 22, 1801, and then on December 23, 1801, mentions "The Ruined Cottage," [8] after which there is no mention of either for some time. It seems unlikely that she would refer to the same poem by two different names on successive days. The natural inference is that the poet had stopped work on a poem called "The Pedlar" and had undertaken some revision of his earlier poem "The Ruined Cottage." Three days later he was working on *The Prelude,* which seems to suggest that he had temporarily abandoned work on both of the earlier poems. Nevertheless, it remains possible that Dorothy's mention of "The Ruined Cottage" on December 23, 1801, was simply an accidental recurrence on her part to the earlier name of a poem now usually called "The Pedlar," as the editors of the new edition assume.

b) After Wordsworth's arduous labors on "The Pedlar" in the winter of 1801–2, Dorothy copied it on March 6 and stitched it up on March 7. In the succeeding months Wordsworth apparently made some further changes in the poem, for on July 8 Dorothy wrote: "William was looking at *The Pedlar* when I got up. He arranged it, and after tea I wrote it out—280 lines." [9] This is the last mention of "The Pedlar" in Dorothy's journal, and it certainly seems to refer to a poem separate from "The Ruined Cottage," which was already over 900 lines long in 1798. The "280 lines" seems to be clearly a description of the length of the whole poem, but the possibility of course remains (though her words make it seem remote) that Dorothy meant she had copied 280 lines of a poem which in its entirety was considerably longer. The Oxford editors omit this entry in Dorothy's journal entirely from their consideration of the history of the poem.

c) Wordsworth's letter to Sir George Beaumont of December 25, 1804, states that "The Pedlar" is to be part of *The Recluse* and adds that *The Recluse* is "about 2,000 lines" long.[1] Before this time Wordsworth had written the "1,300 lines" of 1798 and "Home at Grasmere," which was 1,047 lines long. It is far from certain that "The Ruined Cottage" constituted part of the "1,300 lines," for if so, and if "The Pedlar" and "The Ruined Cottage" were the same poem, it seems strange that Sir George should have to be told that "The Pedlar" was to be part of *The Recluse,* for Coleridge had recently read "The Pedlar" to him and could hardly have avoided telling him it was a part of a larger poem if it had actually been so regarded since 1798.[2] If, then, the 1,300 lines of 1798 did not include "The Ruined Cottage," Wordsworth had already announced the composition of well over 2,000 lines of *The Recluse,* exclusive of "The Ruined Cottage," before 1804. Therefore it seems probable that the "2,000 lines" of 1804 are the 1,300 of 1798 plus "Home at Grasmere" and a shorter poem called "The Pedlar." The 900-odd lines of "The Ruined Cottage" would swell the number of lines to a total which could not, even in round numbers, be referred to as 2,000.

8. Dorothy, *Journals,* I, 95.
9. *Ibid.,* I, 168.
1. *EL,* p. 424.
2. *Ibid.*

d) The time apparently required for Dorothy to copy "The Pedlar" seems more appropriate to a poem of 280 lines than to one of over 900 lines. See, for example, the entry in her journal for March 6, 1802, when she sat down to breakfast at half past one in the afternoon and subsequently copied "The Pedlar," finishing it before going out to tea.

The newly published material from the manuscripts adds another bit of evidence which seems to me to point strongly to the possibility that "The Pedlar" was for some time an independent poem. The manuscripts show that Wordsworth at one time (?1799) decided to divorce the character of the Wanderer from "The Ruined Cottage," and with this in mind he had Dorothy make a copy of "The Ruined Cottage" ("MS D") from which 262 lines on the Wanderer were omitted, these lines appearing in a rearranged order as addenda to the poem, "evidently reserved for use in some other place." [3] It is tempting to infer that this marks the birth of "The Pedlar," especially since the number of lines involved so closely approximates Dorothy's "280 lines" of 1802. The editors find, however, that these lines were restored in a manuscript ("E") dating from the winter of 1801–2.[4] But their dating of this manuscript is based on the assumption that "The Pedlar," on which Wordsworth was engaged at that time, was really "The Ruined Cottage." Therefore it is still possible that the restoration was made later, and of course the lines could have been developed experimentally in the two different poems at the same time, even after their restoration to "The Ruined Cottage."

The only other bit of evidence brought forward in the new edition to support the identity of the two poems is the fact that Dorothy speaks of "The Pedlar" as a poem in three parts, and in some of the manuscripts "The Ruined Cottage" is divided into three parts. The only supporting reference provided by the editors is to Dorothy's journal, December 27, 1801, where she says, "Mary wrote some lines of the third part of Wm.'s poem, which he brought to read to us. . . ." [5] But it is clear from the preceding entry that this refers to *The Prelude* and not to "The Pedlar" at all, as De Selincourt himself indicates elsewhere! [6]

It is of course quite possible that "The Pedlar" was used, at least occasionally, as an alternative name for "The Ruined Cottage." However, the evidence now available still seems to me to point to the probability of the existence of an independent poem on the Wanderer, called "The Pedlar," composed of lines extracted from "The Ruined Cottage" (and subsequently returned to that poem for use in *The Excursion,* I), or of additional lines dealing with the Wanderer (subsequently used in Books I, II, IV, and perhaps VIII and IX), or of a combination of both. As this poem was disengaged from "The Ruined Cottage" and subsequently recombined with it, the name "The Pedlar" may also have been used on some occasions to refer to "The Ruined Cottage."

3. Wordsworth, *Poetical Works,* v, 404.
4. *Ibid.,* v, 409.
5. Dorothy, *Journals,* I, 96.
6. *The Prelude,* De Selincourt, ed., p. xxxv.

Further corrections to be made in Chapter II above:

a) Pages 13–14: The Oxford editors regard it as probable that the 1,000 lines of *The Recluse* Wordsworth mentioned in a letter of September 8, 1806, are additional to the 700 lines mentioned on August 1.[7]

b) Page 13: It appears that "Home at Grasmere" was designed for *The Recluse* from the first.

7. Wordsworth, *Poetical Works*, v, 371.

Index